A Twofold Life

by

Wilhelmine Von Hillern

Double 9
BOOKS

A Twofold Life
by Wilhelmine Von Hillern

Copyright © 2024

All Rights reserved.

ISBN: 978-93-68094-76-0

Published by

DOUBLE 9 BOOKS

2/13-B, Ansari Road
Daryaganj, New Delhi – 110002
info@double9books.com
www.double9books.com
Tel. 011-40042856

ABOUT THE AUTHOR

Wilhelmine von Hillern (1836-1916) was a German novelist and playwright known for her works that often explored themes of gender roles, societal expectations, and personal identity. Born into a literary and artistic family in Munich, Germany, she was the daughter of the celebrated actress Charlotte Birch-Pfeiffer, which greatly influenced her literary career. Hillern's works often focused on the struggles of women in a patriarchal society, highlighting issues of gender inequality, personal freedom, and self-discovery. Her writing is characterized by detailed character development, emotional depth, and a keen insight into societal norms and their impact on individuals. Hillern's novels and plays were significant in the context of 19th-century German literature, particularly for their focus on women's issues and societal critique. Her work remains an important part of discussions on gender and literature. Wilhelmine von Hillern's contributions to literature provide valuable insights into the challenges faced by women in her time and offer timeless narratives that continue to resonate with readers today. Her ability to weave compelling stories with strong, independent female protagonists marks her as a pioneering figure in literary history.

CONTENTS

I
MENTAL STRIFE

In an elegant apartment which luxury and wealth had adorned with everything that the fantastic industry of our times affords, two stately figures were pacing rapidly up and down: a lady no longer young but still magnificently beautiful, a true Parisienne and *lionne* of society, and a young man with an aristocratic, though somewhat stern, bearing, dark hair, and strongly marked features. At times they eagerly approached each other with flashing eyes, then turned away to resume their restless pacing to and fro.

"It is useless, we must part!" cried the youth, after a pause. "My passion for you is destroying my whole life: my studies are neglected, nothing has any charm for me unless connected with you; my fancy is unceasingly busied with your image. I can no longer work, no longer think, no longer create anything, and unless I can break loose from this conflict I shall become a dishonored wretch, or consume my strength in endless torture and go to destruction! We must part forever!"

There was no answer. The lady had thrown herself upon a causeuse which stood just under a niche overgrown with ivy and lighted with lamps that gleamed through crimson shades, and was gazing steadily into the soft gloom, while a tear rolled slowly down her cheek. Our hero turned, after vainly waiting for a reply, and looked ardently at the beautiful picture.

The deepest silence pervaded the elegant apartment, only interrupted by the low plashing of a tiny fountain which fell into a marble basin filled with goldfish. Countless hyacinths exhaled their fragrance amid tall exotic plants, and between the heavy silken curtains and portières gleamed marble statues, which in the dim purple light seemed instinct with life. Everything breathed love and secret bliss. Allured by some magnetic attraction our hero knelt before the silent figure, and kissing the hand that hung by her side, whispered: "Great Heaven, if you weep how shall I find strength to conquer this moment? Oh, do not condemn me to suffer all the torments which only a fiend can devise for feeble human beings! If you have a heart that can weep, in mercy soften this farewell. If you really loved me, you would not by every alluring art seek to place me in a relation where your better self must renounce and despise me."

"What do I desire?" was the reply. "I wish to keep you, you who are the sole happiness of my life. I will not, cannot, see you leave me so coldly, cannot loose you from these arms, which in your person hold my very life. What will my husband lose if through you he receives what he does not know how to win himself: a happy wife? what will he lose if the smile I *feign* for him becomes *real*? What has he made me? A doll to amuse society, a puppet to minister to his empty vanity. What does he lose if the doll receives life? He has never asked for my heart,--do I rob him if I give that which he neither knows nor prizes to another who longs for it, and whom it can make happy?" She paused and pressed a light kiss on the listening ear of her friend. Bewildered by her musical whisper and warm breath, he leaned his burning cheek upon her breast and could find no reply.

She clasped him in a closer embrace and continued, in a tone of reproachful tenderness, "Now that our relation must be decided, you are so stern, so coldly conscientious, and yet--who woke this love in my frozen heart? Who implored me to prolong my stay in Germany? Who increased my passion by a thousand sweet nothings? Was it not you, who now reject me?"

"Alas! my wretched frivolity, it punishes me heavily," he murmured, with a deep sigh; "but as it has brought me to this pass, it shall at least lead me no further."

He tried to rise, but she still clung to him. "Do you no longer love me?" she cried, bursting into tears.

"Yes, my heart is glowing with love for you!" he exclaimed, clasping her in his arms. "But shall I become unprincipled because I have been thoughtless? Because I have taken peace from your heart, shall I rob you of a quiet conscience? Because ennui and ignoble desires have led me to form an unworthy friendship with D'Anneaud, your mindless, heartless husband, shall I now become traitor to his honor and my own?"

"Go, then," murmured the beautiful woman, removing her arms,--"go, if you have the strength to do so."

"You give me the power yourself, for you do not understand me. The more firmly you cling to me, the more surely my nobler being finds the strength to escape you. I am aware that I have two natures within me: one longs for you, but the other turns resolutely away, and at this moment solemnizes its greatest, most agonizing victory, since it compels me to resign you. Yes, its most *agonizing* victory," he repeated, clasping the angry woman to his heart with passionate love. "You weep, but my very heart is bleeding, beautiful, lovely woman; no tongue can express what I suffer."

For a moment they stood with their lips clinging together; at last with a violent effort he tore himself from her embrace and rushed out of the room without another word.

"Henri!" she cried, faintly.

In vain: Henri ran down the staircase, sprang into his carriage, and shouted to the coachman, "To Ottmarsfeld!"

Ottmarsfeld, Heinrich von Ottmar's family estate, where he lived alone with his servants, was a two hours' drive from the capital. While within the limits of the city Heinrich looked incessantly back towards the tempting house, but when the carriage rolled through the gate he wrapped himself in his cloak and sank into a profound reverie.

The keen night air blew sharply upon him, and he shrank back into one corner of the carriage with a shiver. The trees along the highway towered stiff and bare in the darkness. Now and then one of the horses shied at the sight of some strange shadow. A muttered oath and the crack of the whip followed, then all was silent again except the regular beat of the hoofs as the horses trotted forward. *Heinrich's* heated fancy compared this cold, ghostly drive with the hour he had spent in the elegant perfumed boudoir, by the side of the fair, frivolous Parisienne. He closed his eyes to shut out the surrounding gloom, and conjured up the statues, flowers, and the moment when the graceful, weeping woman reclined before him on the silken causeuse.

"I am a fool," he said to himself; "to what phantom am I sacrificing myself? What object, what reward, can I hope for in return for my superhuman self-denial? None, save curses from the lips which offered me blissful happiness, and tears of sorrow in my own eyes. Yes, she was right. Who will lose anything if we are happy? Shall the fairest hours of my youth pass away in consuming, unsatisfied longing?--shall I allow my studies to suffer from this secret struggle, and draw upon myself the disgrace of failing in the examination? Are all these things outweighed by the imaginary duty imposed upon me by the title of friend, with which I have honored her fool of a husband, and whose violation he will notice as little as the most conscientious fulfillment of it? Will they be outweighed by the preservation of one's self-respect, and is not this, after all, a matter of opinion?--is it not a sort of coquetting with one's self? What will all my self-esteem avail, if the world calls me a simpleton because, under the ban of my passion, I neglected my studies and social interests? If I am pointed at as an incapable man, shall I not sink in my own eyes?" His blood grew more and more fevered as his reason coldly analyzed what a short time before had seemed to him an inviolable duty. The moral stand which he had taken in his conversation with Madame d'Anneaud was not sufficiently powerful to protect, him from the relapse which had now come. "I shall never rest," he thought, "until the beautiful woman is *mine*, then only I shall be myself again! My father always said that we could find no better way of defending ourselves against the power a woman obtains over our hearts than by degrading her. How the cold, shrewd man of the world would laugh if he were alive, and could see how I am toiling to keep this woman in a position from which she herself wishes to descend!--if he could see how my love hallows one who does not desire to be held sacred! And her husband! Well, if he discovers it I would give him satisfaction by a few ounces of blood, and none of my acquaintances would despise me for the scandal half as much as I might perhaps despise myself."

He drew out his watch: he would turn back if there was still time. It was too late: it was already past the hour when he could see Madame d'Anneaud alone. He clinched his teeth and hid his face in his cloak, as if shivering from a feverish chill. The carriage entered a thick wood, and at last stopped before a large iron gate.

"You are ill, Herr Baron," said the old valet de chambre as Heinrich entered the castle, trembling violently.

"Yes, yes, I feel very ill," he replied, passing an to his sleeping-room to wait with burning impatience for the following day, which would afford him an opportunity to atone for his previous reserve in the arms of the beautiful Madame d'Anneaud. But the next morning brought a farewell letter from the lovely Parisienne, who informed him that she should return at once to her home in France. It was written with all the pride and anger of a woman who has experienced the deepest possible humiliation; who, having offered more than was desired or accepted, now wishes to make amends for her too great willingness to yield by a double measure of coldness and harshness. The youth of twenty was still too great a novice in a woman's words to perceive that this cold reserve had as little real foundation as the pride from which it sprung, and which with such ladies too often supplies the place of true honor. Heinrich was hopelessly crushed, and as everything that is denied us doubly excites our desires, the indignant woman who had cast him off was far more charming in his eyes than when she had pleaded for his love. Remorse and passion strove in his heart with all the fury of the hot blood of twenty. It was the first connection of such a nature that

Heinrich had ever formed, the first great feeling of his life. Such periods, with their secret resolutions, are those in which the elements of the inner life are analyzed, separated from each other, or harmoniously blended. They are the standard for the guidance of the whole life.

Heinrich von Ottmar had been educated entirely without love. His mother died before he reached his fifth year; his father, a heartless aristocrat, was Grand Steward of the Court of the Principality of H----, where Heinrich was now to commence his career, and all the efforts of the haughty, ambitious noble were directed solely to the one object of inoculating his son with the ideas which, as he believed, had made him great, and might prepare a similar destiny for Heinrich. He was one of those tyrannical persons who make even those they wish to benefit unhappy, because they take no account of individuality, and compel the victim of their anxiety to be happy, not in *his own*, but *their* way. He brought only discord into *Heinrich's* young soul, which was already sympathetically attracted by the development of the times, for while he succeeded on one hand in rousing and directing it entirely towards one object,--that of obtaining power and position on the loftiest heights of society,--he could not suppress his leaning towards the struggles for freedom peculiar to the times, which were an abomination to the man whose inclinations tended towards ultramontanism. Here also, influenced by the illusion that everything could be done by force, there were many violent scenes, in which he threatened the young defenseless boy with expulsion from his home, a father's curse, and disinheritance. But no opinions are changed, no convictions uprooted, by menaces and blows; they are at most forced to conceal themselves where it is impossible to struggle with them. Heinrich accustomed himself *to be silent* and to *dissimulate* at an age when he was incapable of understanding the moral wrong and evil of these qualities. Thus, under this father's tyrannical sway, every budding germ of manly truth was suffocated, and shot forth unavailingly. There are two results from such a course of training. When the parental authority asserts itself also in the petty details and interests of life, a most independent and rugged character is often developed, firmly determined to exchange a hated, tyrannical present for a free future, however dark it may be. This was not the case with Heinrich von Ottmar; on the contrary, his worldly-wise father allowed him full liberty in all the trifles on which youth sets so high a value,--greater liberty than a more conscientious man would have done. He knew how to make his home-life pleasant enough to him, induce him to fear expulsion from it as the greatest misfortune; thus he always retained his influence, and the youth, spoiled by the glitter and pleasures of life, bore the intellectual tyranny of his father because it allowed the most unlimited personal freedom, and learned to yield and submit. He was naturally generous and warmhearted, capable of enthusiasm for everything good and beautiful; but under these circumstances only his intellectual, not his moral, powers could develop, and his affections were forced to pine for the lack of food. But his hot blood asserted its rights, and as it found in his soul no lofty ideal against which its strong, youthful waves might dash, it lost itself in the broad, shallow stream of sensuality. His father held the opinion that there could be nothing more disadvantageous, more injurious to the thinker, as well as to the man of the world, than a deep feeling; and as he desired to make his son both, if possible, he wished to save him from the evil. He also knew that there is no better protection from it than the habit of frivolous, careless intercourse with insignificant natures, and therefore cheerfully endured this phase of *Heinrich's* character. He had no esteem for women himself, and it seemed to him a matter of indifference if the impulsive youth turned where favors were granted most speedily, and where he unconsciously lost his reverence for the sex. Thus the blinded father, with his inexorable sternness on the one side, converted a noble, many-sided nature into an ambiguous, varying character, and, by his unprincipled indulgence on the other hand, transformed a heart-craving love into a disposition of unbridled license; and when, in *Heinrich's* nineteenth year, he closed his eyes, he left his son entangled in a confusion of inextricable contradictions, with an incomprehensible impulse towards goodness and beauty in his breast, and without any compass to enable him to obtain them, *desiring* the right with the yet undestroyed power of a noble nature, but defrauded of the power of *doing* it; in spite of his father's influence a philanthropist, and through it an egotist. Thus he was a mystery to himself, whose solution he expected to find in life, not suspecting with what sacrifice he should be compelled to purchase it. Tortured by this secret conflict, he sought refuge and support in science, and devoted himself to the study of political law. He was too deeply imbued with the spirit of the times to find satisfaction for his ambition solely in the prerogatives of the nobility and a mere court office. True, he desired a position near the throne, but it must be one which should have some political importance, and deal not only with the organization of the court, but of the state. This was the highest aim which appeared before him, and he labored with honest zeal to reach it. Then he made the acquaintance of Madame d'Anneaud, who was visiting a married relative in H----. She was the first highly cultured woman he had ever known, and the impression made by her beauty, united to the polished manners and dainty coquetry of an aristocratic Parisienne, exerted an intoxicating influence over the mind and imagination of the young man. Her sudden departure inflamed his passion to the highest pitch; but in order to approach the beautiful woman he had formed a friendship with her husband, and the very bond which had brought the lovers together now formed a wall of separation between them. To mislead the wife of a confiding, unsuspicious friend was an act of dishonor from which his skeptical reason recoiled. In this conflict month after month elapsed in idleness. It was the year in which he was preparing for his examination; he felt that he should fail if he did not conquer his inertness and return to his studies. He had been too long accustomed to receive all the favors of love to be able to endure a hopeless wish and longing for any length of time. He must either possess Madame d'Anneaud or avoid her. He had chosen the latter ere he knew how difficult it would be to deny himself anything he ardently desired. He wished to do right; but when he felt the bitterness of such self-denial his strength to carry out the impulse failed, for he was already far too great an egotist to make any sacrifice, and without sacrifice there is no virtue.

Thus his first victory over himself was transformed into a defeat when Madame d'Anneaud's implacable letter robbed him of the ground on which he expected to enjoy with her the fruits of a shameful peace. Now, as he fancied, he had lost all, committed a wrong both against his beloved and himself, for which he must strive to atone with all the energy of passion. He drove into the city to see Madame d'Anneaud, but she refused to admit him. He wrote a despairing note and sent it to her by a confidential waiting-maid, but it was returned with the seal unbroken.

He spent three days in the most terrible excitement. The blood coursed madly through his veins; his brain burned and whirled with plans to regain the lost one and prevent her return to Paris. On the third Monsieur d'Anneaud called to bid him farewell, complaining bitterly of the caprices of his wife, who had suddenly dismissed her whole household, would see no one, and wished to set off at once for Paris. Everything around him grew dim as he heard these words; his heart throbbed as if it would burst, and when his friend had taken leave he turned deadly pale and sank exhausted upon the sofa. Now for the first time he felt what, in the suspense of the last few days, he had not heeded, that he was ill; but he dared not yield to it. Madame d'Anneaud was to set out that very evening. The thought drove him back to the city, that he might at least watch her window and witness her departure. She saw him, and as she entered her carriage cast a long and, as it appeared to him, sorrowful glance at him.

He returned to the castle wild with despair. What was he to do now, follow her, perhaps to be again repulsed? sacrifice his scientific studies at the decisive time of the examination to rush around Paris imploring love, perchance in vain? It seemed too useless and degrading for him to resolve upon it without further reflection. He strove with superhuman exertion to busy himself in his work; in vain, his thoughts refused to obey his will. Day and night he sat over his books, gazing with burning eyes and bewildered brain at the letters, to him so unmeaning and disconnected, while the maddest longing raged in his panting breast. In this torturing, mental struggle his bodily health failed more and more; the illness which he had felt ever since his first great emotion made itself the more apparent the less he spared himself. At last he yielded, and became the prey of a most violent feverish attack. The physician who was summoned shrugged his shoulders thoughtfully, for the young man's condition afforded every symptom that nervous fever was to be apprehended.

II
DUAL APPARITIONS

The fever increased day by day. Heinrich became very delirious and required incessant watching. On one of his worst nights the nurse, overpowered by fatigue, fell asleep. The patient seemed to become more quiet for a few minutes, and gazed with half-closed eyes at the dull glimmer of the night-lamp. For a time in his stupefaction followed a fixed train of ideas,--it was the conflict between duty and inclination which had made him so ill. His imagination incessantly painted pictures which his conscience destroyed. He lamented that he did not possess that thoughtless frivolity which receives every enjoyment as a gift from the loving Father, without doubt, struggle, or conflict with what we term conscience, duty, honor. "Oh, God! Thou who hast given me life," he murmured, "what didst thou bestow in putting me under the dominion of a power which feeds upon the blood of my murdered joys, and absorbs the sweetest marrow of this existence! The only happy natures are those which can so divide intellect and feeling that they can no longer bias each other. Oh, would that I might also!"

Amid such thoughts be fell into that feverish, half slumber in which dreams and reality are often so strangely blended. We know that we are in bed, know that we are dreaming, and yet cannot prevent the creations of our fancy from appearing before us, surrounding us like substantial forms, and arbitrarily forcing their existence upon us. Such was the case with Heinrich. His mind was busily weaving the torn threads of his thoughts into fairy-like figures, at first quaint like arabesques, but by degrees revealing a strange secret connection. The faces became more and more distinct as his consciousness of the outside world grew dim. He still felt vaguely that egotism and ideality were waging a fierce battle in his heart, and by degrees the ideal he could no longer think of in the abstract assumed a bodily form. There seemed to be something in the room which terrified him,--something that crawled and glided over the floor. "Do not fear," it whispered hypocritically. "I do not come to destroy but to aid. I am the impulse of self-preservation, and when in aristocratic society I cultivate my mind and call myself Egotism." The shape writhed and glided nearer, while over *Heinrich's* head sounded a melodious yet powerful rustling of wings, and a voice from above rang like the low notes of an organ, "Fear not, I am the Genius of the Ideal, and will save you."

Heinrich gasped for breath, he feared the whispering, ghostly apparitions that surrounded him, his breast and neck seemed bound with heavy cords, he strove to cry out but his voice refused to obey him, he tried to open his eyes but in vain; he only felt the overmastering presence of the two original elements of humanity, and his ear thrilled at their words. "See what cowardly monsters you men are!" laughed the fiend on the floor. "You carry hideous forms within you and think you imperiously rule them, but recoil in horror when you have conjured them from the secret depths of your hearts. I was nearer to you when in your own breast than I am now, yet you fostered and cherished me; now that I appear before you, you fear me."

The voice above murmured: "Compose yourself, we are only the powers you have felt struggling within your soul, but now we have united in the common object of gratifying your wishes, for your folly will never be satisfied until you perceive the vanity of your desires. Your wishes shall be fulfilled, that you may learn to perceive in what the end of life and true happiness consist."

"Oh, mighty beings!" groaned Heinrich, "we are so proud of what we accomplish by your aid, and yet it is we who serve you while you do everything. What sustains us, that in our weakness we do not fall helpless victims to one or the other of you?"

"The Hand which rules over all things and appoints to each its bounds," answered the Genius of the Ideal. "It has so wisely apportioned the powers of evil that we exert an equal influence over the human race. As the law of attraction holds worlds in their courses, our opposing strength maintains the right balance in your minds if all the elements are properly blended; but sometimes that is not the case, then your lives take their direction from the strongest, for spirit strives towards spiritual things, outweighs the earthly nature, releases itself from the world, and follows my guidance above."

"But the earthly nature tends towards the earth," grinned Egotism, "and more frequently you sink down."

"Thus," said both, "you human beings preserve the equilibrium between mind and matter,--therefore you can neither withdraw from the world," cried Egotism,--"nor be dragged down by it," said the Genius of the Ideal.

"Oh, you are right!" murmured Heinrich; "but I have lost this equilibrium."

"You have not lost it," replied the Genius of the Ideal, "the divine and earthly natures are striving in you with equal power: that you may not arbitrarily crush either, we wish to *separate*. You shall lead a twofold life. Passion shall not disturb intellect, and intellect shall not destroy pleasure."

"Yes, yes," cried Heinrich, eagerly, "has the dear God sent you to me to bestow the whole precious substance of life? How has such favor fallen to my lot?"

"You will learn some day that God has reserved greater mercies than these," was the reply.

"And now, you crawling creature, what do you want here while this divine being is holding converse with me?" said Heinrich, proudly.

"You will henceforth have little use for *him*," replied Egotism; "it is *my* service you need first, and *I* must gratify your wishes. I am a merry companion: you need not shun me. I appear in constantly varying forms: now a usurer paying like a hardened miser, now an elegant spendthrift throwing money away with lavish hands; now secretly murdering a helpless enemy, now wrapping myself in the shining armor of duty and slaying thousands; now with an honest, enthusiastic manner gliding through the darkness to the innocent young maiden, ruling over hearts and nations, kneeling before thrones and altars,--who knows all the myriad forms I assume? If the spirit above your head did not work against me, the world would be filled with my masks. Where the heart and intellect are equal I prosper least, for then man is a harmonious creature, as his Maker intended. Still, I often succeed in separating them, and then my power is strengthened. It shall be so with you. Soul, divide into two portions! Part, mind and feeling, move asunder and form two wholes! Heinrich, have your wish, possess a double nature with a mind destitute of sensibility, and a soulless heart."

Heinrich's breast heaved violently, his heart throbbed with redoubled speed, every vein swelled to bursting. Pleasure and pain thrilled his frame; by degrees something within him seemed to be tearing itself away, inexpressible grief overwhelmed him. A voice in his heart murmured, "Farewell." "Farewell," answered every nerve; the chasm in his soul yawned wider, as if a burning wound had passed through his nature. Tears of inexplicable sorrow gushed from his eyes, and a cry of agony at last burst from his lips as he felt that he was leaving his body. He now stood face to face with *himself*, exchanging glances of astonishment. All anguish was over, and he felt free and careless. "I have been born again!" he cried, in delight.

But the Genius of the Ideal answered,--"You have only divided your nature. Your desire is accomplished, and will last until you no longer wish it. Woe betide you if you remain in this condition and no longer call upon me for aid! Egotism has produced this separation, he will henceforth be your companion; cold reason and coarse sensuality will make you their prey. But if from beautiful eyes the pure ray of a noble soul falls upon you, let it enter your heart, it is I who command it to shine upon you. If an earnest voice strikes upon your ear in tones of warning, heed it, it is I who speak to you; and if you are at last convinced that everything done and enjoyed without me is empty, turn to me and I will guide you back to the source of happiness." Then turning to the divided natures, the vision cried "Be friends; you are now two forms, but you possess but one life, therefore remain at peace, and take my blessing," exclaimed Egotism. "Enjoy," he cried, turning to sensuality. "Attain," he said to intellect. "But remember," said the Genius of the Ideal, "that the end of life is neither to enjoy nor obtain, but to be useful and accomplish good works." With these words the apparitions disappeared.

The two shapes were alone. The first at last broke the silence. "I shall dub myself *Henri*, that is what Madame d'Anneaud used to call me, and French names give one better luck with women."

"I will remain *Heinrich*," said the other.

"Give me your hand!" exclaimed *Henri*. "I will enjoy for you, you shall labor for me, and when I am about to commit an act of folly you can warn me." So saying be merrily compared himself with his image. "I don't doubt that we shall make our fortune. To be useful and accomplish good works the object of life! Bah the object of life is to be happy, and only success and pleasure can give happiness. 'For *myself*,' is henceforth my motto!"

"And mine," cried Heinrich: "it is the only sound philosophy."

Just then the nurse awoke, and sprang from his chair in terror, for his patient was not in bed, but standing before his long dressing-glass, looking into it and talking to his reflected image in the greatest excitement. It was with the utmost difficulty that he would allow himself to be led away from the mirror and put to bed. His delirium had reached its height, and showed him the true state of his own soul in the form of an allegory. That which his reason had never been able to solve was depicted before him in bodily form, by the divining power of the instincts of feverish hallucinations; and thus this vision was the true picture of his life, and the separation he had witnessed only the symbol of his own secret struggles.

After three months of great suffering, Ottmar at last recovered, but so slowly that the physician forbade him to resume his studies, and advised him to seek health and diversion for his thoughts in travel.

As he heard that Madame d'Anneaud was still living in Paris, he hastened thither to resume his former relations with her. But here, for the first time, the signs of his twofold nature became apparent. The glittering, alluring form in which materialism clothes itself on the one hand, intellectual suggestions on the other hand, and French frivolity, did not fail to produce their effect. The man of reason and sensuality developed such rude contrasts of character that he became what he had beheld in his dream, *"Heinrich"* the cold thinker, and *"Henri"* the careless *bon vivant* in one person, changing as often and as suddenly as if they were two separate individuals forced to inhabit the same body. He was proud of this transformation, for he could now enjoy and obtain everything: but happy he was not. The same thing befell Ottmar that has happened to so many others in whom the strange wonder of a secret rupture has taken place. Where intellect reigned it required only cold knowledge and understanding; where feeling ruled it degenerated into a burning fire, which, when the moment of extinction arrived, left nothing but emptiness and indifference. Thus by turns both extremes took possession of the pliant body, and his beautiful features, gradually moulding themselves according to the division in the soul, now bore the impress of the astute thinker, and anon the winning charm of the lover. He possessed one of those temperaments at which one gazes as a "marvel of genius," which exert an alluring charm over women, who perceive in them a "demoniac spell," a tempting enigma which irresistibly occupies their thoughts, but in whose solution many a woman's heart has slowly bled to death.

At the same time he was what the world calls a man of honor. As social integrity may be a result of cleverness, he never allowed himself to be in fault in his civil or social position, for there the intellectual *Heinrich* ruled. The errors which the sensual, elegant *Henri* secretly committed, if detected, were not ascribed to him. There were and are too many such natures for society not to stretch its very relative standard of morality for the sake of their good qualities.

Everywhere he was the centre of interest,--sought, petted, and honored. His many-sided character attracted the most opposite temperaments; yet he was unhappy, life was shallow and wearisome.

There is an invisible something, on which human happiness depends. We have soul organs, by means of which we receive and impart the inner world of sensuous feeling,--organs which we call organs of the heart; and those of *Henri* were very active when passion was once aroused. We have also organs to unite us with the spiritual world,--organs of thought,--and *Heinrich* possessed them in the highest perfection. But we have besides these an organ that forms the bond between the other two, like a connecting vein, through which the streams of thought and feeling flow into each other, and which carries the mingled tide through the entire being. This is the emotional nature. Where the heart and intellect are not peculiarly disunited, the emotional nature must exert an influence; it is the organ by means of which we make our simple every-day life pleasant, endurable, if possible poetical. This tie between the heart and intellect was of course torn asunder by the division that had taken place in Ottmar, and thus he not only felt painfully the eternal dissatisfaction of both natures, but quiet every-day life lost all charm and value, and found him cold and unsympathizing. He desired great contrasts, great passions, or great problems. It was only when these occupied his thoughts that the two extremes of his nature could assert themselves. Then only he felt at ease.

Henri sought the material pleasures, which are always the same, and always result in emptiness. *Heinrich* unceasingly pursued the course of ambition, which is ever renewed just as we believe we have reached the goal. Between the two Ottmar found nothing but satiety. He now had what he had so eagerly desired,--two lives, two natures, in one person. True, he could no longer suffer, but neither could he enjoy; he could neither love nor hate. *Henri's* feelings were only instincts, and his thoughts the refinement of sensuality; to which *Heinrich* sometimes lent a loftier language when in the presence of noble women, in whom his shallow frivolity would have excited only repugnance. Ottmar, as on the night of his delirium, fancied, with vain satisfaction, that he had been born again; but he had, in truth, only divided himself. It seemed to him as if he possessed a twofold nature, and must now enjoy life doubly. But the law of true humanity cannot be denied without rebuke. He had erred. Instead of two natures there were only two disjointed halves; instead of enjoying a double share, he enjoyed but half, for what pleased *Henri Heinrich* did not feel, and what *Heinrich* obtained was useless to *Henri*.

This was not yet clear to Ottmar. He only knew that the apparitions had given what he desired, and did not understand why he was not happy. He had not comprehended their sneers, like all who, in the impetuous whirl of life, hear the prophetic voices of their own breasts, and first understand them when their predictions begin to be fulfilled.

In Paris, Ottmar gave free course to his inclinations, and for some time lived in intimate relations with Madame d'Anneaud. But the beautiful woman soon became wearisome to him, and he deserted her for a fairer face, for faith, as a matter of course, had become an impossibility to this nature.

Then he hurried from face to face, exhausting one empty pleasure after another, until at last, after a year of idle dissipation, ambition obtained the upper hand, and intellect asserted its claims. He would, as he said, try philosophy for a time, and returned to Germany. Another life now began. "Quick! You must do something,--accomplish something," he said to himself. "But how? of what nature?" In the whirl of empty pleasures he had become too superficial and frivolous to recommence his neglected scientific studies with the redoubled industry which, after so long an interruption, they required; he could no longer adopt any regular profession. By means of his great ability, favored by his position, he did and learned what and where he pleased. As he began too much at the same time, he acquired nothing thoroughly, and obtained that so-called cosmopolitan education which dabbles in all colors, is skilled in all branches, whose variety often excites admiration, but cannot be of any practical value. For five years he visited universities, heard lectures from the most distinguished professors, and passed in review the various sciences. None satisfied him, for none aided him to reach the goal of his ambition with sufficient rapidity.

At last the years of his early youth passed away, and he had as yet obtained nothing. Insignificant fellow-students went out into the world to enter upon the honorable career of government service, while he did not even know to what branch it would be best to devote himself in order to become a man of mark.

He wrote several semi-scientific, semi-poetical works. The critics acknowledged their merit, but they were not read. The scientific portion was too commonplace for learned men, the poetry too dry for ordinary people; for, in spite of his genius, *Heinrich* was no poet. His nature lacked that which alone can carry away the masses, and which no thought can supply,--heart impulse; and he did not succeed in becoming popular. An earnest, uninterrupted course of study would, in a very short time, have made him competent to enter upon some settled career; but too frequently *Heinrich's* assiduous industry yielded to *Henri's* pursuit of pleasure, and the wearied frame threatened to give way under this constant change from one extreme to the other.

When he had at last exhausted all the intellectual and material treasures of his native land without the slightest profit to himself, some secret power again drove him forth to seek in a foreign country the happiness he could not find at home. He went to Italy.

III
FROM FALSEHOOD TO FALSEHOOD

On the way to Rome he met a gentleman whose striking appearance attracted his attention. *Heinrich* thought he had never seen a handsomer and at the same time more intellectual countenance, and a conversation arose between them which greatly interested *Heinrich*, and very soon led him to make disclosures about himself and his course of life, to which the stranger listened with an attention extremely flattering to Ottmar's self-love, and entered, with affable condescension, into every subject introduced by the latter. He appeared to be so familiar with every sphere of life, all the relations of European courts, that *Heinrich* took him for a diplomat, and eagerly gathered up all the information he communicated, because it always bore the stamp of accurate, positive knowledge. But the stranger had so much noble enthusiasm, his language was often so eloquent, that *Heinrich* frequently felt tempted to think him an artist, and his curiosity increased more and more when he baffled, with consummate skill, every effort to turn the conversation upon himself. The hours flew by *Heinrich* like the scenes through which he was passing, but he noticed nothing to which the stranger did not call his attention. He had eyes and ears only for him. He knew not which he most admired,--the comprehensive knowledge of society, the elegant modes of expression, or the aristocratic, yet winning, manners of this mysterious man. The latter himself felt an increasing interest in his young companion, and when the gigantic dome of Saint Peter's rose before them *Heinrich* eagerly expressed his regret that the delightful journey was over.

"Will you seek me out in Rome?" asked the stranger.

"Most gladly!" cried *Heinrich*, with delight.

"Very well; then promise me to come to-morrow after early mass."

"Certainly; but how shall I find you?"

"Ask for Father Severinus, the Prefect of the Collegium Germanicum."

Heinrich gazed at him in unconcealed amazement.

"You are----"

"A Jesuit," said the priest, laughing; and left *Heinrich* to his speechless astonishment.

The short disenchantment the latter experienced very soon yielded to redoubled admiration for the remarkable things this man had accomplished in spite of the narrow sphere to which he was limited by his position as a priest. His father's predilection for the Jesuits recurred to his mind, and many tales of the wondrous labors and successes of this order no longer seemed so incredible and exaggerated as before. He felt a desire to know more of the institution which cultivated such remarkable charms of mind and person, and did not fail to go to the Casa al Gesu the following day. The reception he met with far surpassed all his anticipations.

Father Severinus introduced him to the other chiefs of the order, and when at last the General himself requested him to pay him a visit there was not a single point in which *Heinrich's* vanity was not flattered and his curiosity excited to the utmost.

The visit to the General ended with an invitation to dinner, and during the meal the latter appointed a certain day upon which *Heinrich* should be his guest every week.

Ottmar had never before been so well entertained among men, and soon found himself nowhere so agreeably situated as when with Father Severinus and his companions. The holy fathers procured for him every pleasure that a stranger can enjoy in a new place. They showed him an admirable selection of the glories of Rome, afforded him an opportunity to see many curiosities which are usually inaccessible to strangers, were always at hand when he needed them, and did not appear to be in the world when he did not require their services. Under their guidance he obtained a sight of the treasures in the library of the Vatican, and they also afforded him a glimpse of their own archives; but as soon as his desire for knowledge was excited, and he wished to penetrate farther, the interesting matter was withdrawn because it was allowed only to the actual adherents of Jesuitism. Yet the fathers imparted much confidential and extremely useful information, by means of which they gave him to understand that they were in possession of still more important secrets, into which, however, only actual students of the institution, whose loyalty to the order had been severely tested, could be initiated.

Heinrich at last could not resist inquiring into the conditions upon which he might be considered a tried servant of the order and be permitted to share these favors. For their agents in the world, these consisted of a novitiate of one year for the trial and practice of obedience, and another year of voluntary residence and study in the college. As he already knew more than was taught in the Germanicum and Propaganda, he, of course, did not think of going through a school course; but the thought entered his mind that at the cost of a novitiate, which he already perceived would not be too strict, he could obtain information which might be of the greatest use to him in his career. He did not doubt that no one knew the world and mankind better than the all-observant, inquiring Jesuits; and they did not neglect to represent the principal European states and courts as a department of their restless and manifold branches of labor. He was assured that he could graduate from no better school of diplomacy than the quiet Jesuit convent, and it seemed to him well worth the trouble of shutting himself up here for a year, to emerge such a brilliant personage as his admired Severinus. The priests gave him plainly to understand that his novitiate would be only a name, for they had too much knowledge of human nature to repel a young man of the world, like Ottmar, by the prospect of monastic austerities. This promised indulgence was by no means contrary to the rules of the order, since Ottmar was not to be trained for priesthood, but the world, and therefore must be considered as a guest rather than a pupil of the Germanicum. He possessed the entire confidence of the fathers, for first from courtesy to his hospitable hosts, and afterwards from prudence, he had been silent in regard to his differences of opinion, but showed a sincere appreciation of some of their institutions, which they naturally mistook for devotion to the order. The principal reason was that his father was known to have been a devout Catholic, a circumstance which so completely deceived the holy fathers, that *Heinrich* had no occasion to do anything but keep silence and submit patiently to the rules of the order to enjoy all the advantages of this rare confidence. The temptation was too great, he had been too long accustomed to yield to every caprice, every fancy, to be punctilious about the concessions of his own convictions he would be compelled to make, and decided to enter the Casa al Gesu. The Jesuits were extremely delighted with their new conquest; for they hoped to make the unusually gifted young man an agent for Germany, particularly the Protestant court of H----, which had hitherto been closed against their influence. They willingly acceded to *Heinrich's* desire to enter the college under another name; for it was of importance to them that his stay should remain unknown, that he might afterwards act in their cause with fewer impediments.

Thus the first step was taken on the path of deceit which his blind egotism considered the speediest road to the goal, and upon which a man always enters when he lacks the self-denial to make his opinions his rule of conduct. Many a favorite of fortune is a miserable egotist, and passes for a man of honor only because his fate has never chanced to bring him in conflict with his selfishness; had such been the case he would quickly have lost his cheaply-won fame. Thus it fared with *Heinrich* at a time when his acts and conduct were not yet burdened with any responsibility or visible result. His proceeding had no objective importance because he had not as yet gained any influence as a public character, or formed any political relations. In his view he committed no treason against the party to which in his own mind, though not formally, he belonged, by depriving it for another year of the man who was nothing to it. The point in question did not concern an actual change of opinion,--for when he once entered the world he would be faithful to his long-chosen colors,--but the attainment of a purely personal advantage. It did not occur to his inexperienced mind that, as a member of the party, he would be responsible to his followers not only for his future but the past. He did not shrink from abusing the confidence of the holy fathers, because he thought himself morally justified in using for his own advantage men who merely wished to make him a source of profit to themselves. It was doubtless repugnant to him to feign a faith he did not possess, but he was filled with admiration for various different individuals of the order, always felt happy with them, and in truth was indifferent to what religion they belonged, for he had, as previously mentioned, the toleration of carelessness. To him all confession was a mere phenomenon of historical culture. The pious exercises were empty pantomimes, on whose performance nothing depended except the approval of the fathers, and they were all the easier because he had grown up among Catholic ceremonies. The political and social influence of the Jesuits he considered too feeble for him to fear that he should ever be placed in a situation where he would be compelled to oppose it. But he was to learn too late how terribly he had erred.

Thus his novitiate began, and what he had once undertaken he carried into execution most persistently. He appeared to be a most obedient, zealous pupil, and succeeded in blinding the good fathers so completely that, to serve their own ends, they gave him instruction in everything that could win him esteem at courts,--the most accurate information about all personal and diplomatic relations, the royal families, reports made by the emissaries of the Jesuits in every country, a quantity of secrets whose judicious use must procure him a great influence, and, in short, impressed their whole sophistical moral teachings upon his mind. But with these things, so important to him, he learned something which was to destroy the anticipated result of their efforts,--to undervalue the order more and more. The more equivocal and selfish these motives seemed to him, the more he thought himself justified in deceiving them and casting aside the claims of gratitude. He perceived with terror what an influence the Jesuits exerted over everything; how relentlessly, with a thousand weapons, they subdued everything that he numbered among the greatest intellectual blessings in the world. The farther he penetrated into their mysteries the greater his repugnance became, and the more distinctly he saw the wide gulf which lay between him and Jesuitism.

When the first year of study was drawing to a close, he formed the resolution to seize upon the first good pretext to release himself from the distasteful bonds into which, with youthful carelessness, he had entered. He did not wish to burden himself with any further obligations, which he now knew he should never discharge. But he was too familiar with the power to which he had committed himself, not to be aware that an open breach with the Jesuits might make his career impossible, perhaps destroy his whole future. Therefore it seemed to him unavoidable to keep friends with them for the present, and under his father's authority he had already learned to submit to such "necessities."

Thus he must find a pretext which would apparently compel him to sacrifice the second year of study and leave the Casa al Gesu before its commencement. The moment was favorable to him. It happened that the government of H---- took certain decisive steps against the Jesuits' intended settlement in that principality, which aroused the greatest excitement among the whole order. *Heinrich* took advantage of this opportunity. With remarkable address he induced the fathers to send him to H---- in order to ascertain the actual state of affairs, and in their interests begin as quickly as possible the career for which they considered him sufficiently mature. The expectations which the priests placed upon him justified this step; for he had increased and strengthened them by an act which usually requires the greatest readiness for self-sacrifice, he had at the expiration of his novitiate presented to the order a sum of ten thousand thalers. The holy fathers did not suspect that it was the payment by which he wished to relieve his conscience from every burden of gratitude, that with it he paid for his residence and instruction as he would have defrayed the expenses of his studies at a university, because, as a man of aristocratic disposition, he wished to be in debt for nothing. So they took for an act of devotion what was really an effort to obtain moral freedom, and their confidence in the man who had made such a sacrifice for them became as great as is possible for the cautious, circumspect Jesuits. So they allowed him to set out.

"Become a diplomat and act for us; practice the arts of the world to serve the cause of Heaven," they said, when they bade him farewell. And he thought, with a sarcastic smile, "I will become a diplomat not to serve Heaven, but myself." On returning to his home, his rank and striking character made it easy for him to begin a diplomatic career.

The government of H---- was Protestant and liberal. He therefore carefully concealed the fact of his stay in the Jesuit college, and, with his large means, succeeded in a few years in raising himself to a lofty position. He became councillor of the legation, a friend of the minister, a favorite at court, and now stood upon the height from which he could begin to discharge his debt to the order, and the admonition was not delayed. The point in question, of course, related to procuring admittance into the country for, and also extending the privileges of, the ubiquitous Jesuits.

Ottmar was to introduce these claims--and did not. The moment had arrived when he must break with the order openly and forever. Now, for the first time, he perceived the danger resulting from the step. Ought he to become the representative of a faith which he denied, and during his stay in Rome had found utterly irreconcilable with his opinions? Was it to become the shibboleth, which would betray the earlier associations he had so carefully concealed, perhaps forever crush his aspirations to obtain a portfolio in the government of H----? At this price the year of study in the college had been too dearly bought. Should he, on the other hand, forfeit the powerful assistance of the Jesuits, and make unrelenting enemies where he had formerly possessed trusting friends?

The outward advantages of the two courses to be chosen seemed tolerably equal; his convictions of right must turn the scale, and did so. In vain were the more and more vehement warnings that followed. He wished to make the unfettered tendency of his intellect the guide of his life, and deserted the teachings and struggles of the order; for there still remained in him a remnant of that feeling of duty which commands men to oppose what they consider false and pernicious.

But vengeance was not delayed.

Heinrich soon felt that his position in the government and at court was no longer the same. While hitherto, from the prince down to his humblest subject, the greatest respect, even admiration, had been paid him, he now suddenly found himself eyed distrustfully, and even avoided, without being able to discover a reason. Formerly no important measure had been taken upon which the minister had not privately requested his counsel, now the latter enveloped himself in a cloak of cold reserve. Thus days and weeks elapsed, leaving him in a most distasteful position.

But one person at the court remained the same towards him: his patroness, the niece of the widowed prince, Princess Ottilie, an ethereal vision, who combined the haughty grace of a born aristocrat with the charms of a feeling soul. In her he possessed a true friend, whom he honored as a higher being; nay, he was often inclined to believe he loved her, although not even the faintest wish to possess her had ever arisen in his mind. All real merit was attracted to the princess, and she won every one by her poetic mind and clear intellect, as well as the charms of her maidenly character, although she had already passed her first youth. She had distinguished Ottmar beyond all others at the court, but for some time she had been unable to receive him. It was reported that Ottilie was ill, and in his very uncomfortable situation he was totally bereft of counsel and consolation.

IV
A GUARDIAN ANGEL

At last a court ball was given, and *Henri*,--for it was *Henri* who went to balls,--who was always the star that dazzled all eyes, found himself as much neglected as ever. Only the members of the court who were suspected of ultramontanism approached him with mysterious cordiality; and whenever a number of observers were present, some persons whom he knew to belong to the ranks of his worst enemies cast strange glances at him which could scarcely fail to be noticed. Infuriated by this irritating and to him incomprehensible conduct, he turned to the young girls to pass away a few moments in their society; but the first whom he approached, a distant relative, drew back with mingled sorrow and alarm. He laughingly seized the little finger of her outstretched hand and drew her into a window corner. "Why do you avoid me, little Elsie? What have I done to harm you?" he asked.

"Oh, go away, you are a Jesuit!" whispered the girl, half timidly, half sullenly.

"Ah!" A flush slowly mounted into *Henri's* face, but without the slightest change of countenance he pushed a gold bracelet which had slipped down to the young girl's wrist so far up the rounded limb that for the first time in her life she shrank from the sight of her bare arm.

"Do you know that a Jesuit is something so very bad?"

"No," was the embarrassed reply. "I only know it is--must be--something you ought not to be; or else you would not do it so secretly." The young girl paused.

"Well, and who told you this?" asked *Henri*, in the greatest suspense, gazing so steadily and firmly into the large childlike eyes, that she continued in the greatest bewilderment.

"Why, Herr von Neuenburg told my mother so, and she was very unhappy about it, and they both said you could not be trusted any more. Now you know, let me go. Oh, dear, I ought not to have said anything about it!"

With these words she ran away, and his smiles fled with her. It was no longer the careless, jesting *Henri*, but *Heinrich* who stood haughtily erect in the alcove surveying the assembly with cold, contemptuous glances.

"These people wish to be diplomats, and discuss such important matters before children! Fortunately, I know you well enough to perceive that this rumor proceeds from you Jesuits. Oh, to be chained to such a life! to be forced to sacrifice all one's power for an honor the miserable breath of a liar's lips can blow away like dust! Is this life worth the trouble?"

"Not this life," murmured the fiend who was to help him "obtain." "You must enter a wider field, and mount higher and higher to a sphere where these petty intrigues can have no power over you; then only will you find rest."

These reflections, which were not by any means the first of the kind, were disturbed by the rustle of a dress, and when he looked up Princess Ottilie was standing before him. She gazed at him for a long time in silence, while he bowed low, murmuring a few words of apology for his absence of mind.

"Not so, Herr von Ottmar," she interrupted; "we already know that even when surrounded by the bustle of a crowd, you sometimes hold intercourse with your own thoughts; in any case, a much greater source of entertainment than society could offer you."

"Ah, your Highness, if society consisted of the elements united in my gracious princess, it would be the highest enjoyment to devote to it every power; but when people are compelled, like me, to wander perpetually, held aloof and misunderstood, through this labyrinth of pretensions, disappointments, and prejudices, they are sometimes glad to take refuge in the unsubstantial world of thought."

"But why do you not release yourself from surroundings so distasteful?" asked the princess. "Why do you not find strength to withdraw, if not to the world of spirits, at least to that of the intellect?"

"Your Highness," replied Ottmar, after a slight pause, "if I could take with me to that realm what has hitherto chained me to the court, how gladly would I resign this whirl of society! But so long as the object of my holiest longing is still clasped in the arms of the world, so long I will at least maintain a place near her, and fill it as well as I am able."

With these words he cast upon the princess one of the glances whose power he had so often tried. She involuntarily turned her head to see if any one could hear her.

"Herr von Ottmar," said she, and her voice became lower, her expression more sympathetic, "may I speak to you frankly?"

"Oh, my most gracious, benevolent friend!" murmured *Heinrich*, in a tone whose submissive devotion produced an irresistible influence upon the impressionable soul of the princess.

"Do not imagine that I have not perceived your design of winning me by flattery; I have read that, as well as your whole character. I am gracious enough to forgive you for placing the same estimate upon me as upon every other woman whom you may have misled by similar speeches. I forgive you, because I believe you to be greater than such arts would make you appear; you possess no false nature, and if you deceive it is only in cases which have no connection with your secret life, and no reality for you. Where you have to answer for yourself, your own established convictions, you will be true. I have this confidence in you, and therefore can calmly look on and see you make sport of the men and circumstances which, from your lofty stand-point, must appear so small; nay, I can even see you test your superiority over myself; and while I know all you say is false, am unable, I frankly confess, to resist the charm which your masterly acting exerts over me, and feel attracted towards you as the ignorant man is drawn to the artist whose skill he admires. Do not deny the truth of my assertion. Be noble; or, better still, show yourself to me as you really are, and confess I am right."

"Princess," cried Ottmar, "you are right. I grant that you have understood me; but I must oppose you in one thing, that I have been hypocritical to you. Ten minutes ago you might perhaps have termed me a flatterer, but now everything I said has become simple truth, and I should have far more to say to you if time and opportunity favored me." "I fear this is the last opportunity I shall have of speaking to you undisturbed, and therefore I speak now. I know you will not remain here under existing circumstances, and was not willing to have you go without taking with you on your weary way a word of conciliation, perhaps of warning; for you do not deserve the sentence passed upon you, and it grieves me deeply to see a noble, great-hearted man so misunderstood through his own fault."

"Has it already gone so far?" asked Ottmar, in surprise.

"Unfortunately, yes, my friend. You are considered a very dangerous man. Your enemies have decried you as a secret agent of the Jesuits, and at last placed before the prince proofs that you spent a year as a student in the Jesuit college at Rome. Your whole secret is betrayed." "And do they not suppose," replied Ottmar, "that the Jesuits would know how to guard such a secret better, unless it suited their interests to reveal it?"

"You must consider that you are at a *Protestant* court. You have hitherto passed for a free-thinker, now you are discovered to be a pupil of the Jesuits. Thus one or the other must be false; people find themselves mistaken in you, and are so blindly enraged that they will believe your enemies rather than you. They consider everything you have done and are doing against the Jesuits to be merely a mask. The cordiality which several gentlemen, who are known to be adherents of the order, showed you this evening confirmed the prince still more in his opinion. You know his passionate temper; I have just heard a conversation between him and the minister which I have neither time nor inclination to repeat; but my conscience urged me to warn you, and--"

"And your heart, princess; it tells you that, spite of the equivocal part you see me play, I am a man of honor, who at any moment can cast aside hypocrisy and deceit as contemptible tools, and whom you can trust."

"I know not whether I may venture to do so. You were sincere with none, and I can only entreat you always to remember that falsehood is as dangerous as a poisonous dye, by means of which men often color things of trifling value, but which by constant use so pervades the atmosphere that they at last can no longer breathe in it themselves."

"Your Highness," whispered *Heinrich*, "let me at least know why, in spite of my faults, you can still feel so much sympathy for me."

"Because I have recognized your great talents, the conflict, the want of peace, in your soul; because I know that the contradictions which make you suspected by the world at large are rooted in the contrasts of your own nature; and because I cannot help feeling the deepest compassion for you," she said, at last, with an outburst of feeling, laying her hand carelessly upon his. Her voice rang upon *Heinrich's* ear in tones of strange warning, and tears were glittering in her deep blue eyes as she continued: "Oh, there is something so noble, so godlike, in a true human soul, that when I see one struggling and battling in the prison of this earthly body, ensnared and tortured, my heart bleeds and I would fain extend my hands protectingly over the wildly fluttering wings, until the hour when it can free itself and soar away unfettered! We are observed. God be with you! Farewell!" She glided away and disappeared among the crowd.

"My Ideal spoke from her lips," said Ottmar, gazing after her.

A strange conflict now ensued between the opposing elements in his breast.

"She loves me; she, this noble creature, so full of intellect and feeling," said *Heinrich*. "She could not speak more distinctly, and what she concealed

I read in her eyes, which absorbed my image in their blue depths and reflected it again, as the sun paints a Fata Morgana upon the clouds."

"And I," *Henri* rejoined, "I feel ashamed and miserable when in her presence, for I can give her nothing in return for the treasures she brings me. I do not love her."

"And why not?" asked *Heinrich*. "Can she not make a man happy for his whole life? Does she not hold a lofty position, is she not as noble as she is intellectual, and has she not sufficient strength of mind to accept my hand, if I offer it, in spite of all intrigues?"

"True," replied *Henri*; "but she is neither young nor blooming, and is an invalid. How can I bind myself forever to one who has not the slightest personal charm for me? A beautiful soul and noble mind are phantoms, but a sickly body is the most comfortless reality, and a burden which I must drag about with me during my whole life. No: so long as I am still young I wish to enjoy this miserable life; when I am old and decrepit I shall have enough to do to bear my own ailments without the addition of an invalid wife."

"Ah, I could love her!" said *Heinrich*. "You should not extend your arms to me vain, beautiful soul; I would foster and cherish you as my most sacred possession; but it is impossible. Even if I should give her this man, what would she possess? A cold intellect and a sensuality which this poor ethereal nature would be unable to attract, and by which she would sooner or later be betrayed." Absorbed in these thoughts, he walked through the rooms to take his leave. He wished to go home, for he had lost all inclination for the entertainment. When he reached the last apartment a new dance had just commenced and drawn every one into the large salons. The room was silent and empty, only the lights in the candelabra burned with a low crackle; fans and withered bouquets lay scattered over the tables, and cloaks that had been carelessly cast aside were thrown upon the sofas. Everything bore witness to the bright and joyous life that had reigned here a few minutes before, and now the deserted chamber with its marble columns and gilded arches seemed like a mausoleum, where the soul might take a last farewell. He paused an instant. "Ottilie!" he murmured, half unconsciously, and the solemn mood he had felt a short time before again overmastered him. It seemed as if beneficent spirits were floating in the waves of light that surrounded him and trying to whisper something, but he could no longer understand them. Just then he suddenly heard a low rustle: some living creature was near. He looked around him and saw the princess standing in the doorway gazing at him with deep earnestness.

"Ottilie," cried *Heinrich*, "God has sent you here! The angel of my life called me, but I could no longer understand his words; for in the tumult of the world I have grown deaf to his spirit voice. He dwells in you; become his oracle, let him speak to me through your lips."

"Herr von Ottmar, my heart is filled with the thought of your welfare, but how to help you I know not. I will pray your good angel to show me some means of fathoming the trouble in your soul. I know of no way unless"--she hesitated, less from embarrassment than to seek the right word,--"unless you can find a nature which will understand and have for you the patience of true love. Only the anxiety of a heart entirely devoted to you will discover the means of restoring your lost peace. That you may win such a being is the hope and desire of my soul."

"Princess," cried *Heinrich*, whom Ottilie's lovely enthusiasm had deeply charmed, "if I now say that I find such a being in you, that there is no woman to whom I will intrust my life except you--"

"No, my friend," said Ottilie calmly, though she turned pale. "You are deceived in yourself at this moment. You do not love it is the longing for the right which, thank God, always lives in you, which attracts you to my--I may be allowed to say it--pure soul. This is not love; I know it, and would never strengthen you in an error which would defraud you of the best portion of your life. Yet I thank you for your confession. It makes you appear still more lovable in my eyes; not because you have made it to me, but to the ideal to which I would so gladly see you rise."

"Ottilie, let me thank you on my knees for the light you have poured into my darkened soul, and let me swear I will do everything good and great of which I may be capable in your name, your spirit!" *Heinrich* impulsively threw himself at her feet and clasped her hands. "Oh, my soul loves you, Ottilie, with a love which--"

"Which is not of this world," interrupted Ottilie, bending over him. "Another love will enter your heart, and you will bless me for having had strength to refuse what does not belong to me! And now I entreat you to rise and leave me to myself."

Heinrich rose and started back as he looked at Ottilie. She was standing proudly erect, struggling for breath, as her tears flowed more and more violently; her eyes were closed, her delicate lips firmly compressed, she was a most touching picture of agonizing self-sacrifice.

"Poor heart! you love me, and yet are noble enough to reject me?" asked *Heinrich*.

"Yes, my friend," murmured Ottilie, "so truly as God will sustain me in my last hour, so truly I desire your happiness more than my own, so truly I resign you. You must be free, and choose freely. God grant you may find the right!"

"After this vow I have nothing more to hope," said *Heinrich*. "Farewell, my friend! One who has power to exercise such self-restraint has also strength to conquer her sorrow." He kissed her cold, pale brow, and hastily left the room.

"Thank God it has turned out so!" whispered *Henri*; and *Heinrich* also uttered a sigh of relief: he felt that he had escaped a great danger. He had been hurried on by a momentary impulse and Ottilie's unconcealed love to a step which he would have bitterly repented; for he was equally convinced that no one would ever understand him like Ottilie, and also that her appreciation alone would not satisfy him. As *Henri* desired more sensual, *Heinrich* demanded greater intellectual, charms. He wished to be excited, kept in a state of suspense, enlivened, amused: Ottilie's uniform, quiet earnestness would not have afforded him this, and he thanked her for having rightly understood his hasty enthusiasm and been generous enough to reject him.

Meantime, the queenly Ottilie stood motionless in the glittering apartment, her hand pressed to her heart and her eyes raised towards heaven. "Which of us is most to be pitied, he or I?"

V
MASTER AND PUPIL

On his way home, Ottmar remembered that he had appointed this very hour for a tender meeting, and gradually the solemn impression made by the last few moments faded before the charming picture which now obtained the mastery over his soul. When he returned home his old valet, who had served him from childhood, met him with a pale, sleepy face, and slowly lighted the candles.

"Has not the little girl come yet?" asked *Henri*.

"Who?"

"Who should it be? Röschen," he added.

"Röschen, Marten the beadle's daughter, do you expect her?"

"Of course I do; I persuaded her to meet me in the garden. Keep watch at the window, and when she comes take her into the pavilion," he said, absently, throwing himself into a chair.

"Permit me to warn you, Herr Baron," said the old man with sorrowful earnestness. "Röschen is an innocent maiden, the only daughter of an honest, poor man, whose sole joy is in this child. Have you considered this?"

"Don't bore me with your reproaches, man!" cried *Henri*. "Don't grudge me this little pleasure; life with these frivolous, coquettish women is already gradually becoming so shallow that it is no longer endurable. I must have something pure and simple, which can refresh my mind and interrupt the everlasting sameness; and she is really a charming creature!" he murmured, admiringly.

"Herr Baron," said the old man, with deep emotion, "I promised your dying mother to watch over you as far and as long as it was in my power. In former days my influence often prevailed; but since your severe illness and residence in France you have become a different person; still, I did all that was possible in my limited sphere to keep you from evil of every kind. Of late I have feared more for the safety of your soul than your bodily welfare. I have had occasion to perform services of which I have been ashamed.

To carry letters and attend light-minded ladies home is not the business of a respectable man; yet I did it out of affection for you, and because no innocent person suffered. You gave me no thanks for my obedience, but took it as a proof that I shared your views, and probably secretly despised me for it. I bore all patiently and did my duty. But today, Herr Baron, it is time to hold you back from the path on which you have entered. To ruin an innocent girl is a crime of which I would not have believed you capable, and to which I will lend no aid."

"Old fool!" muttered *Henri*, looking at the clock, "if you were not so useful I would have dismissed you to some quiet place long ago. Don't pretend to be more silly than you are, Anton. I've already heard so much morality to-day that I was on the point of doing a very foolish thing. Do you suppose I shall begin again with my valet? Go, and let me alone!"

"Herr Baron," replied Anton, firmly, "I am sorry to be obliged to tell you that I must leave your service if you insist upon seeing the girl, and beg you to discharge me to-night."

"Anton," cried *Henri*, in a furious passion, "I have borne with you for a long time! You were faithful to me, even resisted the temptations of the Jesuits, and always attended to my welfare. All this I have recognized and rewarded; but I can no longer keep a servant who wishes to set himself up as a judge of my conduct, were he ever so indispensable to me; so remember your place better, or go!"

At that moment the door-bell rang gently. "Ah, she is coming!" exclaimed *Henri*, exultantly; and forgetting everything else, he turned to Anton, calling, "Lights!"

The old servant did not move, but stood with clasped hands praying, under his breath, "Dear God, save this young soul!"

Henri rushed down the staircase on which the moonlight lay in broad bars; his hands trembled with joyful impatience. "Wait, my Röschen! my little pink rose! I will admit you, my darling!" he whispered, as he turned the key and threw open the heavy door, half bending forward to embrace his angel; but a tall figure, on which the moon cast a ghostly light, entered and fixed a pair of dark, searching eyes upon the astonished *Henri*.

"Oh, Christ! what is this?" he exclaimed, staggering back as if overwhelmed with terror and disappointed expectation against the door, which he closed again.

"It is not Christ, but one who comes in his name," replied the stranger's deep voice in the purest Italian.

"By all good angels, Father Severinus!" murmured *Henri*, recoiling a step. A low knock sounded from without; the young man's blood mounted to his brow, and he hesitated a moment in the greatest embarrassment.

"Here are my companions," said the Italian. "Allow me to open the door." He threw it back, and two figures, clad in the same dress as his own, entered, accompanied by one of the Jesuits who had spoken to *Henri* that night at the ball. They greeted him respectfully, and he was man of the world enough to instantly accommodate himself to his painful situation as well as the torturing disappointment of the moment.

"You are welcome, reverend sirs," he said, smiling, and led the way up-stairs.

Old Anton stood upon the landing with a light, and one of the priests saluted him with his "Praised be Jesus Christ."

"Forever, amen!" replied the old man, with a deep sigh, as he placed chairs for the strangers and left the room, casting a sorrowful glance at his master.

"We have been looking for you at the ball, my son," Father Severinus began; "because I only arrived from Rome this evening, and must set out again early tomorrow morning. I am taking a journey through Germany, and thought it my duty to see you, my favorite pupil, and look after the welfare of your soul. But, unfortunately, I was compelled to learn that the soil which so readily received our lessons was a mere sand-heap, whose best harvest is blown away by the wind."

Heinrich, who had taken *Henri's* place, quietly listened to the priest's words with his usual satirical smile. "Reverend sir, I must first observe that I am no longer in the mood to allow myself to be treated like a schoolboy. There are times when a peculiar fatality seems to pursue us; to-day appears to have been set apart for giving me moral lectures, and I assure you the more of them I hear the less successful they are; so you perceive you will not be able to accomplish much in this way, especially with a man who has returned at one o'clock in the morning, weary and heated, from a ball."

"Perhaps Princess Ottilie also belongs to the number of those whose 'moral lectures' have been so unsuccessful," sneeringly remarked Ottmar's ball-room companion, Geheimrath Schwelling.

"What do you know about that?" exclaimed *Heinrich*.

"Enough, I should think; the noble lady did not speak so low that any one in the adjoining window corner could not hear everything, and it is really a duty to inform her how useless her admonitions are, that she may not trouble herself vainly in future."

Heinrich cast a glance of inexpressible contempt at the sleek, fat face and restless eyes of the speaker. "Princess Ottilie is the noblest woman I know," he exclaimed, with deep emotion, "and is too lofty to lend her ear to such vulgar insinuations. If, however, you succeed in betraying me to her, remember that you will do me no harm, but only inflict useless pain upon a noble heart."

"Or heal it," replied the Geheimrath, contemptuously.

"Cease this aimless conversation, gentlemen," said Severinus. "I am astonished, Herr Geheimrath, to hear what language you employ towards a man whose great talents, even as an enemy, should command your respect. Surely these are not the means worthy of so great an end; and if our affairs in Germany are managed thus, I can understand why the word 'Jesuit' is here used as a bugbear to frighten children. *In majorem Dei gloriam*, never forget that. Unfortunately, I see you men of the world must be reminded of it more frequently than our dead General has done. It was time a more powerful hand should seize the reins; I perceive that more and more at every step I take upon this soil."

He had risen from his seat as he uttered these words, and there was something so menacing and imperious in his bearing that the Geheimrath exclaimed, with mingled fear and anger, "By what authority do you use this language towards me, Father Severinus?"

"By the authority the General, who sends me, gave me over every worldly coadjutor who enjoys the advantages of our alliance without showing himself worthy of them."

The word General and Severinus's majestic bearing utterly crushed the Geheimrath, who sank into a chair in silence, passing his hand over a brow bedewed with cold perspiration.

"Take me to a room where I can speak to you in private, my son," said the priest in a very different tone, turning to Ottmar. "We alone have understood each other, and we shall come to an understanding again."

"As you please," said *Heinrich*, hesitatingly, and was about to take one of the candlesticks from the table.

"Nay," observed Severinus, checking him. "You know my habits; do not refuse me the favor of being allowed to speak to you in darkness as in former days. The soul can collect its powers better when external objects are concealed."

"As you please," Ottmar repeated, while a faint smile played around his lips.

He led the priest into the adjoining library; then left the room a moment and said to Anton, in low tone, "Examine my study, remove the papers lying around, and bolt the door leading into the dining-room. If Röschen comes, I also rely upon your faithfulness to take her into the garden and shut her up in the pavilion."

Then he quietly returned to his guest. The library was dimly lighted by the moonbeams. The books towered aloft in immense cases, and from the most exhaustive works of the *intellect*, bound in these lifeless cases to arise again in spirit, the eye wandered to the most perfect works of *nature* imperishably imprisoned in stone and colors to refresh the weary thinker, and gently win him back from his dizzy heights to this world and its lovely forms. Statues and pictures of every kind stood and hung around.

If a moonbeam shone upon the gilt letters of the names of the greatest poets and learned men, it also revealed the mute embrace of Cupid and Psyche, and brought out in strong relief the marble shoulder of the Venus de Medici. In a niche filled with palms and climbing plants, it cast flickering shadows upon Schwanthaler's nymph, which seemed to be lamenting that she was stone, and glittered upon a marble basin at her feet. Then its pale gleam struggled with the vivid hues of the exquisite copy of a Titian, or glided over a table filled with charts, sketches, and plans, whose half-rolled sheets fluttered gently. The room revealed a strange, mysterious life and nature. Ghosts seemed to be gliding to and fro,--the tall, chastely-veiled ghosts of philosophy and poetry,--the nude, caressing genii of love and pleasure. Now all appeared to have gathered curiously around the dark, tall form of the priest, who stood leaning thoughtfully against the pedestal of a Hebe.

"This study, or library, is characteristic of you, my son," began Severinus, when Ottmar returned. "I see everywhere the results of the two dominant powers of your nature,--intellect and sensuality,--but no piety; a worship of the mind, a worship of nature: but where, where are the traces of religion? Have you, then, utterly cast aside what you adopted when with us?"

"Father Severinus," said *Heinrich*, advancing until he stood face to face with him, "we are alone. Be frank; do you ask, *you*, that I shall become a devotee?"

Severinus gazed at him bong and earnestly. "That you should become a devotee? No! What I ask of you is consistency! When with us you apparently became deeply imbued with religious feeling, and openly displayed it an all occasions. Now you deny it; therefore you have either *lost*--in which case you are to be pitied, or never *possessed* it, when you deserve great blame for the deception you have practiced in relation to the most sacred things and towards us."

Heinrich was silent. He felt the justice of the priest's reproof, and found no reply; at the same time he was stupefied by the dim, flickering light and the excitement of the last hour, and could not suppress a slight yawn. Father Severinus was also silent, and waited patiently for a reply. At last *Heinrich* said, impatiently: "Most reverend father, you might spare a great deal of your pathos. I do not deny the truth of your reproach; the only doubt is whether it specially concerns me, for I must confess to you that it is a matter of comparative indifference whether you have cause to be indignant or not. I have released myself from your authority, and belong to another party, so I have nothing more to expect or endure from you. True, you have succeeded in making me suspected at this court; but I shall find means to justify myself, and then we will see which of us has most occasion to fear the other."

"I am deeply grieved to hear this language, which, by my faith in Christ, I have not deserved," replied Severinus. "I am guiltless of the measures the hasty, newly-appointed agent for Germany induced the Father General to employ against you. Will you believe me?"

Heinrich bowed. "I am well aware that you are too proud to adopt such a course."

"Well then, for what wrong can you upbraid me, which justifies this inconsiderate, heartless language?" He paused and looked at *Heinrich*, who bit his lips and drummed on the arm of his chair. "What wrong has the order done you that you take upon yourself the task of entering upon a contest with it?" repeated Severinus. Another pause ensued. "What could induce you to commit such a breach of faith?"

"I have committed no breach of faith!" exclaimed *Heinrich*, "for I never belonged to you; I am and was a free-thinker. For a long time I admitted your great and manifest excellences, but the longer I remained among you the more I learned to hate you and the principles of your order, whose sole aim is the subjection of the mind to your dogmas, or rather your authority, an object to attain which you know how to employ every conceivable means, good as well as bad. Do you really ask a man of my nature to submit to become the tool of such plans? If you could expect it, it was your fault, not mine, if you now find yourselves deceived."

"To that, my son, I have two answers," replied Severinus, after a short pause of reflection. "If the principles of our order, which the hand of God has hitherto wonderfully protected, seem to you so worthy of blame that you consider it a duty to oppose them and prepare a better fate for your nation by your own ideas, I can say nothing against it in my own person, except that I pity your error, while I can pay a certain respect to the man who has at heart the welfare of his people, even though his views may be mistaken. But you, *Heinrich*, do not oppose us from the necessity of preserving your country from a supposed evil, nor from the sanctity of a firm though erroneous conviction, but merely out of vanity, that thereby you may play a prominent part before your revolutionary party. You know nothing more sublime and imperishable than the worldly admiration bestowed upon you, because the reward and recognition of Christ, promised by his vicars throughout eternity, are incredulously scorned by your narrow soul. Vanity and egotism are answerable for your actions towards us, and even destroy the paltry merit of having sacrificed yourself for your convictions."

"Oh, Ottilie," *Heinrich* suddenly exclaimed, in bitter wrath, "gentle, innocent angel! How much better you understood me!"

"That is not all I have to say in reply," continued Severinus, without permitting himself to be at all disturbed by the interruption. "If, as I have just seen, the reproach of acting from selfish impulses wounds you so deeply, tell me what noble motive induced you to remain a year with men whom you abhor, receive every possible proof of friendship from them, and feign enthusiastic interest in a faith which seems to you pernicious and criminal? Pray answer this, if you can."

"I can," replied *Heinrich*, quietly. "Chance and ennui threw me into your hands. You took me to the college. The genius of your system attracted me; I wished to penetrate the mysterious nimbus which surrounded you, to investigate you and your nature, as people desire to examine every curiosity. You interested me, and I very soon perceived that it would only cost me a little hypocrisy to acquire knowledge which would be useful all my life. I looked upon it as a necessary entrance-fee, and paid you with it. Why did you not see that the coin was false? You trained me for diplomacy, and drilled me in the arts of dissimulation, to which you gave the noble name of 'self-command.' As I learned them I tested them on you, and thus you see that my diplomatic career began by making you the first victims of your own teachings, and by deceiving you. Truth will pardon my year of faithlessness for the sake of a lifetime of repentance."

"That sounds very strange," said Severinus. "Did we teach you hypocrisy? To *conceal* the truth without *telling a lie* is the art we communicated to aid you in your diplomatic career. But granted that it was so, granted that we taught you dissimulation to obtain certain necessary ends, should not common human gratitude have withheld you from betraying in such a despicable manner the men who trusted you?"

"Gratitude," laughed *Heinrich*, "for what? Did you receive me cordially and bestow your instruction upon me for my own sake? Certainly not. Why did you expel poor Albert Preheim, who was miserably poor, dependent, and sincerely devoted to you? Because he had not sufficient ability to serve you, because he was a man of limited intellect. You did not keep me for my good but your own, because you expected to find in me a useful tool, because a skillful agent for this country was necessary. Tell me yourself, would you have done all this for me if the matter had only concerned my welfare?"

"No," said Severinus; "our mission is to serve God alone. This claims us so entirely that the interests of individuals must be excluded. We cannot trouble ourselves about any one who is not in some manner useful to this end; he must apply to those orders whose sole vocation is the practice of Christian charity. If he cannot find among them the benefits he seeks, he would not be worthy of ours."

"Well, for what do I owe you gratitude?" asked *Heinrich*.

"Because you were afforded an opportunity to advance the holiest cause, to become a fellow-laborer in the service of the Highest Being. What are we men, what is our feeble influence? Only when we belong to a great band, unite our strength, direct our manifold powers towards *one* lofty aim, do we feel strong and have real weight. And the more we enter into the struggle of the whole, the more petty cares for ourselves disappear, then only do we obtain true contentment."

"My noble Severinus," exclaimed *Heinrich*, "do you not suppose that I too belong to such a band, like all who are imbued with one great aim? Do you not suppose that there are sacred interests in the world and among nations, whose representatives are united by an invisible bond of common activity? Are you not sure that in our world also there are such associations which, without compulsion or vows, without being bound by time and space, or ruled by statutes, have an eternal existence?"

"What you say sounds very noble; I know these are your philosophical catch-words, but it is untenable," said Severinus. "Your union, supposing that such an one might exist in fancy, is too diffuse to produce the consciousness of mutual dependence, which can alone suppress selfishness in individuals; you gentlemen, who desire to promote the happiness of the world, always have room enough within the limits of your imaginary union to cherish your individual cares and interests, and make war upon yourselves. Even though your object may perhaps be the same, you are always at variance about the means of attaining it; nay, you are often, from purely personal motives, most bitter enemies. You may have an association, but you have no unity, and your efforts are unsuccessful in consequence of your want of harmony. You lack positive legal consolidation, which is the secret of our power; and while you win at tea-tables men of superior minds to join your confederacy, we deprive you of the masses. You can undoubtedly belong to such a band without injury to your egotism," he added, smiling; "but you will always feel discontented and solitary." He paused and gazed at *Heinrich*, then continued: "How differently you would labor with us! My son, is there no way of bringing you back? Is there no feeling of devotion which binds you to me? You say you are free from every obligation to the order; are you also free from all obligations to me? I think I have done more for you than even our purpose would have rendered necessary. As prefect of the college, all manner of claims were made upon me; yet when my days were occupied I sacrificed my nights to initiate you into secrets which the order confides only to a chosen few. I have borne with your thousand caprices, smothered your passions with inexhaustible indulgence, and unweariedly labored to develop your great talents. I wished to obtain you for our cause, not only because we needed remarkable powers, but also because I knew of no greater happiness for yourself. In you I learned to love men once more; for your sake, I have become tolerant, for your sake I have come from Rome. My chilled heart warmed towards you as towards a son. Does this deserve no love,--not even forbearance?"

"Love!" said *Heinrich*, impatiently. "What do you desire? Men do not love each other. I honor you, for you are the best and noblest of all in the college, and if we had a common interest I would gladly join you; but I do not deal in useless feelings, and frankly confess that I don't understand how people can have them, except towards women."

"Is it possible?" exclaimed Severinus. "So you believe you love only what you desire to possess. You love nothing at all, *Heinrich*, and I resign all hope of moving you by gentleness and kindness." So saying, he started up and again leaned against the pedestal of the marble Hebe, who vainly held her goblet of joy above his head. His delicately cut features were slightly flushed, and his dark eyes flashed an imperious glance at *Heinrich*. "Here stands a man who has devoted his whole life to the service of a divine idea.

Educated in a Jesuit college, sent into the would as an ecclesiastical coadjutor, and finally promoted to the rank of assistant, I learned to share all the joys and sorrows of our order, and have become a Jesuit from the crown of my head to the sole of my foot. I have felt every passion struggle within me and subdued them all: for the honor of God was the object unchangeably before my eyes; I used my life only as a preparation for eternity, and therefore proudly approach death without blanching. Will you meet the annihilation in which you believe as calmly?"

"I hope so," said *Heinrich*, coldly.

"And if, instead of your deities of sensuality which beckon to you here, a bleeding Christ should appear before you in his chaste mother's lap, pleading, 'Turn back to those who will guide you in my ways--'"

"I would say to him, 'Lord, guide me in thy ways *thyself!*'" exclaimed *Heinrich*, with a forced laugh.

"And if we threatened you with the curse of the church?"

"I would become a Protestant."

"Misguided, accursed son of the flesh, with which you defile the vessel of divinity, your joys shall one day be shivered by the hand of the Lord like this idol!" cried Severinus in an outburst of fury, seizing the Hebe and dashing it so violently at the feet of the startled *Heinrich* that the room shook and the graceful head rolled a long distance. The dust rose from the floor in clouds.

For a moment *Heinrich* stood petrified with astonishment, gazing regretfully at the beautiful broken limbs. "So you intend to close our conversation with this resounding crash, father?" he asked at last, when he had recovered his former sarcastic mood.

"Close? Oh, no; we have not done with each other yet," said Severinus, as he paced up and down the apartment several times, and then suddenly paused with quiet dignity before *Heinrich*. "This is the most disgraceful trick my impetuous temper has ever played me. Fortunately, I can replace your broken property. It would be far more difficult to repair the moral loss you have sustained in this hour. We will come to an understanding quietly. My recent violence was the last outbreak of my sorrow for your loss, but your cold derision has chilled my affection forever. Ascribe it to your own conduct if my dealings with you are henceforth destitute of all consideration. The *man* is dead to me, you are now simply the enemy of my church, whom at any cost I must disarm."

Heinrich looked at him in astonishment. "Indeed, I am curious to learn in what way you will propose to effect this."

"You shall know at once. We must first determine the relations in which you will in future stand towards our order."

"That would be useless labor, father, since for a long time no relations have existed between us, and none will ever be formed again!"

"They will, they must exist! The tie was formerly a voluntary one on your part, now it will be compulsory: that is the only difference. You have proved to me that you have secretly deserted us, my care will be to prevent your making it public; and since persuasion is unavailing, this must be done by force."

"Force?" cried *Heinrich*, starting up. "What do you mean?"

"Simply that I possess means to compel you to that which you will not do of your own free will."

"Father Severinus, we intimidate children in this way, but not men!"

Severinus looked him steadily in the face. "Have you ever seen me employ empty threats?"

"No," replied *Heinrich*, with visible anxiety.

"Very well; then let us come to the point without further circumlocution. You must first of all be fully informed of your present situation. That you are pointed out as our agent, and consequently in disfavor here, you know, and also that you must take leave as soon as possible, if you prefer an honorable voluntary resignation to a disgraceful dismissal."

"And why must I do this? Who can dismiss me on the ground of such vague accusations?"

"These accusations will be proved."

"They cannot be, for I shall find means to justify myself. Although I cannot deny having been for some time connected with you, it does not follow that this is still the case."

"That too is provided for. We possess the most irrefutable proofs that you still maintain an intercourse with us by letter." He drew out a small portfolio. "Now I will ask you for a lamp." *Heinrich* lighted the candles, and saw two envelopes, which Severinus held out to him, addressed in his own hand. "You see,--these envelopes contained the replies to the General's requests concerning the erection of a private institution in H----. We shall know how to conceal the fact that these answers were refusals. It is enough that the postmarks on envelopes addressed by your own hand will afford proofs of the recent existence of a secret correspondence."

"And of what use will they be if you are forced to conceal their contents? Suppose you are asked why you do not produce the letters themselves?"

"It will be sufficient reason to say that they contained important secrets which we cannot reveal on any account."

Heinrich passionately struck his brow. "Oh, could I suspect that I had to deal with men to whom no measures are too petty, and who are not ashamed to collect pitiful envelopes and use them to aid their designs!"

"Nothing is so trivial that it is not worth the trouble of keeping, if it can serve the honest cause. Our Lord Jesus Christ was not ashamed to pick up a piece of old iron; why should not we, his servants, make even the most trifling things useful for his designs?"

"I hope, father, that you yourself feel the humorousness, not to say absurdity, of such logic at this moment."

"Let us not digress. I am aware that our proceedings can in no case meet with your approval, and bear you no ill will for it; therefore I have not submitted them to your judgment. Every word which does not directly concern the matter in hand is a mere waste of time."

"Well, then, father, we will use very few. Tell me exactly what you require."

"That you should bind yourself to contend with us no longer."

Heinrich burst into a loud laugh. "And by these untenable threats you wish to induce me to take such a step! No, father, we have not yet gone so far. Although I have no proofs that our correspondence was a hostile one, you are equally unable to show that it was confidential and friendly; far less, that I have failed in my duty towards my own government. Our risks are equal."

"If they are, I need only throw in these papers and your scale will sink!" held aloft a roll of manuscript. "Here are the proofs of the offenses you committed against your government and court during your stay in Rome. Whoever sees them will no longer doubt that you are a traitor now as well as then!"

"Severinus!" cried *Heinrich*, fairly beside himself with fury.

"Be calm, my friend; we are only weighing our comparative advantages and disadvantages. If you compel me to make these papers public, your honor and all your ambitious plans are destroyed!"

"If you rob me of my future career as a statesman, woe betide you! Do you see what an enemy you will find in me? I, too, am in possession of secrets which you would not desire to have revealed!"

"As we know this, my friend, we do you the honor of treating with you. Towards any one else we should have adopted a shorter course. The only point in question now is which of us has most to lose, and it is you!"

"What do those papers contain?" asked *Heinrich*, in a hollow tone.

"In the first place an article in your own hand, which you prepared at the rector's command, containing the characteristics of this court and those of the most influential persons who surround the prince."

"That can only compromise me personally," said *Heinrich*, with forced composure.

"It can be displayed by a malevolent person as an act of treachery to your court in favor of the Jesuits' designs,--and in fact it was intended to aid us in our first steps here."

"It failed, however, for the characteristics were not correct. Any one who is familiar with the relations existing here will instantly perceive that they are intentionally falsified, to mislead any one who might wish to use them."

"This may have proceeded from want of judgment quite as much as design."

Heinrich suppressed a smile. "Oh, father, pardon my lack of modesty if I doubt that any would impute want of judgment to *me*!"

Severinus bit his lips. "You were a very young man, whose penetration could not have been so well disciplined as now. Meantime, where many proofs are brought together the number turns the scale, and I possess one which will weigh heavier than all the rest." He drew a printed document from his breast and pointed to the title. "Who is the author of this pamphlet written in favor of the Jesuits and against your government?"

"I," said *Heinrich*, coldly. "But, fortunately, you can create no proofs of the fact."

"We can procure them."

"*No*, father; there was but one, the manuscript written by my own band; and this no longer exists, for I threw it into the fire myself, and saw it burn with my own eyes. I knew you crafty gentlemen too well to allow such a dangerous document to fall into your possession."

"You burned the manuscript, but not the proof-sheets," said Severinus. "When you asked for them you were told that they had already been destroyed. Here are the corrections written in your own hand! You wondered at the time that we should have such miserable compositors in our secret printing-establishments, because you found whole words wrong. You were unsuspicious enough not to perceive that the errors were only made in order to obtain as many corrections as possible in your handwriting; no one who knows its peculiar characteristics will doubt the authenticity of this document." *Heinrich* turned very pale. He cast a glance of deadly hatred at Severinus, who was quietly watching him. "Moreover, here is also the letter you sent to Father K. with the pamphlets he had ordered; and although you took the precaution not to name the title, no one will believe that you submitted to the judgment of the General of the Jesuits any other manuscript than one written in the interests of the order." expression of bitter irony played around the priest's delicate lips. "It seems to me that you were not aware how 'crafty' we are! You can now proceed to make public all these 'contemptible coercive measures,' as you call them; you may perhaps thereby injure us a little, but you will not justify yourself. As soon as this secret is revealed you are lost. Suppose you hold psychological discussions with your court and government concerning the transformation which has taken place in you, and the causes that induced you to deny your convictions for an entire year,--you will be laughed at, and your name will be handed before all parties."

Heinrich trembled with rage. The painful dilemma into which he found himself hurried without the slightest warning, the incomprehensibility of his situation, the priest's crushing dialectics, and his own physical exhaustion--all these combined causes so bewildered him that he lost all control over himself, and following only the blind impulses of his instinct, he vigorously rushed upon Severinus, who had just replaced the document in his breast. "Hold!" he cried, seizing his arm. "Do you really suppose I will voluntarily leave these papers, which decide the destiny of my whole life, in your hands?"

Severinus remained perfectly calm, and measured him with a contemptuous glance. "Ottmar, I could defend myself if I did not have sufficient confidence in your good sense to know that I am safe from violence."

After a long pause, Severinus approached him; his expression became more gentle, his harsh tone softened, and it seemed as if sorrow was mirrored in his eyes as he laid his hand gently upon the young man's shoulder and in a low tone murmured his name. The latter looked up sullenly.

"Ottmar, I do not act for myself, but for my church."

"It is a matter of indifference to me for when you act if you destroy my career. Oh, it is despicable! I have robbed you of the labors of a year, but you are defrauding me of a whole life! Woe to him who rashly ventures within your charmed circle! He can never break through it without being crushed."

"Ottmar, I do not understand how you could ever have imagined we would send such an invaluable power into the world without holding in our hands the leading-strings by which we could draw you back at any moment. Let us come to some conclusion. I have the most positive orders not to leave here without the security I have already mentioned. If you do not promise to-night that you will voluntarily send in your resignation, to-morrow I must commence proceedings which will make you a dishonored man."

"And I am to allow my hands to be tied, I am to mount to this height, and in the zenith of my success to be hurled back to every-day obscurity, laughed at and dishonored! No, I will not and cannot be ruined by you! You recognize only the fanaticism with which you incessantly pursue your own aims. I too am a fanatic; but it is in the cause of ambition, and to this everything must yield, good and bad. You shall perceive that I have not been your pupil in vain. You have impressed upon me the stamp of your society to brand me in the eyes of my party; but what will injure me at *Protestant* courts will aid me in *Catholic* ones. If I am reported to be a Jesuit, I will make the rumor profitable. I will enter the service of a Catholic country under the guise of being in accord with you. You cannot contradict yourselves so far as to decry me here as an ultramontanist and there as a liberal. I will go to N----, where you are sure that I am powerless against you. If this is not sufficient security, let the battle begin,--I can do no more!"

"It is the only expedient that you still have, if you seek your happiness solely in the brilliancy of a diplomatic career; and it is not our intention to exclude you from it, for we do not wish to drive you to extremities unnecessarily. N---- is at least the only place where you cannot injure us. On this condition we will mutually spare each other and keep the peace, but if you succeed in obtaining influence in N----, and should ever attempt to use it against us, we have the power there to crush you at once: not by stratagem, but by our firmly-established might. Do not forget this."

"Ottilie," thought *Heinrich*, "you spoke the truth. I have so poisoned the air with my falsehoods that I breathe nothing but corruption, and am rightly served." "Well, then," he said to Severinus, "your holy object is attained by the noblest means. You thrust a man, who has hitherto made only a short digression from the path of right, into a course of wrong and hypocrisy, careless whether a soul is destroyed, so that appearances are preserved."

Severinus cast down his eyes. "The cause must be saved; the individual must be sacrificed to the cause. May God have mercy upon his soul, if that which should lead him to good turns him to evil! Come, we will repeat our agreement before witnesses." Severinus opened the door, and they entered the drawing-room, where the others were waiting with anxious faces.

Heinrich's offer was discussed in detail and confirmed by his word of honor, after which he took a formal leave of the gentlemen.

Severinus turned in the doorway and clasped his hand. "I do not know what mysterious impulse of affection binds me to you, that, while treating you as my worst enemy, tears of sorrow dim my eyes, although I have only faithfully obeyed my orders. For Christ's sake forgive me, as I pardon you, and if ever you need me call upon me!" He gazed at *Heinrich* with all the strange meaning of his wonderful eyes. It seemed as if their brilliancy was shadowed by tears as he asked, "Shall I not see you again when I return to H---- in a few weeks?"

"No," said *Heinrich*. "I shall send in my resignation to-morrow, and depart as soon as possible."

Severinus suddenly clasped him passionately to his breast. "Farewell, my lost son! From this hour I will love nothing but God!" Then he went down the staircase with a steady step, without casting another glance behind. Old Anton lighted the way, and then returned, pale but calm.

"Where is Röschen?" exclaimed *Henri*, who was longing to forget the tortures of the past hour in the arms of love.

"She is not here," said the old man.

"Not here?" asked *Henri*, in amazement. "Where is she?"

"Forgive me, Herr Baron! I could do nothing else,--I took her home to her father."

"What! what!" cried *Henri*, fairly beside himself with rage. "Did you dare to oppose your master? Leave this house early to-morrow morning before I am up! I will never see you again!"

He threw a heavy purse at his feet. The old man burst into tears, and his knees trembled under him.

"Herr Baron," he said, in a choking voice, "may you never regret having driven such a faithful servant from you! Farewell! may God preserve you!"

With these words he tottered out of the room, while Ottmar threw himself upon his couch in a mood of sullen discontent; for the first time consciousness of his marred existence came over him with crushing distinctness.

The second step was taken; he had fallen one degree lower. The warning voice had not failed him, but Egotism must complete his work at the cost of everything else.

The first act *Heinrich* had committed against his conscience, under the influence of this terrible demon, was the game he had played for a year with the Jesuits, in order to obtain knowledge which would be useful in his career. When he afterwards came to the decision, where he had an equal amount to lose or gain, he chose the path of truth; but now he again encountered the necessity of sacrificing his ambition or his convictions, and principle was compelled to yield to egotism. He would henceforth choose the path of falsehood, of worldly advantage, instead of the only one which could lead him to higher things.

He had bound himself to appear in N---- as an enemy of progress,--to aid in oppressing an impoverished nation. He must persuade his conscience that all his ideas of right and freedom were dead, and not worth the sacrifice of a whole life of honor and influence,--that the philanthropy which, in the guise of an earnest sense of duty, had lived his cold intellect, was an eccentricity of his youth, and must yield to his own advantage; in truth, it could not be otherwise. Only the emotional nature makes all ideas so living that we weep, suffer, and bleed for them as if they were real sentient beings, and gives us, for men whom we cannot draw within the circle visible to our senses, that warm feeling of sympathy which we call philanthropy. But he had lost this power, and with it a true sense of honor, yet to-night he found no repose. He was formed by nature for noble ends, and although he no longer felt as he had done in former days, he knew what his emotions were once. He knew the difference between right and wrong, and that he was choosing the latter, and looked back with shame upon the preceding day.

Both *Heinrich* and *Henri* had fallen equally low. If *Heinrich* had crushed his sense of right and yielded to ambition, *Henri* had gone so far in his pursuit of pleasure that he had sought to destroy a young, trusting heart, and angrily driven away the old man who had opposed his design. *Egotism had completed his victory over both natures.* Haunted by these and similar thoughts, he at last fell asleep just before dawn.

It was late in the forenoon when he awoke. The rays of the winter sun were shining upon the bright, blooming landscapes on his window curtains; a few freezing, starving birds were twittering loudly; everything bore a delusive semblance of spring, which had as little existence in the outside world as in his own breast. He opened his eyes, looked around him, and with a deep sigh murmured those words of painful disappointment: "Thank God, you have only been dreaming!" He sank back upon his pillows for a moment; it seemed as if his soul had not yet opened its eyes and was still slumbering, while he watched the bright colors upon his curtains. It seemed to him as if the door would open and old Anton come in to wake him. "Yes!" he called aloud, and started up. But he found himself alone. He rubbed his eyes and remembered that for the first time in his life Anton had failed to rouse him at the right hour. He had sent him away that very night! It was no dream: he had really done and experienced everything! "What has been begun must be finished," he said, with gloomy resolution, and rose to enter upon his sinful new career.

VI
THE PRISON FAIRY

Six years afterwards, on a cold, dreary November day, a grumbling, discontented crowd was waiting before the building in which the weal and woe of the country of N---- were decided. An important conference had just been concluded,--a consultation concerning increasing the severity of the punishments inflicted upon political criminals. Carriages drove up, and ministers and councilors entered them. At last a brilliant equipage, drawn by two snorting, spirited gray horses, dashed up so quickly that the crowd shrank back in terror, and looked at the door in eager expectation. Two servants hastily let down the steps. A slender man appeared who had not yet reached middle life, but on whose pallid face sharp lines were already visible. He did not vouchsafe to cast a glance at the throng, but as he entered the carriage he heard those near him whisper, "That is Ottmar; he is one of the worst of them." The door was closed, the footmen sprang back to their places, and the impatient steeds dashed through the crowd like griffins.

"Do you hate me at last?" murmured the cold man in the carriage. "It is well; if I once see I am hated I shall be able to shake off this remnant of conscientiousness that still tortures me, and henceforth live only for myself and my own aims."

The carriage stopped before a castle-like building, the state prison. Ottmar had for some time been commissioner of one of the revolutionary provinces of the country, where of late a new uprising was feared, and had therefore received orders to try to draw from the political prisoners, who were natives of that region, disclosures which might place some clue to the conspiracy in the hands of the government. The prince had selected him for this office because his cold watchfulness, smoothness, and skill in dealing with different natures seemed to make him peculiarly fitted for it. During the short time that Ottmar had been in the employ of the N---- government he had risen to the rank of privy councilor and member of the council of state, and displayed his talents in the widest spheres. He was the trusted friend of the young prince, over whom he exerted an inexplicable power, executor of the most secret measures, not unfrequently employed to deal with the agents of foreign courts, and his enemies began to fear him more and more when they perceived too late that his influence had already pervaded the whole court.

What it had cost him to submit and cringe to a system which his inmost soul abhorred, though with the longing to be or strive for something better he had violently crushed down every other feeling, as egotism and ambition had always suppressed the better emotions of unbiased convictions, was stamped in terrible characters upon the haggard, pallid, but still handsome face, the frail but haughtily erect figure.

He walked in gloomy silence behind the guide, who was taking him to the worst criminals in the lower story. A cold breeze blew over him, chilling his breast, and he involuntarily said to himself, "Yet men are compelled to live here!" It seemed as if the sound of despairing sobs reached his ear through one of the iron doors. He paused and listened. A low, soft voice appeared to be speaking words of solemn warning.

"Open this cell," he said to his guide; but the latter did not move.

"Oh, Herr Baron!" he said, imploringly, "shall we not go to the others first?--the man in there is very violent."

"Open the door!" said *Heinrich*, imperiously.

"Have mercy; we are all ruined men if you do not have mercy upon us!" stammered the guide, in the greatest confusion.

"What is the matter with you?" asked *Heinrich*, extremely perplexed. "I will be merciful if I can, but open the door at once."

The man hesitatingly unlocked the low door, and *Heinrich* stood in the entrance as if spell-bound. A young girl, thoughtful and beautiful as artists paint the Muse of History, was sitting on a stool holding in her lap a book, from which she had apparently just been reading aloud. She was bending over the prisoner, who had thrown himself weeping on the ground at her feet, and speaking to him consolingly. *Heinrich* motioned to the guide to be silent, and hastily retreated behind the door that he might not be seen.

"You have come too early, surely. I have not yet spent half an hour with Sebastian," said the young girl. A pale sunbeam fell upon her as she raised her head and shook back from her face a mass of luxuriant curls. Her full lips pouted a little as she asked the jailer, "What is the matter with you to-day? why do you look at me so?"

"You must come out now," said he.

She rose slowly.

"Stand up, Sebastian; be reasonable."

She bent over the despairing man and tried to help him rise; but he pressed his face still more closely to the damp ground.

"Stand up!" she suddenly commanded. "Behave like a man, not like a child, if you wish me ever to come here again."

The prisoner rose. He was an old man, decrepit and thin, with the staring eyes peculiar to those who for years have vainly endeavored to pierce with their glances the dungeon walls that surround them.

"Oh, do not be angry!" he pleaded. "I am calm now."

"Farewell for to-day, my poor Sebastian!" she said, returning to her former wonderfully gentle tone, and walked quickly along the passage to the next door. As she looked round to see if the warden was going to open it for her she perceived *Heinrich*, who could now no longer conceal himself. He advanced towards her, and she watched his approach with surprise, but very calmly. Her gaze had only been fixed upon his breast, which glittered with orders; but as he stood silently before her in his manly dignity she raised her dark eyes to his, and their glances met like electric sparks. A flush slowly suffused the young girl's clearly cut face, and she involuntarily cast down her eyes as if she had received a shock.

"I am very much surprised to find such charming society in these inhospitable apartments, Fräulein," *Heinrich* began.

"I do not think it so very astonishing if the jailer's daughter seeks to aid her father in his arduous duties."

"Pardon me, Fräulein, if I take the liberty of doubting the accuracy of that statement," said *Heinrich*. "A jailer's daughter does not use such language; besides, the alarm displayed just now when I wished to enter the cell was far too great for me not to attribute more importance to your incognito. I am, unfortunately, compelled to look at your romantic appearance here through the extremely prosaic spectacles of an official, whose duty it is to obtain information in regard to every unusual event; therefore, by virtue of my office, I must inquire your name as well as request an explanation of your object."

The young girl looked at him with a long, steady gaze, while an expression played around her lips which *Heinrich* had never before seen on a woman's face,--a slight shade of irony.

"Very well, sir; if these people have already betrayed me I need use no further deception. I did not employ it for my own sake, but on account of these poor employees whom I have estranged from their duty. My name I hope I may be permitted to conceal; but I owe you an explanation about my object: it is only to do good. As others go to hospitals to heal diseased bodies, the majority of which can no longer be saved, I come hither to aid sick souls, where often the best and highest results may be effected. Do you think that so romantic? I have surely done no wrong in bribing the officials here, partly by money, partly by kind words, to allow me to make a daily round through the cells. In charitable institutions the doors and gates stand open to all who wish to bring aid and consolation to the sufferers. The thrice wretched unfortunates in our prisons are refused all means of cheering and ennobling them. No account is taken of individuality here, where individuality is the sole standard of measurement. A chaplain is sent to admonish criminals to repent, who is to convert them all in a lump according to his own theories; but people trouble themselves very little about the result of this manufacturing method of conversion, and when at the expiration of their imprisonment the criminals are sent back into the world, they begin again just where they stopped years before."

"Oh, Fräulein, you go too far! The punishment itself does most, for it terrifies them," replied *Heinrich*.

"Some, but certainly by far the smallest number. Many in the course of years become so hardened to it by custom that it loses its terrors, and the only moral the majority draw from imprisonment is--to manage more cautiously in future. There is only one guarantee for the permanent harmlessness of the criminal who cannot be imprisoned for life--amendment; but this principal object of punishment is always made subservient to the principle of avenging the insulted law."

"Well, and can you tell me also how this amendment is to be effected?" asked *Heinrich*, with increasing interest.

"I think by the admitting of judicious, trustworthy persons who can understand these different characters, and influence by advice and instruction, where the latter is needed."

"I admire your sanguine, philanthropic ideas," replied *Heinrich*; "but tell me yourself, my honored Fräulein, would not the state have too much to do if it was compelled to take into account the peculiarities of each individual criminal, and establish and pay a whole corporation of amendment officials?"

This jeer wounded the young girl, and a deep flush crimsoned her noble, intellectual brow for a moment; but after a pause she continued, undaunted: "Such a task would perhaps be too visionary and comprehensive for the government; but the citizens would come to its aid in this as well as in benevolent institutions, and from the hearts of the populace a corps of volunteer amendment officials would arise, in which our noblest patriots would undoubtedly be associated. But I have no intention of discussing a subject upon which folios have been already written, and which you understand better than I. I only wished to give the motive for my actions; and your recent sneer," she added, in a slightly defiant tone, "has fully convinced me that you will at least consider these 'sanguine philanthropic ideas' in the mind of a fanciful young girl too harmless to put them on official record, so my examination is doubtless over."

"Not yet," said *Heinrich*, firmly. "Your ideas and language do not seem to me quite so harmless as you suppose. I cannot help desiring to obtain more exact information concerning the motives of your acts and the bearing of your influence. I must and shall find means to do so. You stand too proudly and firmly before me for me to be able to believe so implicitly in the purposelessness of your enthusiasm. I am a servant of the government; as such it is both a duty and a right to ask, 'Who are you? in what relations do you stand towards the prisoners? what is your object?'"

"Who I am I shall not tell you; in what relations I stand towards the prisoners and what influence I exert you can learn from themselves; as for my object, can you not understand it? I am making myself useful. Do you think it requires another and more important purpose to act as I have done?"

"Making yourself useful?" repeated *Heinrich*, thoughtfully. "Do you really imagine you are of much use here?"

"*How much* is not for me to measure, I make myself as useful as I can. If every one only did this the world would be happier. It is not the success, but the will, that determines the value of an act. Vanity asks only about the result, honest purpose is satisfied with the doing."

"Indeed!" said *Heinrich*. "Are you so totally free from vanity?"

"Oh, no!" She suddenly burst into a merry laugh, and a ray of bright healthful enjoyment sparkled in her eyes. "I will not say that. God forbid that I should surround myself with a false halo. I am as vain as every other young girl; it is only where the sphere of my earnest labor is concerned that I am humble and modest, then my own person retires completely into the background, and I live solely to accomplish my purpose. But in the outside world, where I am least useful, I am vain, assuming, and selfish. I have often thought of this contradiction."

"I understand that," said *Heinrich*; "you feel small in comparison to your ideas and wishes, because like all gifted human beings you always desire more than you can accomplish. But when, outside of this sphere, you meet with commonplace, petty natures, you feel great, because you desire and accomplish so much more than they. Am I not right?"

The girl raised her eyes in astonishment, and looked at him earnestly. "You are right, and must have studied psychology more than one would have expected from a 'servant of the government.'"

"There is a singular blending of jest and earnest in your disposition," said *Heinrich*. "I have never before witnessed such rapid transitions from gay to grave and grave to gay in any one. Yes, I might really believe you followed only your own impulses without motive or purpose."

"Indeed, indeed you can! Believe me, I am doing nothing and want nothing, except to prove my love for mankind in every possible way. You seem to give me credit for political intrigues and dangerous connections. Oh, go to the prisoners, and convince yourself whether the spirit I instill is a revolutionary one or one of humility and repentance! By the manner in which I have taught these people to bear their misfortunes you will see whether my intentions are good and pure; and then you will give no information, but permit me to continue my office here, will you not?"

Heinrich made no reply; he was gazing earnestly into the sparkling eyes of the suppliant. Suddenly he pointed to the nearest door. "Go in to the prisoner there,--unobserved; I will watch how you discharge the duties of your office and then decide."

The warder opened the door, and the young girl quietly entered. A shrill cry of joy greeted her. "Oh, Prison Fairy! dear Prison Fairy! have you come at last?" exclaimed a young man.

"Why does he call her that?" *Heinrich* asked the turnkey, in a low tone.

"One of the prisoners gave her the name, and since then we have all called her by it, because we know no other, and this suits her so well."

"Oh, dear Fairy, I have passed another terrible night! So long as you are here I am as good as a child," continued the prisoner; "but when you go away, the old sorrow bursts forth again in all its fury. Oh, if I could go out into the world and satisfy the impulses of my own heart! Something might be made of me now, but after five years it will perhaps be too late. I felt that last night. True, the power to do evil may perhaps be broken in a ten years' imprisonment, but so is the strength to do well; and when I am sent out of this place, crippled in body and soul, an outcast from society, robbed of all civil honors and ability, it will get the dominion over me again. Then I shall be a mere idiot, who can no longer think of or feel anything except the greatness of his own misery; and for the assault I committed in a moment of passion, a twofold murder will have been practiced upon my body and soul during these ten years!"

"Albert, why are you in such a horrible mood to-day?" asked the young girl, in alarm. "You have not been so for a long time."

"Because I have been obliged to wait for you during so many painful hours; because I thought you were not coming again, and felt that in you alone is rooted the power which has upheld me for the last three years, that I should be lost if you remained away. No, I have not deserved this punishment."

"Albert, shall I repeat what I have always told you? Repeat it yourself."

"You said I was aware of the punishment, and voluntarily drew it upon myself by my crime, that I must bear what was the result of my own guilt; but I assure you again and again that if that terrible moment I had been sufficiently master of myself to be able to think, I should never have committed the crime; not from fear of the punishment, but of the sin."

"That excuses you in my eyes, but not in those of the law. Will you never be able to perceive that a man of such blind passions must be made harmless? Who will guarantee that the next instant, spite of all good resolutions, he may not be attacked by the same madness and commit a second murder?"

"Harmless! Yes, yes, I have been made harmless!" he groaned. "Why do you conjure up all the stings of conscience when I so greatly need consolation?"

"Because I see more clearly than ever that only the memory of your guilt makes your misery endurable; because you complain of the injustice of your punishment, and always become calmer when forced to acknowledge that, if not deserved, it was at least necessary and unfailing. And has not God sent a comfort to you in your sorrow,--a soul which understands you, which brings news of your beloved into your dungeon, and keeps the heart of your betrothed bride faithful to you? Is not this a divine mercy which can cheer you?"

"Yes, yes, I acknowledge the blessing, and for the sake of this mercy will strive and hope that I may procure for you the only reward you can receive, noble, wonderful creature!--the consciousness of having saved a soul!"

"Yes, my friend, give me that reward; it is the noblest gift which can be bestowed upon me for my efforts; and if I live to see the day when, purified and ennobled, you return to the world, I shall thank God more fervently than ever for having given me a heart to suffer with others, and also make them rejoice."

"And some day I will tell my children of the 'Prison Fairy!'" cried the young man, transported with hope.

Just at that moment *Heinrich* appeared in the doorway. "Well, sir," said the young girl, "is any other motive needed for my conduct? Do you now believe that such a moment would outweigh years of fruitless toil?"

"I understand and believe you, for you are a perfect enthusiast," said *Heinrich*, seizing her hand.

"Do you call this enthusiasm?" she said. "If so, every great act of love, from Christ's down to our own times, has been enthusiasm, and nothing is true and real except enthusiasm and its results. I confess, sir, that if all mankind shared your views, I would rather live with my prisoners in this dungeon than in the outside world!"

Heinrich gazed in astonishment at the proud, girlish figure, with the natural dignity of a pure, unshaken self-appreciation on the undaunted brow, and the alluring grace of true womanhood in the soft, undulating outlines of the whole frame; and an admiring reverence overwhelmed him, such as, for many a long year, no woman had inspired in his breast.

"Do not misunderstand me, Fräulein. You take the word in a different sense from the one intended. Where enthusiasm is united to such energy as you possess, it has always accomplished the noblest deeds the world has ever known; but we usually give that name----"

"To what we have no power to feel ourselves," involuntarily interrupted the excited girl; and it seemed as if her glance rested sorrowfully upon *Heinrich's* beautiful, expressive features.

Heinrich stood speechless. He felt as if a burning brand had suddenly been cast into the dark recesses of his soul, and his spiritual eyes were following the light as it penetrated deeper and deeper.

Just at that moment the prisoner's voice interrupted his reverie.

"Pardon me, sir," he began, timidly, "have I not the honor of seeing Herr von Ottmar?"

"Albert!" exclaimed *Heinrich*, "is it really you? I thought I recognized you, but doubted it, because I should have expected to find you in a monastery rather than a dungeon, and besides, you are very much altered. How did you, of all the world, happen to be placed in such close confinement?"

"Oh, Herr von Ottmar, you were so kind to me at college, may I tell you the story of my misfortune?" said Albert, the person who had been at the Jesuit college with *Heinrich*, and of whom he had spoken in his interview with Severinus.

"Will you allow it, Fräulein?" asked *Heinrich*.

"Certainly," replied the young girl, joyfully. "Perhaps the tragical history may for once arouse even in you the enthusiasm of compassion."

With these words she glanced at *Heinrich* with a pleading, inexpressibly charming smile. The latter could not turn his eyes away from the wonderfully changeful face, but murmured, as if in assent, "Prison Fairy!"

Meantime Albert had commenced his story. At first *Heinrich* gave it very little attention; gradually, however, he became attracted and listened eagerly, even anxiously. Albert related how, after being expelled from the order in the second year of his novitiate, he had for some time earned a scanty support, and at last lived several years as a tutor in the family of a wealthy German merchant. Six years before, this family removed from Italy to Germany, and in fact to the very capital where Ottmar had lived before his departure for N----. "There," said he, "I became acquainted with a young girl,--a girl who was really as pure and blooming as a rose. I had never loved a woman before,--the dark, ardent Italians were repulsive to my quiet nature,--but when I found the thoughtful, golden-haired German maiden, I clung to her with fervent affection. She loved me; and I, who had been tossed about the world from a child, was intoxicated by her tenderness, as if it were the aroma of some costly wine. I gradually neglected my pupils, my duty, and several times received censure; but in vain. Passion, so long repressed, was aroused, and locked me, the novice, completely within its magic circle.

"But now I became the sport of other feelings, which were more dangerous to me,--I grew jealous. My beloved suddenly seemed changed. She became timid, absent-minded, embarrassed, and day by day colder. I spoke to her father. The old man asked me whether I doubted the virtue of his child. The fever of jealousy and suspicion increased. I had no thoughts for anything else, and no longer knew what I was doing. Then one day my employers dismissed me. They had grown weary of my indolence and absence of mind, and I was penniless. With an agonized soul I hurried through the gathering twilight to seek my betrothed. I wished to find her heart once more,--the heart for which I had sacrificed and lost all. She was deeply moved when I told her of my misfortune and the tortures I had suffered for her sake; and as in decisive moments a long-concealed truth is often revealed, her innocent breast in this agitation could no longer hide its secret. She confessed, amid tears of agony and remorse, that she was on the point of being lost to me forever; that an aristocratic, handsome, brilliant gentleman had tempted her, and she was too weak to withstand him; that he had loaded her and her father with favors of all kinds, and she had thought gratitude made it her duty to obey him; nay, he had even persuaded her to come to his garden, but there, heaven be praised! she had been saved from disgrace by his old valet. The gentleman must have gone away an a journey, for she had heard nothing more from him.

"So I had sacrificed everything, and this was my reward. I stood silent, trembling from head to foot, as I leaned against the window in the little dark room on the ground-floor. I was not accustomed to say much, but I felt all the more. A cold perspiration trickled down my forehead; my clammy hands clinched the sill; the lights out-of-doors cast strange, unsteady shadows into the room, and dim, restless shadows settled upon my brain. At last I asked with difficulty, 'Who is the scoundrel?' The young girl had been standing beside me pale and trembling, with her eyes fixed intently upon the street. Suddenly she screamed and retreated from the window alarm. There he comes! so he hasn't gone yet! It is he! he is coming!' I saw a tall, slight figure, closely wrapped in a cloak approach the house; heard that it was he! The blood rushed to my brain! I seized an axe that was lying near the stove, dashed out, and felled the approaching figure to the ground! The young girl ran after me terror, saw the wounded man, and screamed, Jesus Maria! it is not he! You have killed an innocent person!' I felt bewildered and unable to move. Just then the man opened his eyes, looked at me, and gasped my name. My heart seemed to stop beating! I had killed Father Severinus!"

A long pause ensued. The prisoner was living over these scenes again, and needed a moment to collect his thoughts.

Heinrich gazed fixedly at the floor in silence. The Prison Fairy, in her dark dress, leaned calmly against the wall, her eyes resting on *Heinrich's* agitated face.

"What is the young girl's name?" asked *Heinrich*.

"Röschen, the daughter of Martin the beadle," replied Albert.

"And you do not know the name of your rival?"

"I have never learned it," continued Albert "I said no more to Röschen that terrible evening. She was the first to regain composure, and made me understand I must go home. Her father returned immediately after, and procured assistance for the wounded man, who did not again recover his consciousness while in his house. The old man stated that he had found him in the street. He could swear to this deposition, for he did not suspect the true state of affairs. So no one thought of me except Röschen. She thought he would never open his eyes again to betray me, and before the police came to Martin's house, to avoid a possible cross-examination, went to one of Princess Ottilie's maids. The latter instantly took her to the princess--"

"What, to Ottilie?" eagerly interrupted *Heinrich*.

"Certainly," replied Albert; "the princess has known her for a long time through the maid, who was well disposed towards Röschen, and often gave her work. The princess, gracious and benevolent as she always is, had once told her if she had anything to ask to come to her. So on this terrible day Röschen told the noble lady all her troubles, and the princess induced her to take an oath never to reveal to me nor any one else who her tempter was."

"Did Röschen mention his name to her?" asked *Heinrich*.

"Yes; and the princess must have been very kindly disposed towards the gentleman,--she insisted so earnestly that it should remain concealed. Then she gave Röschen money to aid me to escape and enable me to support myself for a long time, and promised to take her under her protection. In the firm conviction that Severinus could not survive the blow, I was mad enough to fly to N----, my native country. But although the doctors gave him up, he recovered his senses sufficiently to denounce me as the criminal. He expressed the most positive suspicion that I had made the murderous assault solely from revenge towards him because he had been the first in the college to declare me useless. A warrant was issued, and I was arrested and brought up for trial."

"But how did you happen to receive so severe a punishment, when Severinus escaped with his life and you had no premeditated design?" asked *Heinrich*.

"But I had no means of proving the fact!" cried Albert, despairingly. "I could do nothing but protest that I did not wish to punish Severinus, but the man who had tempted my betrothed bride. I could not tell who this tempter was, for I did not know; and I wished to conceal the name of my betrothed, for I would have died rather than bring the hitherto blameless girl into a disgraceful trial and brand her for life. Thus I could not prove the circumstances which might have placed my act in a more favorable light, and consequently my whole defense was rejected as a mere subterfuge. The statements of the angry Severinus were far more clear and positive than mine, so I was sentenced to ten years' imprisonment in irons, and would gladly bear my misery, nay, even death," he added, gnashing his teeth, "if I had only struck down that scoundrel of a seducer instead of the innocent Severinus, or at least could ever discover who he is!"

"Who he is? Look at me, Albert!" cried *Heinrich*. "I am that *scoundrel*!"

"Sir, you only tell me so because I stand before you in chains," cried Albert, starting like a wounded animal. His veins swelled, his fingers tore at his fetters, his breast heaved convulsively.

"Do you think so, unhappy man?" cried *Heinrich*. "Now let us see whether you will venture to lay hands upon me."

With these words he led the young girl out of the cell, and ordered the jailer to remove the irons at once.

"I command it, and will be responsible," he said, imperiously, as they hesitated, "and then lock us both in from the outside." The fetters were taken off, and the turnkeys withdrew, locking the door behind them.

"Now summon up your courage; you see that I am unarmed and your chains are removed," said *Heinrich*, standing directly before him, and gazing at him with an unwavering glance.

The unhappy roan stood motionless for a moment, engaged in a most violent struggle with his emotions. At last his whole frame trembled, his hands fell as if weighed down by fetters of double weight, and he sank at *Heinrich's* feet, unable to utter a word.

The latter gazed at him a moment in silence, and then knocked on the door. The turnkeys came in anxiously and raised Albert, but his knees still trembled so violently that he was obliged to sit down on his bed. The Prison Fairy, with a sublime expression of sympathy, stroked his burning brow, and gazed at *Heinrich* with imploring expectation.

The latter quietly approached the group. "Albert, I have convinced myself that you can subdue your passions. You are worthy of the freedom I shall now help you secure. You shall no longer suffer for my frivolity, and both you and this lady shall be convinced that I am no scoundrel. Farewell for to-day."

Albert suddenly clasped his hands over his brow, and a flood of tears relieved his oppressed heart. *Heinrich* looked for a long time at the young girl, who, with pallid face, was gazing silently at the floor, then begged her to follow him, and left the cell.

When they were outside, he asked, "What do you think of me now?"

"If you go on and give yourself up to the law, as the best proof of Albert's deposition, I shall think well of you."

"I have determined to do something of the kind," said *Heinrich*, "and I hope you will then be convinced that I am not so entirely destitute of all enthusiasm."

"I shall be very glad, for the sake of my prisoners."

"Only for your prisoners? Why not for your own sake too?"

"Because it will principally concern the welfare of the unfortunate men who are now apparently dependent upon your compassion. I, thank God, have nothing to hope from you."

"Indeed!" said *Heinrich*, in an irritated tone. "But if, after those words, I refuse you permission to go to your *protégés* again?"

"You will not do that," replied the young girl, firmly. "If you really feel compassion, you will not, merely from an irritable whim, deprive the prisoners of the only comfort that can be afforded them in their cheerless situation."

"Fräulein," said *Heinrich*, with his usual winning courtesy, "you certainly do very little to bribe the government official; yet this very course wins me still more, and I do not merely permit, I entreat you to return and accept me as your assistant."

"So long as you are with the prisoners, sir, they will not need me. Permit me to come here at a time when you are absent."

"You have become suspicious of me; we are farther apart now than at the first moment of meeting. My candor in your presence was over-hasty. Forgive me, and mingle a little of your kindness of heart with the austerity of your youthful ideas of virtue, that you may not utterly condemn. Will you? You forgive, and try to reform even criminals: reform me too. Why are you so intolerant to me alone?"

She gazed at him with gentle earnestness, and slowly shook her head. "When I enter a prison, I know I shall find a criminal, and am prepared for arguments about sin which are not too difficult to disprove. But with you I am disappointed and embarrassed, for your face promised something better, and I cannot enter into your delicate sophistry. I am an 'enthusiast'; you a 'servant of the government': the two characters are not easily harmonized. Farewell. Allow me to choose the time of my visits here, and forgive the poor jailers whom I have outwitted." With these words she hastily ran up the stone staircase.

Heinrich stamped his foot angrily on the floor. "Willful, haughty witch!" he murmured, as he hurried after her.

She paused on the upper step and nodded to him with all the winning charm of heartfelt emotion. "Be kind to my prisoners, Herr von Ottmar, and I will be kind to you!" Then, turning a corner, she disappeared before *Heinrich* could follow her. He gazed into vacancy, as if he wished to trace in the air the shadow into which she seemed to have dissolved before his eyes.

The jailers timidly approached him with their petition for pardon. "You shall be forgiven for the sake of this lady's eloquence, which is difficult to resist. But on pain of losing your places let no one hear of what has taken place to-day, or may occur in future," said *Heinrich*, sternly, and left the building.

The two turnkeys looked at each other a long time in silence; at last one said, as the result of his meditations, "It's the Prison Fairy!"

Heinrich's astonishment was raised to the highest pitch by the appearance of this young girl. Even the thought of the strange fatality which had made Severinus the innocent victim of the sensuality he had denounced so bitterly, a few weeks before, could not long fix his attention. He was convinced that Severinus had discovered to what "rose" he had wished to open his doors, and had gone to Martin's house with the intention of obtaining his daughter's confidence, and using it against him. "Poor Severinus!" said he. "You were compelled to pay dearly for your efforts to save souls. The ghost of the artist whose Hebe you so mercilessly shattered has revenged itself upon you; but the innocent tool of this vengeance was the very person whom you had most deeply injured, the poor, rejected Albert! Oh, the wonderful justice of fate!"

Then he returned again to the remarkable apparition of the young girl, which unceasingly occupied his thoughts. She had such a peculiar, changeful temperament that she had pleasantly affected every chord of his being. A deep earnestness gleamed through the naïve coquetry by which she had sought to bribe him to favor her *protégés*. He perceived that hers was a kindred spirit, that she too, like himself, was under the influence of supernatural powers, but in her childlike soul had unconsciously united these forces in harmonious, changeful action, instead of, like him, being their sport.

This perception awed him. He felt that he would be understood by this nature if he showed himself openly to her, and rejected a thousand plans to discover who she was. "What strength is it that, in a feeble woman, rules powers which have crushed and conquered me--a man? Would not this strength exert a blissful influence over me also? With what joyous pride she said, 'I am making myself useful.' She is happy in the thought, and wants nothing more. Is it possible? Yet it must be. In her character lies concealed that spirit of martyrdom which dies smiling for its idea.

"There is something strange in a philanthropy which rejoices in making others happy. Hitherto I have not desired to give joy to any one except myself! Perhaps she will teach me her art.

"She joyously collects the tears of her dirty criminals as if they were the most precious pearls. I wear on my breast the jewels of various orders,--and yet all have never given me so much pleasure as a single tear causes her.

"Who knows, perhaps I have not yet done as much to earn my orders as she was compelled to do to win her pearls from the secret depths of those hardened souls. Oh, she is a glorious creature! She has the cleverness of a man, and yet is so thoroughly womanly. She proves conclusively that woman can really rise above her narrow sphere of ideas without becoming unwomanly, and that the true emancipation of the mind has nothing in common with that emancipation from principles and forms which so often repels us in those termed women of genius. Yes, such a woman would be capable of obtaining an influence over me.

"But what shall I do to find her again? First of all, I will do what she desired, I will confess the truth to the prince and obtain Albert's pardon. Noble as she is in thought and feeling, she will be touched and conciliated,--will believe in me. So, when occasion offers, I am doing a good deed once more. The prince is a sensible man. He will see the affair in its true light and not refuse me the little favor."

VII
AN ARISTOCRAT

Heinrich went to the palace that very day and requested a private audience. The prince, a young man with stern features and aristocratic bearing, received him in his study. He had just risen from his writing-table, which was covered with a pile of papers, and upon his lofty brow still rested the shadows of thought, which began slowly to disappear at the sight of Ottmar. The large blue eyes seemed wearied with toil, and gazed earnestly into vacancy, as if in search of some ideal country that could be better governed than his own. Long, fair whiskers framed his delicate face. His youthful, earnest character confined itself rigidly to the strict forms of unapproachable dignity. Words flowed from his lips as purely, readily, and smoothly as a cool breeze, and any one who saw him for the first time would be chilled by the frigid reserve which pervaded his whole appearance. He was the very type of the aristocrat by birth and education, who had polished his manners into an impalpable shield against the common herd. The foundation of all aristocratic deportment is economy of time. The aristocrat husbands all personal exertion as far as possible. He chooses the shortest, most indispensable forms of speech, limits his voice to the lowest tone that can be heard, and his gestures to those absolutely unavoidable. He considers this a duty towards himself and others; he speaks curtly and rapidly, because he is always in a hurry himself and is not sure that others may not be also; uses a low tone, because he does not know whether it will be agreeable to others to hear more of his voice than may be necessary to comprehend his meaning; makes few or no gestures, because he does not wish to compel the eyes of others to follow aimless courses and bendings. In intercourse with his superiors or equals, modesty forbids him to intrude more of his personal character than is indispensably connected with the affair, and pride withholds him from revealing to his inferiors anything more than is unavoidable. Thus alone the aristocrat acquires the self-control and delicacy that distinguish him. Only by this silent accommodation to forms, limited to the lowest minimum of personal exertion, does he when a courtier regain the time of which the necessary ceremonials rob him, and only this extreme indulgence and careful use of his physical strength gives him the endurance demanded by the exactions of court-life.

The young prince was a perfect type of these precepts. Whether a warm or cold heart throbbed beneath that smooth exterior, even *Heinrich*, his confidant, did not venture to decide.

"You have come at a very opportune moment, my dear Ottmar," said he. "I was about to send for you."

Heinrich bowed low, in answer to this greeting.

"See, here are a pile of papers and letters which I wish to share with you. So much has come at the same time."

"You know, my prince, that you have no more devoted servant than I. Let me bear a part of your burden," said *Heinrich*, in his most persuasive tones, for his power of imitating the expression of what he did not possess was most masterly.

"I know that you have often proved it. If I can find truth anywhere it is in you. You alone are impartial, and see clearly, while the circle of vision in most men is limited by personal interests and prejudices."

"I have the good fortune to have my prosperity secured by perfectly independent circumstances, and therefore can follow my convictions; but this falls to the lot of very few. Do not judge them too harshly, your Highness, for the majority of mankind are fettered by anxieties concerning their means of livelihood."

"It may be so, but they lack the essential thing,--genius,--the clean, far-seeing gaze which no lessons in state-craft can supply; besides, those who do understand anything rarely possess the art of telling the truth without wounding others or becoming brutal. One cannot well have any dealings with such people.

"There is the new press-law again. Good Minister B---- once took it into his head to carry it through. You know his blunt manner of urging a decision. I must confess that this preliminary, which almost entirely abolishes the right of censorship, is contrary to my feelings and conscience. Shall I permit every revolutionary wretch to scatter poison among my thoughtless, credulous people? Ought I to do so, as a prince, whose duty it is to watch over the nation intrusted to his care as a father watches his children?"

"This question presents only two different points of view, your Highness. Do you prefer to win, by this act of clemency, a transient gratitude? or, by persistently following your better convictions, obtain lasting satisfaction? If the former, make the desired concessions; yet consider that this first favor will draw an immeasurable number of consequences in its train. From the moment this new freedom of the press is fairly established, you will regret having undertaken obligations which you cannot execute without inaugurating a totally different *régime*. Your Highness knows that the intoxication of freedom, caused by the victorious revolution, has penetrated here also, and the fire now and then still glimmers beneath the ashes. Will you, by means of the press, permit air to reach the scarcely suffocated flames?"

"May God have mercy upon my poor country!" murmured the prince, under his breath.

"Must not a moment come when your Highness's duty will compel you to check the progress of this seditious literature? and will you not then have broken your promise and forfeited the transient gratitude which would be paid you?"

"Very true."

"Well, what withholds your Highness from following your convictions, which you have already so often tested, that your own feelings were always the best guides?"

"The doubt whether I can silence and conciliate the discontented masses in a way that will be beneficial to them,--the doubt regarding the means I ought to employ," said the prince, thoughtfully, rubbing his brow.

"But surely this is not the right expedient, your Highness. By granting the freedom of the press you only afford discontented people an opportunity of making their useless complaints and wishes public, and thus making them still more persuaded of hardships, while you neither can, nor desire to, remove their causes. Will not this bring you into a thousand conflicts between your heart and your most sacred convictions in regard to popular education?"

"Certainly."

"If I might venture to give your Highness my humble counsel, I should say that the freedom of the press is the last thing that ought to be granted to a nation. The people must first be contented; then they may be allowed to speak. Pardon my frankness, your Highness; you know I am always truthful."

"That is the very quality I prize in you; but since you are now in the mood to express your opinions even more sincerely than usual, I should also like to hear by what means you propose to content the country."

Heinrich was astonished by this question. He perceived that he had gone incautiously near the verge of truth, and felt he must return, for to-day he had more cause than ever to desire to win the prince's favor, while strangely enough he had never taken less pleasure in deceit.

"Your Highness," he said, at last, "do not ask me whether your subjects are contented, for you must yourself answer the question with a 'no,' without being able to alter the state of affairs. If you ask whether they are prosperous, I may be permitted to reply 'yes.' To make a nation prosperous is within the power of princes; to keep them contented depends upon the power of time. Your country, your Highness, is prospering admirably under your august sceptre. The causes of discord do not come from within, but from without. They do not result from your government, but from the tempest of freedom which roars from foreign frontiers. When this tempest subsides the nation will once more perceive its prosperity. To await this time quietly and indulgently seems to me the only counsel a conscientious man is permitted to lay at the feet of your Highness."

"You are right, Ottmar. I have already said the same thing to myself. If every prince had a friend like you ('Who apparently contradicts him while telling him the very thing he wants to hear,' *Heinrich* mentally interposed), matters would not proceed so far," said the sovereign, extending three fingers of his slender hand to *Heinrich*. "I shall not sign the press-law. I hope my throne, which has outlasted the storms of so many centuries, will also be strong enough to withstand the pressure of these times. If I perceived that these innovations would produce happiness, I certainly would not withhold them from my country. But I cannot. Other nations possibly may be ripe for freedom; my people are not. The men called 'patriots' may say what they like; their intentions are doubtless good, but they wish to raise the masses to a position of which they are not and never will be worthy. No one can see into this matter more clearly than the priests. We must ask them, if we wish to learn to know the people, and the ideal we have imagined will soon vanish. If freedom can be given to these rough natures, it is emancipation from evil by the perception of good, and this only religion and her representatives can bestow. Therefore, my dear Ottmar, I will scorn to purchase a cheap popularity by frivolous concessions, and content myself with fulfilling the duties God imposed upon me with the holy oil. I do not desire to hold the highest place, I only wish to be the protector and guide of the nation intrusted to my care: so, as you have very justly observed, away with all inconsequent and aimless innovations!"

The prince carelessly pushed away the papers and drew out several letters. "Here is this marriage business again. You must do me a favor which no one else can bestow. I have the privilege of choosing between two charming princesses, neither of whom I know, as one has just entered society and the other resides at a court I have never visited. You are prudent and skillful,--a connoisseur in female beauty and character; you must take a private pleasure trip, and make the acquaintance of one of the ladies, that you may be able to give me exact information concerning her, and thus perhaps save me the trouble of a useless journey in search of a wife. But more of this hereafter. I see you wish to tell me something, and have been indiscreet in delaying you so long."

"I have nothing to say which could be more important than listening to you, my prince. However, as you command, I must obey; besides, the matter does not concern me, but an unfortunate man, who is suffering unjustly for my fault, and whom I feel it my duty to aid. Will your Highness graciously condescend to permit me to appeal from the prince to the man, to make a confession which not the prince, but the man, should hear?"

"Speak frankly."

"Five years ago a certain Albert Preheim was sentenced to ten years' imprisonment in irons for having committed a murderous assault upon the present assistant and former prefect of the Collegium Germanicum, who was spending a few days in H----."

"Oh, yes; I remember," interrupted the prince. "The man defended himself by the incredible statement that he had mistaken him for a rival, but could prove nothing and was sentenced."

"Well, your Highness, the man is too severely punished. He is no murderer, and his statements are true. He acted without premeditation, when almost unaccountable for his deeds and under the impulse of the blindest jealousy. The act he committed concerns me, since he had reason to believe me the seducer of his betrothed bride."

The prince drew his breath through his shut teeth like a person whose sensitive feelings have been rudely jarred, and made no reply. *Heinrich* noticed it and possessed sufficient tact to represent the whole affair as if he had himself been the victim of accident. The nocturnal visit he had induced the young girl to make he prudently omitted, and ascribed everything else to the simplicity of an inexperienced maiden, who, in the agony roused by the stings of conscience, had represented the matter to her deceived lover in a very vague and exaggerated manner. In this case, as usual, he succeeded in convincing the prince.

"Make no further apologies about so natural an indiscretion," said he. "True, I confess that, for my own part, I cannot understand how the most tempting opportunity can ever obtain the mastery over the will. As a prince, everything is at my command, but my wishes have never led me to the pleasures of mere sensuality; still, I judge no man who thinks and feels differently in regard to these matters,--you least of all; therefore do not consider it any token of disfavor if I am compelled to request you to make amends for your error, for such it is, yourself. Unfortunately, I am unable to be of any assistance to you."

"Your Highness!" exclaimed *Heinrich*, in astonishment, "will you not pardon the unfortunate man?"

"You ask a pardon for Severinus's would-be murderer. I cannot believe that you have maturely considered this matter. Severinus still suffers from the effects of that dangerous wound, and ought I to release the man who dealt it? Severinus is the soul of the whole reverend order of Jesuits. He has relations with the leading ecclesiastics in my domains. The order, nay, even the whole church, was greatly agitated by this unprecedented crime, whose punishment my confessor thought far too light, and now, after five years, I am to perform a most unusual act of clemency. Tell me yourself, how would it be received? how would it be looked upon by the whole priesthood, which was then deeply offended because I would not make the criminal a terrible example? If you so firmly believe the man's deposition, leave the matter to the regular course of the law; then he will not need my pardon."

"I thought, your Highness, in consideration of the certainty that the unhappy man did not wish to kill Severinus----"

"That is all very fine, my dear fellow," interrupted the prince, with somewhat more animation than usual; "but who knows it? And if I should bring it forward as the cause of my clemency, who will believe it? Can I prove that my private opinion is the correct one, and a sufficient cause for remitting a punishment universally considered to be well merited? My individual opinion ought not voluntarily to take sides with Severinus's assailant, and decide a matter so complicated. Only the calm, unanimous judgment of a court of justice can determine the true meaning of the act, and free him by the power of the law. If you are convinced of the truth of your assertion, you will certainly succeed in persuading the court to believe it, and you doubtless feel that the duty of bearing the punishment for your error rests with you rather than me."

The prince said all this in a low, rapid tone, with a most friendly smile, yet every word fell upon *Heinrich's* soul like a blow. He clinched his teeth even while he smiled, mentally called the prince a smooth, cold egotist, and was convinced that he was a martyr of self-sacrifice in comparison with this man. When two egotists meet, each, with mournful self-satisfaction, considers himself the victim of the other. This was the case with the prince, who also reflected upon the selfishness of *Heinrich's* expectations, and thought himself very noble because he forgave him.

"Your Highness," said *Heinrich*, with the frankness which was his most dangerous mask, "if I avoided adopting the means you mentioned, it was because as a member of the court and council of state I dared not venture to compromise myself by any public transactions in regard to this delicate matter. I thought I was obliged to honor your Highness's servant in myself as well as in any one else. I did not suppose that a powerful prince like my most gracious ruler need fear the anger of the priesthood for performing such a truly Christian deed, and therefore most humbly beg pardon for my indiscreet petition."

"You know you are indispensable to me, Ottmar, and can ask a great deal; but, even though you may feel angered, I cannot grant this request. Even if, as you apparently wished to intimate just now, I need not fear the anger of the priests, I will not rouse it uselessly. If I am the head, the priesthood is the heart of my body politic; shall I wound it if it can be avoided? Of course, something must be done for the poor man; but if one of us is to make a sacrifice for him, it is surely better and more natural for you to do it than for me. Give the information therefore, and after his release I will grant him every favor you may ask."

"So your Highness really commands the affair to be made public?"

"Say yourself. Will it not become so under any circumstances? You know that I could only pardon Albert Preheim by convincing all as well as myself that he was not guilty of the murderous assault upon Severinus. To attain this object should I not be compelled to reveal your acts, first to the priests, and afterwards, for their satisfaction, to the public? You would then be quite as much exposed as if you appeared before a court of justice, and much more harshly judged than if you atoned for your indiscretion by a frank confession in favor of Preheim."

"Of course," said *Heinrich*, bitterly.

"Although the affair will then attract attention, which will be as disagreeable to me as to you, it will in any event be forgotten in the course of a few months. You must take the journey which I just mentioned to you at once,--and when you return no one will give it another thought."

"So, your Highness, it is your wish that a man whom you openly honor with your confidence, who has a voice in the council, and with whom you deign to share your cares concerning the weal and woe of the state, should appear before a court of justice and a curious public to make confession of his youthful errors?"

"Oh," said the prince, "I leave it entirely to your conscience to decide whether you do not consider a man whom you thought worthy of my protection sufficiently deserving for you to perform an act of magnanimity in his behalf. If you are perfectly satisfied that he is too severely punished, I know your sense of honor well enough to be sure that you will act for him. If you are not, you need not expose yourself for him any more than you will ask me to grant his pardon. Give this matter careful consideration; I hope you will not force upon me the alternative of making an innocent man suffer unjustly, or offending those members of my state whom I esteem most highly." He looked at his watch. "It is eight o'clock: I must dress. Shall I see you this evening at the princess mother's?"

"I am at your service, your Highness."

"A pity that it is so small a company. I can have no further conversation with you about that affair of the marriage to-day."

"I deeply regret that I have not better employed the precious moments your Highness condescended to bestow."

"Well, *au revoir*," said the prince, rising, and dismissing *Heinrich* with a gracious wave of the hand.

Heinrich had required all his self-control to avoid making several subtle rejoinders that hovered on his tongue. He was furiously enraged by the failure of his plan and the prince's terror of the priesthood, as he called it. He perceived that the young, strictly religious man was right from his point of view, but rejected his whole standard of measurement with indescribably bitter irony. For the first time since he had lived in N---- this trait in the prince's character had become personally detrimental, and he felt anew the full severity of the fate which had forced him to bend to this hated system.

His longing to win the Prison Fairy and his sense of right struggled violently with his pride. Should he give up the whole affair now? Could he rest satisfied with a single, useless effort, without being ashamed of himself, lowered in the eyes of the prince, and, above all, in the opinion of the Prison Fairy? Must not her pure, noble soul withdraw from him forever, after she had obtained this glimpse of his nature? Was she not the only joy for which he hoped in his cheerless life, and was he to lose it just as he had found it?

Then he asked himself whether she was really what she seemed, whether she deserved the sacrifice he was making for her sake. With deep loathing he saw himself standing before the court, in the presence of the malicious public; his pride struggled against the thought with all its power, and amid these painful considerations *Henri* even allowed himself to be influenced by the fear that, after the confession of his error, the ladies of the court would be implacably lost to him. Would the Prison Fairy outweigh all this to *Heinrich* as well as *Henri*? Would a smile from her have power to compensate *Heinrich* for the sneering laugh on the faces which had hitherto shown only fawning affability? Was her esteem more than the admiration of the court, which would now have nothing for him save the scornful shrug of the shoulders?

While *Henri* was charming the ladies at the court *soirée* by his shallow gallantries, these considerations ceaselessly occupied *Heinrich's* thoughts, and he resolved, cost what it might, to see the Prison Fairy again on the following day.

VIII
IN THE PRISON

Heinrich excused himself from the evening gathering on the plea of illness, and went to the prison. Here be ordered Albert to be removed to another, as he asserted, healthier cell, and remained in his stead in the narrow, gloomy dungeon, which, according to his opinion, the young girl would doubtless visit first. He also gave the most positive orders that nothing should be said to her about his presence or the change that had been made in Albert's cell, and thus hoped that she could not escape him. At eight o'clock in the morning he was listening in the greatest suspense to every step that approached his door. All passed by. His expectation increased to impatience,--his impatience to longing. He, who was accustomed to command, to whom all hastened, sat in a lonely cell like a poor criminal, and was forced to wait patiently until the moment of deliverance approached. He, who had so often been ardently expected behind silken curtains and flowers, now gazed through the iron bars of a little grated window at a the patch of sky, as if imploring that he might be granted what he desired. He had not even thought of taking a book with him, and the most terrible ennui was added to the monotony of the one thought that occupied his mind. The clocks in the various steeples struck the quarter and half hours; to count the near and distant strokes was the sole interruption of his dull reverie. And he had submitted to all this for the sake of a coy young girl, a stranger to him, though he did not even know who and what she was, or what she could ever be to him! He voluntarily put himself in the place of the prisoners, especially that of Albert, who had probably listened with a beating heart for days to hear if she were coming,--she, the only thing he still possessed in the eternal monotony of his imprisonment. His excited fancy pictured more and more vividly how the prisoner must live, year after year, exposed to the most terrible ennui, with only the sight of his four bare walls and his gnawing thoughts; how the only signs of human life that could reach him were a dull roar and the sound of the bells, and the only change in his slowly dragging days the transition from light to darkness. "I can open this door when I choose,--can go out when I please; only the necessity of gratifying an idle whim detains me; and yet the thought of being compelled to spend twenty-four hours here chills my breast, to say nothing of three hundred and sixty-five days and nights, and *five* times,--*ten* times as many!" He drew a long breath, and, merely to employ his thoughts, began to calculate with nervous eagerness how many hours this would be. How often Albert must already have reckoned it! What does such a man *think* during the long years? The soul needs nourishment as well as the body. Albert would doubtless have become imbecile had it not been for the Prison Fairy. She is the one thought that keeps his soul awake. The clock struck eleven. "I have been waiting three hours already. Suppose she should not come? What must it be to the prisoner, when she remains away all day, and he has waited through the twenty-four hours in vain!"

Worn out by involuntary idleness, he sinks upon his couch at night, looks up to the little window, and watches for the thousandth time the motions of the clouds and the gathering darkness; perhaps even greets a twinkling star as a joyful event, compares it to the eyes of the Prison Fairy, and wonders why she did not come to-day, and whether she will come to-morrow, until he falls into his feverish slumber. He wakes early in the morning longing for her, would gladly hasten the hours with his panting breath, urge on the strokes of the clocks by the pulsations of his heart, and yet he has no resource but patience,--continual patience. His soul rises and falls between fear and hope, his head burns, his limbs ache under the pressure of his chains. The sun sends its wandering rays into the cell and shines upon the door; suddenly it springs open, and, as if allured by the rays, bathed in the splendor, the beautiful figure stands in the entrance in all the brightness of her living, loving presence, greeted by a cry of joy as piercing as I heard yesterday from Albert's lips. "Prison Fairy!" She approaches him; she touches the fetters with her flower-white hands, and they become light; her breath cools his feverish brow; she speaks to him a tone thrilling with the melody of enthusiastic feeling; she looks at him with her mysterious eyes, and on her brow is throned that dignity which no bold desire, no injustice, dare approach.

Oh, how longingly he must await such consolation! how he must----

The door opened: a female figure was about to enter; he turned, and the painful suspense escaped in a shrill exclamation,--"Prison Fairy!" The door was closed, and light footsteps rapidly retreated. As in a dream we often vainly strive to reach something with trembling haste, the width of the little space he must pass to pursue the fugitive seemed far too great for Ottmar.

His hands trembled so violently in his hurry that he opened the heavy old lock with difficulty, and when he emerged she had disappeared.

"Where is she?" he asked of a jailer who was just coming up the passage.

"Does your lordship mean the Prison Fairy? I have not seen her to-day."

"That is a lie! She was here just now."

"Yes, your lordship, it may be so; she always bids the Herr Inspector good-morning before she goes to the prisoners."

"Call the inspector here," said *Heinrich*, returning to the cell.

The official, an elderly man, with honest features, obeyed the summons.

"Herr Inspector," said *Heinrich*, sternly, "you have for several years allowed a lady secret access to the prisoners."

"Yes, Herr Geheimrath," said the man, with dignified composure.

"Have you ever received permission to do so from any higher authority?"

"No, Herr Geheimrath."

"And yet you have exceeded the limits of your instructions?"

"I must bear the punishment patiently."

"Are you so courageous?"

"Herr Geheimrath," said the old man, modestly, "I have done what my own heart dictated, and was aware that in following my convictions of Christian duty I was violating only the letter, not the spirit, of my office."

"A prison official, and possessed of a heart! The two do not harmonize, Herr Inspector."

"Pardon me, I did not know it. I cherish the belief that our wise government desires to have the criminal justly not cruelly treated; and to serve the arm of justice is an office which a man who has a heart can hold, although it sometimes falls heavily upon it."

"These are the subtle reasonings of the Prison Fairy, as she is called here. Yet I am disposed to pass over the affair if you will instantly tell me the lady's name, social position, and residence."

"Herr Geheimrath," said the inspector, smiling, "I think if my offense deserves pardon you will be sufficiently just to grant it without conditions, for I cannot possibly fulfill those you have just mentioned."

"Herr Inspector!"

"Herr Geheimrath, I give you my word of honor that I do not know who the lady is, nor where she lives."

"I must believe you; but in that case your course is all the more inexplicable."

"I see, Herr Geheimrath, that I owe you a detailed account of the matter, and am ready to confirm each of my statements upon oath."

"Well?" said *Heinrich*, with ill-repressed curiosity.

"When, five years ago, the jail was filled with political prisoners, a young man named Reinhold was brought in who excited my compassion in the highest degree. He had taken part in the conflicts in the Province of B----, but seemed so feeble and gentle that I could not understand how he had been concerned in such deeds. He was sentenced to death, but the prince commuted the decree to an imprisonment of twenty years. His winning, lovable character aroused the sympathy of all who saw him. Day by day the unfortunate man grew paler and more feeble; but he said nothing. No one heard a word of complaint from his lips, and he always had the same gentle smile for all who entered his cell. Even the jailers pitied this quietly endured, silent suffering, and remarked to each other that the prisoner seemed ill. I went to him, and urgently pressed him to tell me what was the matter. He thanked me and protested that he was quite well; his heart was heavy, but no one could help him there except the one whose coldness had made him rush into his crime and misfortune, and whom he must love till the day of his death. I did not wish to press him with any further questions, because the recollection seemed to exhaust him. One day the young lady of whom we are speaking came to me and implored me through her tears to procure her an interview with the prisoner, Reinhold. I refused. The next day she came again, as she said, to inquire after the prisoner's health, and begged me to allow her to do so daily. This, of course, I could not deny her. She appeared in my little room regularly every afternoon at a certain hour, and I must confess that the young girl soon became as dear to me as if she had been my own child. She did not tell me who she was, but her whole conduct showed that she must belong to a good family, and be perfectly pure in heart; besides, I was too modest to ask what she did not tell me of her own free will. One day I could give her no good news about the prisoner's health. His weakness had greatly increased. She received my communication with so much sorrow that I could no longer doubt some close tie bound her to Reinhold, and that she was the very person for whom he was grieving so bitterly. She clasped my hands in agony and implored me only to let her look at him a moment through the open door of his cell. I could not refuse the poor child this. I led her to the spot, went to the prisoner, and left the door slightly ajar, that she, concealed behind it, might look in. But who can depend upon the unruly heart of seventeen? Scarcely had I addressed two words to Reinhold when she rushed in, and, with a cry of agony, threw herself upon his breast. Neither could speak, and my own tears flowed freely. The unhappy man was so weak that he could not endure this tempest of joy, but fell from her arms pale and lifeless. She sank on the floor beside him and silently took his head in her lap. There she sat as if the Virgin had appeared in bodily form with the dead Christ. Herr Geheimrath, no one worthy of the name of man could have separated them; it would have seemed to me like sacrilege!"

"Go on," said *Heinrich*, in the greatest suspense.

"When Reinhold had partially recovered, a touching scene ensued,--a scene which may be felt but not described. They had never spoken to each other before; she did not even seem to have returned his affection, and implored his forgiveness for her want of love which had driven him out into the world to his ruin. But she would make amends. She called me to witness that she solemnly betrothed herself to him, and implored me in the name of the God before whom I should one day have to stand in the great and final account, to give her once for all free admittance to her betrothed husband's cell. I perceived how she had outwitted me by so completely captivating me during her daily visits, that I could no longer refuse her anything. I was convinced that the prisoner had in her one who would faithfully care for his soul, for she is pure and gentle as a child, wise and firm as a man. So I granted her desire, and up to this moment have never repented it; she has brought a better spirit into the institution, and exerts a remarkable power over the prisoners."

"And the betrothed bridegroom 2" asked *Heinrich*.

"She thought she could still save him by her affection, and nursed him with admirable tenderness. He was happy; but even as grief had once threatened to destroy him, so it was now with love,--he slowly languished.

"After a time she perceived it and attributed it to prison life. She found that the greatest suffering a man can feel is loss of freedom, bore in her heart the deepest compassion, not only for him but his companions in misfortune, and several times assured me that if she did not need all her time for Reinhold she would gladly visit the other prisoners, but she did not wish to deprive him of a moment."

"Just then a political criminal who had been sentenced to fifteen years' imprisonment was brought in, so infuriated by his fate that he tore at his chains with his teeth, and tried to dash out his brains against the heavy irons like Caius Cœlius, as he said; in short, he behaved like a madman. No one could obtain any influence over him; he cursed all who approached him and scoffed at the priests. Then I thought I would ask the Prison Fairy--her lover had jestingly called her so because she forbade him to mention her real name--if she would not try to bring the lunatic to reason. She went to him with the utmost readiness, and the man was so charmed by her beauty and courage that he yielded to her and obeyed her with the greatest devotion. If he ever regain freedom, he will owe it to that girl that he is not lunatic or a reprobate.

"Six months had elapsed, when we heard a cry of despair from Reinhold's cell; and when we hurried to it, found her in the same attitude as on their first meeting,--kneeling on the floor supporting her lover's head in her arms. But this time he was not to wake again,--he was dead. The Prison Fairy wept over the pallid face so bitterly that the jailers crept noiselessly out of the cell, that they might not see her grief. The physician attached to the prison was summoned; said that he had had heart disease, and perhaps would have lived no longer under any circumstances. We talked to her as well as we could; and when she saw how deeply her sorrow grieved us, she composed herself and consoled us. But when the prison door opened and the corpse was borne out, she broke down, and shrieked, Poor Reinhold, now you are *free!*' The tone still rings in my ears; I shall never forget it as long as I live.

"When we were alone she thanked me with touching affection, and entreated me henceforth to grant her admittance to all the prisoners, to alleviate the mental tortures, which often far exceeded the crime and the purpose of the punishment. After witnessing her success with the furious Sebastian, I could not refuse the noble and benevolent wish in which her soul sought consolation; and you must permit me to believe, Herr Geheimrath, that a blessing follows her wherever she goes."

"But does she seem to be entirely consoled now?" asked *Heinrich*.

"For two years she mourned deeply; nay, I often watched her with real anxiety; but at last time and her healthful nature asserted their rights. She grew stronger, gradually became calmer, even gay, and for the last year has been the same vivacious child she was five years ago. Now you know all, honored sir, and can judge for yourself."

Heinrich gazed into vacancy long and thoughtfully. At last he said, kindly, "Under such extraordinary circumstances people must of course make exceptions. You are an honest man, Herr Inspector!"

"I thank you, Herr Geheimrath!"

"But now, tell me, has it never occurred to you to send some one after this strange girl, to see what direction she takes?"

"She always went to the stand of hackney-coaches and drove away in one of them. There is a consistency in everything she does, which would sometimes terrify one if he had not learned to know her kind heart."

"I thank you for your report. Farewell, Herr Inspector." *Heinrich* took his hat and went out.

"Albert must be free! the Prison Fairy must become mine!" said he, as he left the prison.

IX
FRAULEIN VERONICA VON ALBIN

Thus his resolution was at last formed. He perceived that Albert's liberation was the only price with which he could again purchase the confidence of the obstinate girl. The impressions he had received during his voluntary confinement in the cell convinced him of the unwarrantable cruelty he should commit if he allowed poor Albert to suffer unjustly any longer. The useless hours of waiting for the Prison Fairy had increased his interest in her to a longing, and the inspector's story gave him the assurance that she was worthy of a sacrifice. The simple experience of this afternoon had destroyed the web of doubt that overpowered him. He intended to treat the whole affair with the ease of a man of the world, and disarm the malicious public by a display of amiable qualities which no one could resist, and which must of course win the heart of the Prison Fairy. He was conscious of the power of his personal attractions, and, after he became accustomed to the thought of a public examination, took pleasure in the idea of making all his advantages sparkle in the light of her delighted glances. Since there was no other way of gaining possession of her, he ordered the investigation of Albert Preheim's murderous assault to be once more taken up by the courts.

A week passed away before the matter was publicly discussed, and during this time *Heinrich* and *Henri* pursued but one object: to find the Prison Fairy. But all plans were set at naught by the cunning obstinacy with which she eluded him. Ottmar went daily to the jail and showed the prisoners every conceivable kindness, but none of them could tell him anything more than that she had not come of late. The poor men were almost in despair,--it was the first time for five years that she had remained away so long. No one could explain the cause. *Heinrich* knew it and wondered at her firmness,--it could not be indifference that made her avoid him so anxiously; and this thought goaded his impatience to its height.

The day of the examination came. Upon this all his hopes were fixed. The galleries of the hall were crowded. Ottmar, the haughty, dreaded aristocrat, enters the lists to defend a poor, persecuted plebeian, and confesses his own error to prove the innocence of his *protégé*. This was the rumor that ran through the whole city. Every one wanted to see it for himself before he believed it; and instead of the malicious public he had expected, appeared a joyful throng, already half conciliated. A crowd of ladies of all ranks and ages had also assembled to see the famous Ottmar in the rôle of a penitent sinner. It is characteristic that women in general will not pardon the smallest error if it is concealed, while, on the contrary, they will forgive the greatest sin if an appeal is made to their generosity by a frank confession. *Heinrich* hoped to find this experience confirmed by the Prison Fairy, and was persuaded that his conduct on this occasion would completely subdue her defiance. The examination began. All eyes were fixed compassionately upon the pallid Albert, broken down in the flower of his years, as entered the court-room with tottering steps, supported between two gendarmes.

The presiding officer opened the proceedings by a short history of the case, the statements of the absent Severinus were read aloud, and passed on for the assent of the accused and the witnesses. At first no one paid much attention to the course of affairs. They had learned five years ago that the charge against Albert was a heavy one, so they were now only curious about the examination of the witnesses, and that strange, familiar murmur of impatience became distinctly audible after the presiding officer had finished his speech. But, eagerly as the public awaited Ottmar's entrance, he still remained behind the door of the witness-box. At last the presiding officer commanded Baron von Ottmar to be summoned.

A satisfied "ah!" ran through the crowd, as a gust of wind rustles through withered leaves, when *Heinrich* appeared. With all the power of his natural and acquired charm of manner he revealed the psychological causes of the event, and with convincing legal acuteness represented them in their relations to the law. He forbearingly concealed the name of Albert's betrothed, and confessed his fault with the dignity of a man who, on the ground of great and noble qualities, feels entitled to rise above the errors of his youth, and has no timidity in acknowledging a wrong if by so doing he can avoid a greater one. While *Heinrich* was speaking he scanned the galleries, and *Henri* gazed into many a beautiful, joy-beaming face, but the one both sought was absent.

All hearts yearned towards Ottmar; only she for whom all had been done unsympathizingly avoided the sole opportunity which might show him in a more favorable light. And yet he could not believe it; she *must* be there, and had probably only concealed herself from his gaze.

This doubt aroused the greatest agitation. Almost mechanically he continued to play his part as a noble man. He had spoken so admirably that there was very little left for Albert's lawyer to say; but his thoughts were not fixed upon Albert, but the gallery; and the more firmly he was convinced that the Prison Fairy was not there, the more his joy in his good deed disappeared; he no longer dared hope to gain access to the obstinate fairy by any such means.

The court had summoned old Anton from his home to give his testimony; but he had not yet arrived, so another session must be called. If she did not appear then, he had lost the game.

Just at that moment a thought entered his mind which might place him on the right track. She could have obtained her remarkable education only in scientific circles, and had probably been reared in a very intellectual family. Ottmar proposed to make a round of visits to all the prominent literary and scientific people in N----. "She is not a native of this capital, her German is too correct for that, so I will begin with the strangers," he thought. He had hitherto confined himself exclusively to the court circle, and was entirely unknown in the society he now proposed to seek.

Sunday intervened between the first and second session of the court, and Ottmar availed himself of it. He drove around the city in his elegant carriage all the morning, and was everywhere cordially received. Many, beautiful and ugly, forward and retiring, simple and highly educated young ladies were introduced to him. She was nowhere to be found.

When he paid the last visit on his list, and there also met only unfamiliar, commonplace faces, he asked the friendly head of the household, in an under-tone, whether he could mention any particularly interesting people whom a stranger in N---- ought to know.

The old gentleman reflected a short time, and finally inquired whether he had yet heard nothing of old Fräulein Veronica von Albin.

"Oh, you must seek her out!" he exclaimed when *Heinrich* answered his question in the negative. "She is a perfect original, a petrifaction of the period of sentimentality, and withal a really intellectual person, in whose salon you will find every one who has any pretensions to fame, and is enrolled under the banner of poetry and sensibility."

Wearied by his minute explanation, *Heinrich* expressed his thanks, inquired the way to her dwelling, and drove thither. He had made it a duty to follow every suggestion of destiny, but knew in advance that he should not find what he sought in the home of a sentimental old maid.

The carriage stopped before a massive stone house. Two colossal figures on the right and left of the door held lanterns adorned with intricate iron scroll-work in the fashion of the last century. The lower windows were grated with thick wrought-iron bars, and the heavy oaken door did not lack the shining brass lion's head, with the ring in its mouth. Above the door was a somewhat weather-beaten coat-of-arms, carved in stone, overshadowed by a tiny balcony provided with manifold sculptured ornaments and iron scrolls. *Heinrich* pulled the bell. The door was opened, and when he entered a statue placed in a niche in the staircase extended its arms as if in welcome.

A pleasant subdued light fell upon the stone stairs through a tall pointed window, and *Heinrich*, most agreeably impressed by this old-fashioned but massive luxury, mounted the broad stone steps.

A precise, respectable servant was standing on the landing, and silently ushered him into a little antechamber. Ottmar gave him his card, and he went forward on tip-toe to announce him. For a few moments *Heinrich* had time to admire the few but costly articles of furniture, rich carpet, and Chinese vases in the anteroom. His hopes began to sink. The quiet, pedantic spirit which breathed from these carefully preserved relics of a former century could not have trained the original, modern, enthusiastic nature of the Prison Fairy.

At last a pair of richly-carved folding-doors were thrown open. The old servant, with a low bow, silently motioned to him to approach, and *Heinrich* entered a large apartment, furnished in the ancient French style, with silken curtains, and a polished, inlaid floor. The sofas and chairs were of richly inlaid walnut, covered with faded but heavy yellow damask. An old-fashioned screen, ornamented with an embroidered coat-of-arms, stood before a huge stove adorned with Chinese designs. On the clumsy carved tables lay magnificent velvet, covered albums, faded and time-worn, as well as small new books of every description. A gilt eagle extended its wings over an immense mirror, and a pair of sphinxes supported a marble pier-table, bearing a clock. Family portraits, centuries old, stared solemnly from the walls, and fresh roses breathed their rich fragrance over this peaceful image of bygone days.

Almost at the same moment Ottmar entered, the lady of the house, Fräulein Veronica von Albin, advanced through a pair of folding-doors directly opposite to him. She had a slight ethereal figure, whose movements still retained the elasticity of youth, and a pair of beautiful blue eyes sparkled in a wrinkled face, over which at least seventy years had passed. Thin white curls were carefully arranged around the kindly old forehead, and an old-fashioned but dazzlingly white morning dress rustled softly around her. She advanced, or rather floated, towards Ottmar, and held out both hands.

"You are most welcome, Herr von Ottmar," she said, with so cordial an expression that the latter bowed low in astonishment. "You wonder at my affectionate address, do you not?" she continued, offering him a chair. "It is because we always think those whom we know so well must know us.

Since the public legal investigation you have become common property, and indeed such property as every one would most gladly appropriate to himself."

"Have you been present at the examination, Fräulein?" asked Ottmar.

"Certainly; and I can assure you that I became very mach attached to you in the few hours I saw and heard you. Nothing could have afforded me greater pleasure than to receive this visit. Thank God, I am old enough to be able to tell you so without embarrassment," she continued, smiling.

Heinrich found the youthful old Lady possessed very good taste, and involuntarily thought "women are really attractive only at the beginning and end of life."

"My dear Fräulein," he began, "you do not know how happy your kindness makes me. I am a stranger here, and seek those who will understand me. The empty life of the court no longer satisfies me. I long for something else, and come to you because I was told that I should here find what I sought; and indeed I hope if I meet with it anywhere it will be here."

"I think you may be right," said she, looking at him with winning affection. Old age, by relaxing the lids, had drawn a veil over the bright blue eyes, but a glance so full of soul, and pure youthful emotion, beamed from them that *Heinrich* gazed at her with increasing admiration. "Not that I imagine you could find amusement in an old woman like me, but I have the pleasure of drawing young and brilliant people around me, in whom you will surely find something to please you."

"You certainly have some relations?" asked *Heinrich*, expectantly.

"Not exactly relations," she said, shortly; "but it is a great mercy that God gave me the faculty of living with young persons, and that there is at least nothing repulsive in my old age. The young people cling to me, and daily bring new joys into my quiet house."

"Permit me to ask you one question, Fräulein," said *Heinrich*,--then hesitated a moment, and continued in a very different tone: "How is it possible that time has passed you by without leaving more traces?"

"Yes, it is singular. I have really remained twenty years behind my true age. The machinery continued to move, but the hands were stopped by a great shock, and never overtook the time. It is a strange, sorrowful story, and some day when we are sitting by my cozy, singing tea-urn I will tell you about it."

"A sorrowful story?" asked *Heinrich*. "I should have thought you were very happy and contented."

"Yes, I am now. Time effaces everything, and I seem to myself like a transfigured spirit. I have no longer anxieties or wishes, look upon life calmly and impartially, and love all men. My body, as you see, is no very heavy burden, and thus, thank God, I am not so widely separated from the angels."

There was such a depth of earnestness concealed under these jesting words that *Heinrich*, strangely moved, passed his hand over his brow. It seemed as if a good genius with a gentle smile had raised him to a height from whence he could view at a single glance all the perishableness and emptiness of life. "Oh, who could bring heaven so near as you?" he said, at last.

"Dear friend," she replied, with a winning glance, "there is also a heaven upon earth in our own breasts. Do not seek it without, but within your heart; then you will not *come* into heaven for the first time when you die, but *remain* in it always."

"My dear Fräulein'," pleaded *Heinrich*, "permit me now and then to linger a short time in yours until I have created one of my own. Will you?"

"Certainly; with the greatest pleasure. It does you honor that, without any other design, you can take pleasure in spending a few hours with an old lady like myself; and I assure you that your good intention will be rewarded,--rely upon it."

"I do not doubt it," said *Heinrich*; "but I ask no other reward than your favor and counsel in many things that oppress my heart."

"I will tell you,"--Veronica cast a hasty glance at the great clock. "Come and take tea with me to-morrow evening. Some of my chosen friends will be here, and I am curious to see how they will please you. One thing I can positively assure you beforehand: you will find only *good* men with me. Old and independent as I am, I need not receive any except those whom I love; and only such as have preserved a childlike, unassuming character (now, unfortunately, so rarely found) take pleasure in my simple nature."

"Who could be so unfeeling as to find no charm in you?" said *Heinrich*.

"Who? Alas! unfortunately there are many. Believe me, our young people are now very old. When I think how it used to be in my time! There are no longer any illusions,--any enthusiasms. I have often talked to young people who seemed so old that I have asked myself with shame, 'Oh, God! am I really so childlike, or already so childish, that the young people of the present day are so much wiser and more steady?' And that is not the worst. I have always seen that the childlike or childish old woman is much happier in her simple existence than all these hopeful young persons, upon whom life still smiles with rosy hues; and it makes me feel sad."

"She might have educated the Prison Fairy;" thought *Heinrich*, and at last determined to ask her; but Veronica, without allowing herself to be interrupted, continued, with the loquacity of age: "I know they call me the Sensitive Plant, because I have preserved my quick feelings and ready tears; but I do not think they are mocking me, for they know I play no sentimental comedy, but rejoice with those who rejoice, and even follow with sincere interest the struggles of the age, although they do not please me. To me the only true voices are those that speak from sentiment and in its behalf; therefore I must confess that I prefer them to the modern spirit of speculation, piquant as it is, and shall listen to them devoutly until death some day solves for me the mystery of life." She again glanced at the clock and made *Heinrich* a confused apology for having chattered so long.

Heinrich could do nothing but take leave, and was compelled to defer receiving the ardently desired assurance until the morrow; he bowed as low and as frequently as possible, and withdrew from the apartment as slowly as he could. The lock of the door stuck in his hand as if it were bewitched, and he was so absentminded that he was obliged to pause some time in the ante-chamber to remember which was the way out; he did not know where he was or what he was doing. Meantime bitter reflections upon his hasty dismissal, his own strange embarrassment, which had made the harmless question falter on his lips more and more the longer he delayed it, until at last he could no longer utter it; upon the old lady's loquacity, which had not allowed him to speak: in short, the striking of a large cuckoo-clock, which also seemed to jeer at him, first made him aware that he must at last leave the house. With a despairing glance at the different doors he went away, and on reaching the carriage could not help laughing at himself. *Heinrich* scoffed at *Henri*, and *Henri* derided *Heinrich*. An impulse of rejoicing over something, he knew not what, overpowered him.

X
PROGRESS

Early the following day there was a fresh crowd and bustle in the hall where the court held its session. The pressure was so violent that it was already necessary to have police stationed before the building to preserve order. At last all became quiet, for the judges entered. Ottmar, with his eyes fixed intently upon the gallery, looked handsomer than ever. His stern bearing seemed more gentle, his slight figure more elastic, the harsh, rigid outline youthfully soft, and around the delicately modeled lips played an irresistible smile. His dark hair was brushed back, and the peace of a quiet conscience seemed to rest upon his noble brow. His eyes were fixed constantly on the same spot with a remarkably friendly glance, until at last all eagerly followed the direction of the look, but to their great surprise saw no one except old Fräulein von Albin, with several elderly ladies and gentlemen.

"What has he to do with her?" they asked each other.

The examination lasted only a short time. Old Anton arrived and confirmed his master's deposition. The court withdrew to deliberate upon the sentence. An expectant stillness greeted its reappearance. All eyes were fixed upon Albert, who awaited the announcement of the sentence with feverish suspense.

It found him guilty of the attempt to murder while in a passion, and deserving of three years' imprisonment; but, as the accused had already endured a longer and more severe punishment, ordered his immediate release.

Albert seemed confused and did not appear to understand anything.

"You are free!" cried *Heinrich*. But Albert with a deep sigh sank senseless into the arms of the bystanders like a somnambulist suddenly aroused from a heavy slumber. Ere long, however, he opened his eyes and threw himself at *Heinrich's* feet, murmuring, "Forgive me!"

"We have both forgiven each other long ago," replied *Heinrich*, raising him kindly from the ground.

The presiding officer approached him, saying, "Herr von Ottmar, allow me in the name of the whole court to thank you for having given us an opportunity to rescind an undeserved sentence, and changed the sad duty of condemnation to the joy of pronouncing a decree of liberation; permit me to give you the assurance that I have become your sincere friend."

Heinrich took a cordial farewell of the worthy man, whose eyes beamed with heartfelt esteem. But when he came out of the building to enter his carriage the multitude had assembled before it, and for the first time in his life a loud cheer of universal approbation greeted him. *Heinrich* felt every nerve thrill pleasantly at the unwonted sound, and as he raised his hat in acknowledgment murmured, with joyful emotion, "Prison Fairy, I thank you!"

He had intended to play a part; but the seriousness of the matter had laid hold upon him and converted acting to reality. He perceived this fact with a throb of strange elation; and if the joy he felt sprang more from the result than the act itself, the pleasure was so pure, the vanity so legitimate, that even he could scarcely distinguish it from the emotions of an unselfish, satisfied conscience. Enough: he had done a noble deed, felt the happier for it, and formed the resolution to take advantage of every opportunity of procuring this delight again. But of course he thought only of those occasions which would secure him a similar popular recognition; he did not think of the unfortunates he might aid, but of the gratitude he should receive from them and the public. To his heartless egotism no other course of reflection was possible, yet even this was a great advance towards better things.

There are natures which, incited by the love of applause, first do good merely from vanity; but the more frequently this occurs, the more they become accustomed to it, and at last do it, with or without success, from habit. But inasmuch as every habit gradually becomes a necessity, so it is with this, until at last they do right from a secret need.

Ottmar was such a man. Amid all his great faults and errors, it was not the opposition between right and wrong that was the point of controversy in his nature, but that between the heart and intellect. The cause of all the dissensions about right and wrong into which *Heinrich*, as well as *Henri*, had fallen, was that his heart and intellect opposed each other, instead of harmonizing. All *Heinrich's* errors were rooted solely in the selfishness of his cold intellect, as *Henri's* were founded upon the egotism of his material nature. If any great influence could succeed in uniting the two extremes he would become the most noble and estimable of men. Society, therefore, is not so far wrong when it allows itself to be dazzled by the ideal nimbus which such persons understand how to diffuse around them; for beneath it there is always an instinct of good by means of which they may really become what they seem.

There are also noble, sensitive souls which understand such men, and wish to aid them in reaching the right path. The extent of their success of course depends upon their own capacity.

Ottilie was one of these souls, but Ottmar knew that the Prison Fairy would become more, infinitely more, to him if he could succeed in approaching her. That which in the fading, suffering Ottilie had failed to make any deeper impression upon him, because it had appeared in a form too sentimental, too little akin to his own nature, kindled an ardent enthusiasm in him when he encountered it in the energetic, vivacious Prison Fairy. Ottilie seemed to him a distant, glorified ideal; her self-denial, her capacity for self-sacrifice, appeared superhuman, and only rooted in the indifference of a spirit striving to cast off its earthly nature; it never entered his mind to try to imitate, greatly as he admired it. The Prison Fairy, while possessing Ottilie's ideal character, was also in every respect congenial to him, and thus he *could* follow her. He had seen the former suffer from her ideas, which repelled him; but the latter was happy, and attracted him. In a word, the princess gave him the *theory*, the Prison Fairy the *practice*.

He owed Ottilie nothing save a fruitless knowledge of himself; but to the impression the unknown girl had made upon him he was already indebted for this first hour of happiness, and all his hopes were fixed upon this noble, womanly apparition.

Albert, whom he had taken home with him, as he had no friends in the city, gave all the information he could bestow, which was only that she came to his cell very early in the morning of the day before the court held its session and took leave of him, as she was sure he would be liberated. She gave him several louis-d'or to supply his immediate wants, and told him to write a letter containing news of himself every week, addressed to the initial B., *poste restante*. He was obliged to repeat the simple story to *Heinrich* every half-hour. Thus the afternoon passed away, and Ottmar went to dress,--the time appointed for the tea-party had almost arrived. Will she be there?--or will she not?--was the axis around which all his thoughts revolved.

A merry company engaged in eager conversation about Ottmar had assembled in Fräulein von Albin's salon. Veronica was unusually bright. She wore a tight dress of light yellow satin, richly trimmed with old lace, kid mitts, and a cap with a light yellow ribbon. When she sat down she could scarcely be distinguished from the sofa, which had a covering of the same hue; and when she walked she looked like one of the oblique rays of light that fall through old church windows.

"Come, pray do me the favor to stop talking about Ottmar," she said, uneasily. "Can't you speak of something else?"

"Ah! what subject could we have that would be more interesting?" murmured the young girls.

Veronica sent them into an adjoining room, and the ladies and gentlemen discussed a wider range of topics. Just then the folding-doors were thrown wide open, and with his usual haughty bearing the much-talked-of Ottmar entered. A murmur of pleasure ran through the astonished company, but as yet the young girls in the adjoining room noticed nothing.

Veronica received her visitor with the pride with which one sees an agreeable surprise prepared for one's guests safely enter upon the scene. After the first introductions and remarks, *Heinrich's* eyes wandered hastily around the room. She was not there.

"Will you not present me to your young friends also?" he said, at last, turning beseechingly to Veronica.

The latter led him triumphantly into the "second salon," where, unobserved, he paused a few moments in the doorway and scanned the company.

The young girls were playing "Guess by the dancing." One of them was obliged to stand in the centre of the circle, dance blindfolded with a gentleman, and guess his name by his dancing. A young girl whose wonderful figure aroused *Henri's* astonishment was now within the ring. She wore a thin white dress embroidered with crimson flowers, her rich curling hair was arranged in two heavy braids, and a spray of crimson blossoms fell upon her beautiful neck.

Henri would gladly have seen the face concealed under the broad handkerchief. A gentleman was to be led up to her: Veronica took Ottmar's hand, motioned to the company to say nothing, and drew him forward to the young girl. *Henri* threw his arm around her, and they swept round the room in rapid circles. Delighted with the grace and ease of her dancing, he drew the soft, pliant figure more closely to him; her breath fanned his cheek, and his gently stirred the hair upon her brow. The narrow space visible under the bandage became suffused with a deep blush; a magnetic bond was being woven between them. She paused and released herself from his clasp.

"Well, who is it?" cried Veronica.

"I don't know," replied the young girl, panting for breath. "It is none of the gentlemen who were here before."

Henri stood as if spell-bound; surely he ought to know that soft, rich voice, and he removed the bandage himself. "Prison Fairy," he murmured, as a pair of large, dark eyes gazed at him as if in a dream.

She was so much startled that she turned pale and tottered. *Henri* supported her, and the others rushed forward. "Oh, it is nothing," said she; "dancing with my eyes bandaged makes me dizzy." Then thanking *Henri* with a slight bow, she begged to be excused till she had recovered her breath, and went into an adjoining room, where it was cool and quiet.

Henri sought Veronica to request her to introduce him to the charming young girl. "Certainly," said she; "I have anticipated this moment with great pleasure."

They found the Prison Fairy in the tea-room leaning against an open window. She was gazing thoughtfully into the darkness, and did not feel the cold night air that blew over her white shoulders.

"Cornelia," cried Veronica, "you will take cold. How can people be so careless?" The young girl closed the window and turned towards the approaching pair.

"Herr von Ottmar," said Veronica, presenting him. "This is the child of my dead adopted daughter, and therefore my adopted granddaughter, Fräulein Cornelia Erwing. The one sole treasure I still possess in this world!"

Both bowed in silence.

"See, my child," said the old lady, joyously; "this is the surprise I told you about yesterday."

"It is certainly very unexpected," replied the girl.

"Allow me to hope, Fräulein, that at least it was not *undesired*?"

"Oh, no," said Veronica, laughing, as Cornelia made no answer. "You may be sure that she belongs to the ranks of your greatest adorers; but she is an obstinate little thing, and never pays any one a compliment willingly." A glance of earnest entreaty from the Prison Fairy silenced her enthusiastic kindliness.

"Fräulein," said *Henri*, firmly, "you have hitherto eluded me in so remarkable a manner that you will not be angry if I now implore you to grant me a few words of explanation? You will not refuse this satisfaction to the man who rejoices in the favor of your honored foster-mother?"

"Do you permit it?" asked Cornelia.

"What would I not permit to you, my dear child?" replied Veronica. "Speak on; I shall not disturb you, for I must go back to my guests."

The two were left alone. A violent struggle now arose in Ottmar as to *which* of his two individualities should rule this scene. It urged *Henri* irresistibly towards the sofa upon which the beautiful figure had sank, while *Heinrich* was unwilling to lose any of the precious moments he had longed for during the last weeks. The two natures had never struggled with each other so obstinately before. At last *Henri* drew back that *Heinrich* might, so to speak, do him credit with the talented girl. *Heinrich* seated himself in an arm-chair near the sofa, and tried to collect his thoughts after *Henri's* fierce revolt.

"So I have found you at last, wonderful, wilful creature!" he began. "Speak, why have you made it so difficult for me to do so?"

"I would tell you if I did not fear offending you."

"You cannot offend me, for I intend to learn from you how to become a different person; of course the change must begin with my faults."

"Well, then," she said, firmly, "some years ago there was a great deal said here about a certain Herr von Ottmar, whose rapid rise in a foreign country excited general astonishment. People were delighted with his talents, but hated him for the use he made of them, and feared him as the most zealous instrument of the despotic system of our government. They admired his personal qualities, but blamed the want of principle with which he sought to make them win the hearts of women. I never wished to see this gentleman; for, after all I had heard, I felt a deep repugnance towards him. Suddenly a man appears before me in the prison, whose manner and language stir my inmost soul with sympathetic emotion. Without the slightest restraint I yield to this impression as I do to everything good and beautiful,--and learn that this man, with the lofty, noble brow, the earnest, expressive glance, is the notorious Ottmar; learn it at the moment when, voluntarily, in mere arrogance, he confesses one of the crimes so often imputed to him. It wounded me all the more because I thought I had discovered at the first glance something rare, ideal, in your character. I had therefore in your case lost the balance which usually aids my intercourse with men. I became deceived, bewildered, almost irresolute, and wavered between my previous conviction and the impression produced by your personal attributes. The former had its sure foundations; the latter I believed to be treacherous, and therefore avoided you so anxiously. I would not allow myself to be bribed by your manners to excuse and forget what my better judgment must condemn."

"And the step towards the right path which you afterwards saw me take?" asked *Heinrich*.

"Increased my sympathy for you, and at the same time my doubts. A secret power urged me to defend you when you were attacked, and yet I did not believe what I said myself. This is why my adopted mother classed me among your adorers, and thought to give me pleasure by inviting you here; but I do not at all approve of such a step. You are the petted hero of the day; every one is crowding around you. It is bitter to me to be compelled to think that you could charge us with obtrusiveness."

"I understand you, Fräulein," said *Heinrich*; "but you seem to be in error. Fräulein von Albin had an excellent reason for inviting me, for I called upon her yesterday."

"What! did you do that?" exclaimed Cornelia, an expression of joy flashing over her face.

"Did you not know it?"

"No! I suppose Veronica said nothing about it on purpose to surprise me. She certainly desires nothing but to give pleasure, and her simple nature chooses every conceivable means of doing so. But how did you happen to come to this quiet home?"

"Because I was seeking *you*."

"And why?"

"Because I am superstitious enough to see in our meeting the hand of fate, and had an irresistible impulse to follow the hint; because I expect to receive from you the only salvation I can still obtain; because--ah, let me speak frankly!--because you please me infinitely."

"You have probably said that to a great many persons," replied Cornelia, coldly.

Heinrich looked her steadily and frankly in the face. "Certainly I have. Why should I not? I did not say that you *alone* please me."

Cornelia blushed. "That is at least sincere."

"As we always will be towards each other," said *Heinrich*, firmly. "In your youthfully hasty judgment you have placed me in the position of a criminal. I will not justify myself, but afford you the possibility of doing so. To deny my faults would help you very little, but I will teach you to understand them. First of all, let us be perfectly clear in regard to the relation in which we wish to stand towards each other, then you will trust me more. I perceive, by your last remark, that you consider me a universal gallant. You are mistaken, Fräulein; I do not love you, and I desire no such feeling from you. Do not fear that you will be compelled to listen to tender declarations from me; I should not venture to offer you a heart which you know has already loved so often! But I offer you a feeling that hitherto has slumbered in my soul, pure and unprofaned; I offer you the truest, most devoted friendship. If you will neither accept nor respond even to *this*, I ask of you a portion of that philanthropy whose missionary you are,--I ask and demand from you that Christianity which vouchsafes to all the same blessing, and excludes none who truly desire it."

Cornelia sat in silence, with her eyes fixed upon the floor.

"You are silent! you have no answer for me! Prison Fairy, Prison Fairy, must I remind you of your mission? Oh, girl! do not let me be perplexed by you; do not let me think that those eyes,--that the mighty pulsations of a breast animated by a lofty idea,--have deceived me; that you are less noble than they seem: it would be the last, the most terrible disappointment of my life."

Cornelia gazed at the ardent speaker with a searching glance. Her breath came more quickly, her lips parted several times before she could utter the words, "We will be friends, Herr von Ottmar."

Heinrich bent over her with a winning smile. "You are forcing back something that hovers on your tongue, Fräulein! Do you know that on that first meeting you promised to be good to me if I would be good to the prisoners! I have redeemed my promise; but *you*?"

"That is not sufficient; you must abide by it still longer. Keep your word, and I will keep mine."

"Dear Fairy," said *Heinrich*, "cast aside this cold formality, which is ill-suited to you and not at all in place towards me. Be the warm, earnest creature, loving both God and mankind, whom I found in the dungeon, and who, by her rich soul, could transform the prisoner's punishment to reward. Be gentle; you know not how necessary you are to this wounded heart, burdened by heavy chains. We are nearly akin to each other, and you will perceive it some day. I see it in the flashing of those mysterious eyes; in you also slumbers a secret before whose revelation you would recoil in terror did not the faithful arm of an experienced friend guard you from the horrors in your own breast. Come, give me your hands,--so,--now you look kindly at me; that haughty brow grows smooth,--does that mild, thoughtful glance rest willingly upon my features? Say nothing, our souls are talking together, and confiding things of which neither of us has any knowledge. Oh, dear one our souls already understand each other better than we."

"We and our souls are one," murmured Cornelia; "if they understand each other, so do we. Let me confess that I believe I have done you a great wrong; if that is the case, forgive me, for the sake of this moment."

"There is no wrong, Cornelia, for which a single moment of true love could not make amends."

Cornelia pressed his hand with the half-grave, half-friendly smile which had so great a charm for *Heinrich*.

"So I have found you at last, you dear, beautiful child!" he exclaimed. "Cling to me faithfully; you shall not be mistaken in me."

She rose to return to the guests. "Surely you will not deceive me?" she asked, half doubtfully and half firmly, but with charming sincerity.

"Prison Fairy, do you need any other assurances? Only try yourself, and you will refute your doubt better than modesty allows me to do."

"Are you so sure of that?" she asked, smiling; "now I think your modesty does not weigh very heavily upon you." An expression of the most charming petulance gleamed over her face as she glided away.

"You are caught, wild, changeful soul; yet not to cause you pain, only to do me good, I impose upon you this chain, whose weight you shall never feel," said *Heinrich*. "You soar towards the sun; let us see whether you will have the strength to draw me up with you!"

"You can be borne towards the sun on the wings of her aspiring spirit!" cried *Henri*, "if only the lovely form which enthrals me as no other ever did before remains upon the earth. Guide her *soul* whither you please, and leave me alone with its *earthly husk*. Then we can both possess a happiness we have never yet known."

"So long as I can be with her I shall maintain my place," said *Heinrich*; "and this time I do not think you will obtain the victory over me!"

"Indeed! Well, let us see who will first conquer the other," said the aroused spirit of sensuality. "Will you all at once meet me in a hostile encounter, after letting me have my own way so long? What will come of it if the gulf between us should be so greatly enlarged?"

"What will come of it?" asked *Heinrich.* "I do not know; probably merely what has always happened,--a loss of peace; and, although I have hitherto indulged you, it has only been because I could share your pleasures as little as you could find joy in mine. Here, for the first time, we unite in a common desire; our mutual interest is captivated by one and the same object, but it is our curse that the very thing which ought *unite* us *severs* us most violently. Her noble mind attracts me as greatly as her beautiful person charms you, and I will not voluntarily resign to you a single hour I can spend conversation with her. Therefore, we must struggle."

"Yes, we will," said *Henri.*

"Herr von Ottmar," cried Veronica from the door, "will you join the young people's games, or do you prefer the salon?"

"Don't grudge me the privilege of mingling with the young people for a time," he answered, and entered the room where Cornelia, radiant with mirth and mischievousness, was bantering the young girls who were standing around her.

"Veronica," she cried, "the ladies have been industrious; we sha'n't play games any longer. There are poems and essays to be read aloud. Come in, Messrs. Critics; collect your thoughts; we have a severe judge to-day."

"Will you take part in our little college, Herr von Ottmar?"

"I am very anxious to do so," he replied.

"You must have patience and be indulgent to this kind of entertainment," laughed Cornelia. "It is the personal friendship that unites our little circle which makes it interesting to us, and of course that is a thing you cannot yet share."

"You must know," said Veronica, in a low tone, "that my darling child has established among her friends a sort of nursery, in which she wishes to rear clearness of intellect and feeling, noble principles, and independent judgment; and the gentlemen eagerly assist her; they are all more or less in love with her. Every week Cornelia gives the young girls a subject for prose or poetic treatment, or a work to be critically examined. Whoever receives the greatest praise from the majority obtains the prize,--a picture by some one of the artists present, or the dedication of a song by one of our musicians. The young poets criticise the essays and read their own productions aloud.

Finally, the older gentlemen pronounce their ultimatum. You will probably belong to this last and highest court to-day, though less entitled to do so by age than intellect."

"That is a charming idea," said *Heinrich*, "and is in harmony with you both. You thus give society an intellectual seasoning which it usually lacks. Have you poets in your circle?"

"Oh, certainly!" replied Veronica. "Don't you know our young celebrities? See, that one yonder is the tender lyric poet, D----, a sensitive, foreboding soul; the stout, broad-shouldered man is the bold, patriotic bard, B----; and the pale aristocrat, with the bent head, is the poet T----, a very talented person. You have surely heard of the enthusiastic reception of his first tragedy. I only fear his intellect is developing too rapidly. Sooner or later this premature growth will make it sickly, and that would be a pity. There is splendid material in him, which, by the forcing system of our times, would be made to shoot upwards too quickly to form a stout, healthy trunk, from whence the productive power is always freshly supplied. The young man is only twenty-four years old, and his work is already much more massive than Schiller's first attempts; but he accomplishes a remarkable amount in his department, and is a noble, estimable man. These are the poor victims of our times, where the utmost is extorted from every one."

"You are right," replied *Heinrich*. "I am familiar with young T--'s work, and, like you, think it unnaturally mature for his years. Schiller and Goethe themselves won their way by degrees to what is recognized as the highest stand-point. But our young people want to be born upon this height and begin where they ended. It is perfectly comprehensible that they don't wish to remain where they begin, but struggle on and test the powers of their young intellects, as Lessing, Goethe, and Schiller did when they gradually raised themselves above the inferior performances and requirements of their times."

"That is just what I always say," cried Veronica; "and this runs through all circles of society. Our young people no longer have any *simplicity*, and I think this is the glass case beneath which the young plants of the soul should grow, with all their faults and excrescences, until they are strong enough to bear without injury the storms of life and the shears of negation. Without simplicity there are no illusions, and without illusions there is no youth! You will perhaps find here a circle which answers to my demand in this respect. True, there are only a few poets of importance among them, but these compensate me for all the famous, keen, analytical minds which pluck the fragrant rose to find faults its calyx would have concealed, and give us only the purified but empty branch of thorns. You see I am not called the Sensitive Plant without reason."

"Yes, yes," said *Heinrich*, with a kindly smile, "we must learn from you how to keep young!"

Meantime a reading-table had been placed in the centre of the room. With cheeks glowing with embarrassment, a young girl seated herself at it, cast a hasty glance at Ottmar, and read aloud from a manuscript an essay whose subject and title were the justification of sympathy in opposition to the judgments of reason. It was simple, but written in a style free from faults; some of the ideas were not devoid of talent; and it revealed a more thorough culture than is usually to be found in young girls. *Heinrich* perceived Cornelia's influence. His eyes rested steadily upon her; she was standing behind the reader's chair, and often looked thoughtfully at him. It was evident that she had given this subject from a recollection of him.

The following essays, which were read aloud in turn by the young girls, all treated the same idea with more or less talent, and three poems reproduced it in rhyme.

Heinrich perceived with increasing admiration the activity of the Prison Fairy, whose strong, earnest will effected good results, even under the garb of jest, and gave purpose to the most useless things.

The reading ended, and the gentlemen, in mingled jest and earnest, gave a stern criticism. Each sought the lady whose essay had made the most impression upon him,--discussed and opposed the separate points. The authoresses were obliged to defend themselves, and thus the argument continued till Cornelia, who had previously been inclosed in the circle, suddenly started up, exclaiming: "Say what you please against sympathy, it is the only true oracle among us! If our reason enjoined upon us ever so strictly to keep together as we are now, should we not rush apart to all quarters of the globe if it were not for sympathy? And if reason causes a person to appear ever so wicked, and sympathy attracts us to him, we follow the latter, and often convince ourselves that reason, which judges only by deceptive facts, misled us. Reason disjoints and severs, sympathy conciliates. Reason calculates, sympathy discovers; and, what is after all the principal thing, reason does not make people happy,--sympathy does."

"Cornelia," cried the poet T--, "I have never heard you talk so before! What has become of the logic, the clearness of perception, with which you gave these young ladies the guiding threads for their essays upon this subject?"

"If we were permitted to refer to this enthusiasm, we should be greatly delighted, my dear T----; but I fear it is one of her whims," said H----, the novelist.

The gentle poet D---- whispered, softly, "I know what you mean, Cornelia, but I no longer understand you."

"I understand you," a voice which thrilled all the chords in her nature suddenly murmured in her ear. "I thank you, Prison Fairy!" She turned towards *Heinrich* and looked up into his face. She was bewilderingly beautiful at that moment, with the bold, noble profile half turned towards him, the slender neck thrown back, the full lips curved in a smile which made the small, white teeth glitter in the light, and the hair combed up to form a natural diadem above the thoughtful brow. The floating folds of her dress, the drooping crimson flowers, which trembled at every motion, gave her an ideal, fairylike aspect, which was increased by her dark eyes. Those eyes belonged to the class which, the ancient myth tells us, had power to turn to stone any one on whom their gaze rested. The large, sparkling pupils allowed very little of the white of the eye to be seen. They often gleamed like two suns when the long lashes were raised; and softly and sweetly as they rested upon the object of their observation, their expression must be terrible in anger. Ottmar gazed at her with increasing rapture. "Yes, yes," he said, under his breath, "that is the Medusa from whose blood Pegasus sprang."

"How little she knows herself, that she thinks I could see her without coveting her!" thought *Henri*, making a fresh effort to dislodge *Heinrich*; *Heinrich* resisted his attack with unaccustomed strength. He gazed into the depths of those mysterious eyes; and the secrets which, unconsciously to herself, slumbered within them, irresistibly allured him.

"Cornelia," said the young girl who had read the first essay,--and a tear trembled on her lashes,--"they are looking for you."

Cornelia looked up as if aroused from a dream, threw her arm around her friend's neck, and embraced her warmly. "I thank you, Hedwig!" Then she entered the noisy circle and summoned the gentlemen to select the essay most worthy of the prize.

The company voted, and the majority decided in favor of the first one read.

"Oh, I am glad, dear Hedwig!" said Cornelia, hastily, taking the garland of fresh flowers she had woven for the victor and placing it upon her brow.

It was a beautiful sight as the loveliest maiden in the throng adorned the diffident young girl and led her triumphantly into the middle of the room. The gentlemen came forward, bringing the prize upon a cushion. Poor Hedwig, who, in her embarrassment, had by no means the air of a conqueror, received the gift from the hands of the young artist A----, who whispered, gently, "I beg you all not to show it to the original, if it can be avoided. I did not know he would be here."

The young girl did not understand him, and hastily raised the cover, but dropped it again in terror when she saw the sketch, while a burning blush overspread her face.

"Why, what is the matter?" asked Cornelia, taking out the picture. "A study of a head! Herr von Ottmar,--a perfect likeness!" she exclaimed, undisturbed by the young artist's embarrassment.

Heinrich stepped forward and gazed in astonishment at the successful portrait.

"I must crave your pardon for presuming to steal your features, Herr Geheimrath," stammered the artist. "I know you are very highly esteemed in this circle, and could not refrain from robbing my portfolio of the picture, in order to give pleasure to those who assemble here; otherwise this bold attempt of my talent would have remained entirely concealed."

Heinrich smilingly listened to the long apology, and watched, with silent amusement, an old gentleman standing at some distance from the artist, who was accompanying his speech with numerous bows. This gentleman was a certain Archivrath Linderer, an old friend of Veronica's. The worthy man possessed such a wonderful impulse of courtesy that he could not see any one make a bow without mechanically imitating him, and never heard any sort of speech without mentally making one also.

Heinrich's inclination to laugh was so greatly aroused by this sight that he could scarcely utter a few reassuring words in reply to the embarrassed artist. He was about to go in search of Veronica, to question her about this comical man, when he saw Cornelia, who had been gazing at the picture in silence, go to a table and take up a pencil. He went up and glanced over her shoulder at the portrait. She cast a hasty look at him and then fixed her eyes upon the sketch. She felt his beard touch her hair, and shrank back.

"Look, my dear A----!" she exclaimed. "Here are only two false strokes! When these are altered the picture will be masterly! The lines just over the eyebrows, expressing penetration, are very strongly marked in Herr von Ottmar, and you have not brought them out sufficiently. The upper portion of the brow is also remarkably expressive; there must be a shadow here, and here."

"You may be right," said A----, looking at Ottmar's forehead; "make the strokes."

Cornelia rapidly deepened the shadows, and all the bystanders exclaimed, in astonishment, "Ah, that's it exactly! One would think you had studied the head!"

Cornelia quietly compared the picture with the original. "It is a noble work! You have really been carried away by your subject! The eyes and mouth seem as if they were about to speak!"

"Your praise makes me very proud," said the young man.

"And me!" whispered *Heinrich*, almost inaudibly.

"May I ask you to come in to tea?" cried Veronica, from the doorway. "If any one of the gentlemen has anything to read aloud, he must be kind enough to defer it until after supper. It is already somewhat late."

Heinrich was in the act of offering Cornelia his arm when Veronica requested him to take her to the table. He patiently submitted to this duty, and the ill-assorted pair moved on into the tea-room followed by the others.

Cornelia and Hedwig stood together a moment alone. Hedwig threw herself on her friend's breast, and exclaimed, in a low, rapid tone,--

"I will give you the picture, Cornelia. I don't want it."

"You don't want it?" asked the latter, in astonishment.

"What should I do with it? I think you would value it more, and take more pleasure in it than I," replied Hedwig.

"But, Hedwig, you were always so enthusiastic about him."

"Even if I were, it was all in joke. But you know and value him in earnest: I saw that to-day; and if *he* had given the picture, he would have bestowed it on no one but you; so how could I take a thing to which I have no right? Keep it, I beg of you. It is of no value to me."

"But ought I to accept it from you?" asked Cornelia. "Shall I not be robbing you?"

"Robbing me? I owe you so much, and am so poor in comparison with you, that it will make me rich if I can offer anything that will please you. I would give you more, far more, if I had it to bestow."

She pressed Cornelia lovingly to her heart, and the young girls were holding each other in a close embrace when T---- came in search of them, and Heinrich appeared behind him in the doorway.

"Good heavens! Here they stand, kissing each other, while we have been waiting for them so impatiently!" cried T----.

"We humbly beg pardon for having had no one to escort us to the table," laughed Cornelia. "We were consoling each other for the misfortune."

"How malicious you are again! We were so sure that you would be escorted to the table by your lucky Herr von Ottmar that we did not even look for you," said T----, apologetically.

"And you were not mistaken in your belief, sir," said *Heinrich's* voice.

He went up to Cornelia and offered her his arm. T---- stood petrified with astonishment. There was nothing left for him to do except to turn to Hedwig. *Heinrich* led Cornelia to her place, and then went back to Veronica. Cornelia sat opposite to him, and on his right and left hand were the fairest and brightest young girls in the whole circle. Many mothers and fathers looked towards them with almost imperceptible hopes, but everything fell into the lap of the one who neither hoped nor desired anything. *Heinrich's* interest was centred in Cornelia alone.

"You see, my dear Herr von Ottmar," Veronica began, "I have tried to make amends to you for being obliged to take an old lady to the table. My most charming young ladies are around you."

"You would give me far greater pleasure if you would permit me to spend my evenings with you and your adopted daughter, for I must confess that I prefer you to all other ladies, be they ever so charming," he whispered.

"Oh, that you shall certainly do!" exclaimed Veronica, in delight. "Come as often as you please. You will be a welcome guest."

"I thank you," replied *Heinrich*.

Meantime, Cornelia had been conversing with the extremely polite old gentleman, and *Heinrich* now asked who this eccentric person was.

With gay humor she described his peculiarities, and in a low tone related how, on festival occasions and during public speeches, he often disturbed the bystanders by repeating the words half under his breath, and supplying the bows omitted by the orator; how he always most dutifully repeated the last words said to him; how he invariably removed his hat when he saw two persons salute each other in the street, etc. etc.

"Do you know," she said, at last, "I think this proceeds from an excess of benevolence and sympathy! It must be the same feeling that prompts the mother who hears her daughter say a pretty thing to put on precisely the same expression. The mother enters into her child's situation so earnestly that she involuntarily imitates all her looks and gestures; nay, I once saw an actress, starring with her daughter, so carried away by the latter's playing that she unconsciously imitated her darling, and almost merged her own part in her child's. What is this except an excess of sympathy for the beloved being?"

She then, in a most masterly manner, imitated the different mothers and the tragic scene of the two ladies upon the stage, so that those around burst into shouts of laughter.

Yet the gayer the others became the more serious *Heinrich* looked: and she asked, with mingled surprise and anxiety, why they all had so little success in amusing him.

"Oh, you do not know how happy I am!" he replied; "but I am reflecting about something. I see you develop so many different traits and talents that I am bewildered. When I have at last succeeded in harmonizing one of your changeful moods with your whole character, before I am aware of it a new picture appears before me, which I must again incorporate with the whole. You keep me in a perpetual mental excitement, and it seems as if I were compelled to sketch the different waves upon the sea-shore. Scarcely have I fixed my eyes upon one ere it is already swallowed up in another, and I am constantly raising my eyes again to sketch the whole as it spreads before me in its infinite majesty."

He gazed at her with so strange an expression that she looked down as if dazzled.

"Oh, what are you making me?" she said, in confusion. "I am a very simple person, who am merry with the mirthful and serious with the grave. If I am different from others in any way it is because I am always natural. Thousands feel as keenly, change their moods as frequently, as I; but it is not noticed in them, because they have accustomed themselves to a uniform etiquette, an unvarying manner. I have often envied such persons, for they know how to give themselves the stamp of a finished individuality far better than natures like mine, which are sometimes thought gay, sometimes melancholy, now good and then bad, or not at all what they seem, which are sometimes too little, sometimes too much, trusted, and rarely or never understood."

"Oh, Cornelia!" cried one of the guests, the famous actor N----, across the table. "Do you mean to say that we don't understand you?"

"No, certainly not," replied Cornelia. "I had principally in view those whom I consider different from myself. You understand me because you resemble me, and are all, more or less, artist natures!"

"Do you mean that all artist natures are as truthful as yourself?" asked *Heinrich*, doubtfully.

"Certainly; when I trust a man it is the artist, especially those who represent things."

"I am curious to know upon what you found that idea," murmured *Heinrich*, in a low tone. "The actor certainly practices dissimulation as his profession."

"Oh, do not say that! You will surely admit that in every man there is an impulse towards truth and falsehood, as well as good and evil," began Cornelia. "With almost all persons this impulse, like their other good and bad qualities, exerts an influence upon their lives; they lie and deceive in personal intercourse. But there are exceptions, among those in whom this propensity to deceive is decomposed by Heaven knows what process of intellectual chemistry, and becomes objective; that is, forms a power of acting entirely apart from the subject. This power seeks an independent form, and finds it in art, wherein it develops the highest, most artistic structure, and those in whom such a process has been completed are artists, especially actors. Then if the commonplace man can satisfy that strange and undeniable propensity towards falsehood only in real life, in the actor it is to a certain extent *guided* into a higher, loftier region, and he becomes in reality truer and more natural than many who are only considered honest because they are too awkward to feign."

"Your explanation is logical," replied *Heinrich*, "but you cannot carry it into practical execution. Opportunity makes thieves, a capability for falsehood tempts to falsehood. Even the actor will not disdain to obtain an advantage at the expense of truth, and the temptation is all the greater the more he is convinced that the deception will be successful. Nay, I can even imagine that there must be a charm to him in making use of his histrionic skill, not only upon the stage, but off the boards, and I have seen celebrated actors who could not help perpetually performing a part."

Cornelia reflected a moment, and then said, calmly: "There are such instances, of course, but I do not call such people artists; there are two distinct classes of men who bear that name. If this talent we have just mentioned is coupled with more or less mental capacity, the union produces more or less brilliant *performers*; if, however, there is a counterpoise of the great qualities of the soul and heart, it produces *artists*. The performer, it is true, employs the talents at his command in life as well as in art; he knows no higher object than effect. He deceives in life as well as in art when it will make an effect, and in both is true to the same purpose. As he has neither character nor heart, he is neither good nor bad upon principle; he simply turns his talents to his own profit where and as he can. It is this class of people who have in many respects degraded the position of artists. The artist, on the contrary, perceives and seeks something far higher than effect! Like all men of noble aims, he, too, has an ideal towards which he unselfishly struggles-- truth. If he seeks this in his art, often even at the expense of the applause so indispensable to the actor, if he is so conscientious in the realm of illusion, why should he not be equally so in the domain of reality? The power of transforming his whole nature at will he considers as a gift bestowed to serve the holy purpose of art, and would no more turn it to his own advantage than the honorable citizen would obtain an illegal profit from an accidental or fairly won supremacy over others. A keener, more active, sensitive faculty, and the habit of an elevated manner of expression, may give him a peculiar, 'exaggerated,' perhaps 'affected' appearance,--words with which the commonplace man so eagerly points out what he does not understand; but you will acknowledge that a person may be affected and yet possess true, genuine feelings; as, on the other hand, the falsest and most designing men often appear the most artless."

"Certainly," said *Heinrich*.

"You see," continued Cornelia, "that as from the worst and most different materials the brightest, purest flame can be produced, so art transfigures deception with the highest manifestations. Thus in real artists falsehood aspires towards truth! The highest object of his performance is the union of both, and the triumph of falsehood becomes in him a triumph of truth!"

Cornelia glanced gayly upwards towards the jets of gas in the chandelier. In her enthusiastic defense she had involuntarily raised her voice, and did not notice that every one was looking at her. When she paused, all shouted a hearty bravo. *Heinrich* sat motionless, with his head resting on his hand, gazing earnestly at her; he could not smile and applaud with the others,--he was asking himself, "Do I deserve this woman?"

The supper was over; he started up and approached her as the company prepared to take leave. "Cornelia, Prison Fairy, you have opened a new world to me. My mind is so full of all I have heard from you that I cannot speak. Only tell me whether I may come again tomorrow?"

"Certainly, Herr Baron."

"Oh, do not be so formal, Prison Fairy! Let me hear my name from your lips as you bid me farewell, that I may hold it dearer; or my baptismal name. Ah, Cornelia, I should like to hear how it sounded if you would say Good-night, *Heinrich*.'"

"No, Herr von Ottmar, I cannot; you are still too great a stranger."

Heinrich bit his lips as if deeply abashed, and said, with a low bow, "Pardon me, Fräulein, I was indiscreet."

Cornelia held out her hand and looked at him with all her winning charm of manner. "No, no, Herr von Ottmar, I did not wish to cause you pain. I promise you that ere I sleep I will say in thought, 'Good-night, *Heinrich*!' Does that satisfy you?"

Heinrich kissed her hand in a transport of delight. "Thanks, lovely creature! And now good-night, my fairy; send me a pleasant dream."

Veronica approached: he took leave of her; the departing guests pressed him back, and, waving a farewell to Cornelia, he left the house. When he reached the street he raised his hat from his head to allow the night wind to cool his burning brow; and now he was *Henri* again, for he knew he was expected by a beautiful woman who had followed him home from his last journey, and hitherto held his senses in her chains. He mechanically obeyed the force of old habit and turned his steps towards her residence. But when he stood before the house behind whose lighted windows the glittering daughter of sin awaited him in dreams heavy with forebodings, a strange, incomprehensible feeling overpowered him. Cornelia's pure, wonderful charms appeared so vividly before his soul that he turned with repugnance from the desecrated image that allured him. He perceived that no one had any power of attraction except Cornelia, and that nothing could satisfy his longing for her. He went home, and that very night wrote a farewell letter to his purchased love, and freed himself from his unworthy chains.

A ray of light fell through the heavy silken curtains of Veronica's bed, and waked the sleeper. She looked around and saw Cornelia, who, with a lamp in her hand, was noiselessly gliding through the chamber towards the door of the salon. "What do you want there, child?" asked Veronica; "why are you still dressed? I had already fallen asleep."

Cornelia started. "I forgot something," she replied, and slipped out of the room. When she returned through Veronica's chamber she carried a portfolio in her hand.

"What have you there?" asked Veronica.

"Don't be angry with me for waking you, dear," said Cornelia, kissing the white, aged brow, "I only wanted to read Hedwig's essay again; it was left in the parlor."

When she had closed the door of her pleasant bedroom behind her, she took Ottmar's portrait from the portfolio, placed it on a reading-desk, sat down before it, and, shielding her eyes with both hands, rested her arms on the table, and became absorbed in studying the mysterious head. The more she looked at it the more beautiful she found it. "How simple those lines are, and yet how rich, how infinitely expressive! Oh, who could decipher the mute language of that ardent mouth, whose kiss still burns upon my hand? How can people kiss so with such delicate lips? It is not the lips that kiss, it is his heart, which lies between them; that is why his caress is so soft, so warm; that is why it penetrates to the inmost soul. And when he speaks they are again only the beautiful, slender banks over which the flood of feeling streams! And those eyes,--oh, they reveal all the wonders of the soul! He might err, nay, he might even be shattered by life, but the look that shines in his eyes is divine; it will raise him above his lower nature, and everything else. And I,--I will aid him; I will join the good genius that floats above the darkness of his soul like the Spirit of God over chaos, and teach him to perceive his own greatness, his ideal strength."

She sat long, absorbed in thought; but, by degrees, it seemed as if the pictured head moved to and fro, the eyes turned, the lips parted and closed again. She gazed and made the light burn brighter; in vain. Nature asserted her rights, sleep was casting her deceptive veil over her weary head. She rose, removed the flowers from her hair, and released her lovely form from its clinging drapery. Again and again her eyes rested upon the drawing. She paused. "How you look at me, as if you were alive! as if I ought to be confused! Stop, wait! You shall not see me undress." So saying, she hastily placed the picture in the writing-table, went to bed, extinguished the light, and nestled comfortably among the pillows. "Good-night, *Heinrich*."

XI
A NEW LIFE

After *Henri* had written his letter, the exhausted body imperiously demanded rest, and while it slept *Heinrich* hastened to Cornelia and hovered round her slumbering soul as if it were the petals of a folded rosebud. She did not know, but she suspected it; the magic of the soul revealed his presence, and she felt his spiritual kiss.

When Ottmar awoke the following morning he thought he had not slept well, and had been dreaming a great deal of the Prison Fairy. Yet neither had been dreaming; although their bodies slept, their souls were together. *Heinrich* remained in bed some time. He was in the best of humors, and compared this awakening with the one six years before, when he had resolved to yield to the power of the Jesuits. At that time he was in the act of beginning a new but worse life, as to-day he had awakened to a new and better one. He thought of Cornelia with grateful reverence. Through her he obtained a peace of which he had long been deprived; for, while in himself there was naught save opposition and contrast, in her he found the complement of his nature and the full satisfaction of homogeneousness. Thus *Heinrich* already preferred to dwell upon her harmonious character rather than the struggles in his own breast, and this was one step, though scarcely perceptible, towards liberation from the egotism that was constantly throwing him back upon himself. Even *Henri*, the night before, had rejected the pleasure of the moment, and yielded to an ardent love for an object he could never expect to obtain his way. Even in this hopeless submission there was a slight contest with his usual selfish pursuit of pleasure. It was with a certain feeling of abhorrence that he compared the base passions of the past with his longing for Cornelia's intellectual charms, and fell into this temporary self-sacrifice. Thus egotism sooner or later defeats itself. The true egotist ends with a feeling of loathing and disgust, not only towards the world, but himself. Unmistakable tokens of this state were already visible both in *Heinrich* and *Henri*; but, fortunately for him, he was at an age when fresh buds can shoot forth and supply the places of those that are dead. These germs now began to stir with life. Intellect and feeling, with equal power, drew *Heinrich* and *Henri* towards a being whose bodily and mental gifts were equal. In this the two extremes already began to approach; but they did not yet understand each other, and their meeting must still produce conflict instead of reconciliation.

Ottmar lay for a long time absorbed in meditations upon his strange twofold nature. A servant entered to wake him. He remembered how he had expected old Anton to come in that morning, and, for the first time, a strange face appeared instead. "Good old Anton, no doubt he was right," thought *Heinrich*; "and how shamefully he was treated! Now he would certainly have no occasion to be angry about such faults. He was the best servant I ever had. I will take him back again." He rose, ordered a message to be sent to the inn for old Anton, and sat down to write to Cornelia.

"Her name is Erwing," said he; "that is the name of the famous democrat. Can she be his daughter? If so, she can scarcely have known her father, for Erwing must have fled from North Germany to America at least twenty years ago. It must be so. That is why she concealed her name in the prison; she probably knew it would be no letter of recommendation. That accounts for her relations with Reinhold, too. It is decidedly unpleasant! I shall not get much honor at court by the acquaintance. But it need never be known there. It is winter, night shuts in at four o'clock; I shall only go to her house in the evening, so the whole affair can be concealed from the eyes of the jeering aristocracy. My occasional appearance in literary circles will not be misconstrued, as I have the reputation of unusual erudition." He began to write: "Cornelia!" He paused. "Cornelia! It was a lofty spirit that gave her this proud name; is she a true child of this spirit? I almost believe it. That she glides into the cells of the lowest criminals does not spring from humility,--it is the defiance of compassion against the harshness of force, and the consciousness of the joy-giving power of her own individuality. Woe to him who ventured to wound her pride! He would have lost her."

Just at that moment Anton was announced. He threw aside his pen and went forward to meet him. It seemed, as he rejoiced over the return of the old servant, as if some kind of companionship was now a necessity.

"Welcome, faithful companion of my past!" he cried. "Will you share my future?"

"I don't come to force myself upon you as a servant, Herr Baron," said Anton, whose voice trembled with emotion, "but I must give you one parting hint before my return,--it seems to be intended that I am to keep watch for you."

"Well?"

"Your beautiful estates at H----, Herr Baron, really need your oversight again. The steward and inspector are both in league to let everything go to ruin and fill their own pockets."

"What, what! How do you know that? Do you know that during the last few years my income from the estates has lessened so materially that it has caused me serious anxiety, and were it not for my salary I should find it difficult to live?"

"A proof that I speak the truth. On my way here I passed by Ottmarsfeld, and a secret impulse led me into the old castle and the gardens where I saw you, Herr Baron, grow to manhood. But it caused me real sorrow to see how everything had changed for the worse. The stately castle is out of repair in many places, the gardens have run wild, and the cattle are miserable beasts. There are only fifteen day-laborers on the estate, and they are lazy and carelessly watched."

"That is certainly shameful!" cried *Heinrich*. "The inspector has put down thirty day-laborers to my account every year, and charged me many hundreds for repairs on the buildings."

"You will convince yourself that you have been deceived, and your splendid property must soon be ruined if matters go on in this way," said Anton.

Heinrich paced thoughtfully up and down the room, then turned to Anton and held out his hand. "You are the most faithful soul that I have in the world. Anton, you must enter my service again; surely you cannot yet live without me."

"You know why I left you, Herr Baron," he answered.

"I know," cried *Heinrich*, laughing; "but I don't think you will have any further occasion to fear similar cases. I am not quite so bad as you think, and have become much more steady of late."

"Oh, I can never think my own dear master wicked!" said Anton, deeply touched. "But what suits you--is not quite so proper for me. It may be perfectly natural for an aristocratic young gentleman to follow the inclinations of his heart, while it would be wrong for a sedate old man to lend his assistance to things which went against his conscience. So I might be placed in a position where I should be compelled to disobey you, and then you would only send me away again. Let me go home,--I cannot promise unconditional obedience."

"And you need not, Anton," said *Heinrich*, gravely. "I do not wish to make a mere machine of you; I will compel you to do nothing that is against your principles, and you shall even tell me your opinion as much as you please, if it should ever prove necessary. It is tiresome for a man to have no one to quarrel with except himself. I have blessed you a thousand times during the last few weeks for having had the boldness to baffle my wishes, and therefore in atonement I will assure you an inalienable asylum with me as long as you live. Can I do more?"

"Oh, my dear, kind master!" cried Anton, kissing *Heinrich's* hands with a flood of joyful tears. "After such, generosity it is surely my duty to devote all the rest of my life to you, and serve you in all honesty as long as I can. Ah, I really believe you are going to be the dear little master I had thirty years ago!"

He was interrupted by the entrance of Albert, who looked paler and graver than Ottmar had expected.

"Well," asked *Heinrich*, "have you slept off your first intoxication of joy, and do you now feel somewhat depressed?"

"Yes, dear Herr Baron," replied Albert. "It is strange; yesterday I felt nothing, thought of nothing, except that I was free; to-day I already perceive the necessity for me to act, and as the prison was formerly too narrow, the world is now too wide for me. I totter and know not where I can obtain support. Yesterday I only felt that the dungeon had cast me out; to-day I feel that life has not yet received me, and seem so helpless that I could weep like a lost child."

"I understand that, Albert. You cannot yet feel at ease in your new position. Your strength of will has been asleep during your five years' imprisonment, and now, when you need it, refuses to obey your bidding. This, as a matter of course, makes you anxious; but it is ungrateful to consider yourself deserted. Can a man receive more abundant assistance than you have had from me?"

"Oh, my noble, generous patron, my whole life belongs to you! How can you believe me ungrateful? I bless you with every breath of God's free air I take. But ought I to eat the bread of charity in your house, even if you wished it? Must I not go out into the world and earn something, that I may at last make a home for the unhappy girl who has suffered and atoned so truly? But what am I to do? I can accomplish so little, my superficial knowledge makes me so dependent. Who will trust the murderer?"

"Any one who knows you, Albert," said *Heinrich*, kindly.

Albert's frank brown eyes gazed at him doubtfully. "Do you think so? Ah, when I was in prison, among the criminals whose fate I unjustly shared, I seemed like a saint; but now I am free and in the society of irreproachable men, I feel for the first time like a criminal, and scarcely venture to raise my shame-dyed face."

"Albert, in spite of your error, you are a man of more delicate and noble feelings than millions of the irreproachable citizens who pride themselves upon their phlegmatic honesty. That is why there are so few who understand you well enough to disregard your past as I do. I will take you henceforth into my employment. Will you undertake to become my steward?"

"The steward of your estates?" asked Albert, in joyful astonishment.

"Yes; I know you studied agriculture with a landowner in V---- before you turned to the career of a priest, and came to the college. However, if you did not learn enough there, I will send you to the agricultural school at C---- for six months to perfect your education; and then I think you will become a faithful manager of my property. You can marry your Röschen; and the steward's house is so large that in the course of a few years you can tell a number of children the story of the Prison Fairy."

A deep blush suffused Albert's face, and he clasped his hands with an involuntary sigh. "Oh, the Prison Fairy, Herr Baron! You and the Prison Fairy are the noblest human beings the Lord ever made! What shall I say to you? I can give you no better thanks than the wish that destiny may unite you!" With these words he hurried from the room.

Heinrich gazed after him for a long time in silence. "So that is the greatest blessing you can desire for me? Poor fellow! You too, without knowing it, love the Prison Fairy. It is because you must be deprived of her that freedom itself seems cold and barren; and yet she is so far above you that you do not venture to raise your eyes towards her. To me alone you will not grudge her, whom you consider the essence of everything admirable. And I? Does not the blood mount into my cheeks when I think how little I deserve what you wish me; and how, like a thief, I steal the semblance of virtues I do not possess!"

Veronica and Cornelia were sitting in their little tea-room, engaged in needle-work. "Cornelia, you sew very little, and talk still less," said Veronica to the young girl, who was sitting silent and motionless, gazing at the green shade that covered the lamp.

"I can neither sew nor talk: I am thinking of Ottmar," she answered, frankly. "Is not such a soul, which approaches ours for the first time and opens a new world to us, worthy of being received with quiet solemnity? Are we to rest on that day which commemorates a miracle that happened long ago and has never been fully proved? and when the Deity reveals one of its greatest wonders to our eyes, ought we to grudge our souls a time of sabbath repose in which to receive this lofty guest? You must not reproach me if, under this impression, I spend a few days longer in idle dreams. It is my nature!"

"You are just what I wish to see you, my Cornelia. God grant that you may remain so! Give yourself up to your own thoughts undisturbed. Put aside your work and remain silent. People do not hold communion with each other only when they talk."

Another pause followed, and nothing was to be heard except the clicking of Veronica's knitting-needles. But the old lady was not silent long. "You have a deep mind, Cornelia: I could not reflect so long upon any subject; and in spite of my years I enjoy life more unquestioningly than you. What approaches me lovingly I believe in, and when I trust I enter into no subtle inquiries."

Cornelia smiled but made no reply, for these words showed her that Veronica only partially understood her mood; and she did not feel disposed to disclose her feelings any further, though she could not have given a reason for it even to herself. Her large eyes rested affectionately upon the old lady, and she merely asked, "Dear Veronica, are people investigating a subject when they are silently enjoying it?"

"Make the tea, my little angel," said Veronica; "the organ will suit your solemn mood."

Cornelia arranged the tea-table, lighted the wick under an old-fashioned silver tea-kettle, and then sat down to listen to the charming music that instantly became audible. At first one could only distinguish the different tones of boiling water, but by degrees they became more melodious, and blended together not into a confused bubbling, but the notes of the choral song, "Blick hin nach Golgotha!" It was a wonderfully artistic plaything, concealed in the lid, and set in motion by a glass roller, by the pressure of steam. The tones of course were louder or fainter as the water boiled more or less violently, and thus the whole sounded like the singing of a tea kettle, transformed into melody by some invisible fairy.

This tender, mysterious music did indeed harmonize with Cornelia's mood, and she looked up as if roused from a dream when the stiff, precise old servant entered, and, with a doubtful mien, said that Herr von Ottmar wished to see the ladies.

"He is very welcome," said Veronica, joyfully; and the old man, casting a sullen glance at Cornelia's blushing face, opened the door.

Heinrich entered. He apologized for the late hour of his visit by saying that he had received a note from the prince, directing him to prepare for a journey, and expect further orders the following day. Thus it might happen that he would be compelled to set out at once without having any time for farewells.

Veronica assured him that no apology was necessary, and begged him to take tea with them. The old servant, to his great disgust, was ordered to bring another plate, and sternly placed a chair for *Heinrich* beside Veronica, pressing it violently on the floor, as if he would like to make it grow there; but *Heinrich* involuntarily pushed it towards Cornelia, and the old man withdrew, shaking his head.

Cornelia said nothing, and *Heinrich* looked at her inquiringly. In the silence that followed he noticed the singing of the tea-kettle.

"What strange little organ have you there?" he asked, in surprise.

"It is a relic of my sentimental youth," replied Veronica, "and is really closely connected with a portion of my life."

"Why, that is very interesting! What air is it playing?"

"A choral I often sang in my young clays. Tell Herr von Ottmar the words, Cornelia, or he will think you have forgotten how to speak."

Cornelia repeated the well-known strophe:

> "Schau hin nach Golgotha!
> Dort schwebt am Kreuzes-stamm'
> Im Todeskampf dein Jesus,
> Mit deiner Schuld beladen.
> Schau hin nach Golgotha!
> Er neigt sein sterbend Haupt,
> Es bricht sein Herz,
> Selbst Engel weinen:
> Der Welterlöser todt!"

"It is a beautiful choral, but it does not suit a gay social circle," said Cornelia, evidently deeply moved. She had felt that her voice grew tremulous during the recital, and thought herself obliged to apologize. "The profound melancholy of that sublime death overwhelms me in those few lines. They conjure up the whole picture of the saddest hour earth has ever known, and I cannot refrain from tears."

"While you spoke I saw only the angels who were weeping there," whispered *Heinrich*, gazing at her with delight, "and yet your trembling voice touched me strangely. Who gave you this prophetic inspiration, which, after the lapse of centuries, feels agonies perhaps never endured? All the sufferings of Christ were mirrored in your eyes."

"Oh, who could help feeling them?" replied Cornelia. "Who that truly entered into them could help being thrilled with the deepest grief? What a sacrifice, to make himself the bleeding example of his teachings! What a love, which devotes itself to secure the happiness of a world! When I read the history of the passion, it seems as if I had a thousand hearts, so keenly, so painfully, do I feel the death-agony of the One Heart that bore in itself the sorrows of all, suffered for all, bled for all, loved all,--even those who betrayed it,--and was understood and valued by so few. I see him turn pale, and feel how Mary counts his last sighs and dies ten deaths with him. The breezes pause in their course and are silent: the clouded sky bends heavily towards the earth; all creation is frozen with terror, and listens for the fearful moment when the God-man shall die,--when the monstrous murder of the Guiltless One shall be completed. And now he bends his head, and all is over. It is done, and the long-repressed woe breaks forth. The storm rages over the earth, rends the veil, bursts the false temple. The world groans; and the Lord himself, touched even in his unapproachable divinity, extends his arms to his beloved Son to receive him to his heart. Oh, my friend, who can read or hear this story without being moved to the very depths of his soul? Even if you deny this great event and prove that it never existed, and even reveal who invented it,--who subjected a world to the might of this thought,--he too was inspired by a higher power,--he too came from God and has performed a miracle; a miracle that no one can deny, for it uplifts itself in gigantic structures of stone in every land; it stamps its impress upon every grave; it receives the new-born infant with a holy ordinance; it is the last consolation of the dying; nay, at this very moment it fills your own breast with silent veneration: I can see it in you."

Heinrich could scarcely breathe; he did not know what had befallen him. Was it a supernatural creature who was speaking to him? He was obliged to start up and go to the window, so strangely did his thoughts pulse through his brain. Was it the artistic impression of her powerful, eloquent words, her animated play of expression, the capacity for suffering in her nature bodingly revealed in this description, or the effect of the words themselves? He knew not, but he felt as much agitated as if Christianity had just been revealed to him for the first time.

"You could do more good than many preachers," he said, at last, returning to his seat. "You understand how to obtain a hold upon the soul, and I am amazed at your religious enthusiasm. I should have supposed you to have more tendency towards rationalism. Are you a Protestant?"

"Oh, do not ask whether I am Catholic or Protestant! I am a Christian,--that is the principal thing. By faith and education I am a Protestant; but I belong to no creed, for I have no faith in miracles,--at least the miracles the church teaches. I recognize too entirely the divinity of the laws of the universe to believe that God must remove Nature from her usual course to reveal himself. Every deviation from natural laws is an abnormal condition, and therefore unlovely, for all beauty consists in the harmony of each individual part with the whole; but I can accept and reverence nothing that is not beautiful,--far less consider God, the soul of the system of the world, as the author of an anomaly. Herein I am a rationalist. I hate those who bar the progress of science, because they fear the natural explanation of things may destroy the dogma of revelation; but I also hate those who think that by the natural explanation of things they can deny the existence of a higher power. God reveals himself indirectly in the laws of nature, and directly in the soul. The noblest man is to me the greatest wonder of creation; and if I believe Christ to be the son of Joseph, I adore him none the less as the true Son of God, spirit of his Spirit, proceeding from and returning to him. Thus I am a Christian with my whole soul, and, with ardent love, bear my Saviour in my heart as my highest model. What would all my acts be if I had not this fundamental principle of Christianity? if I did not perform my charitable deeds in the spirit of self-sacrifice Christ taught us, what should I be? A sentimental adventuress, a heroine of romance, who has one eccentric caprice today and another to-morrow; is always playing a part, and constantly unhappy because she has no object, no purpose, in life; for selfishness leaves us always empty and unsatisfied, while Christianity is its most powerful opponent."

Heinrich sat for some time in silence, with his eyes fixed upon the floor; when he looked up Cornelia was gazing into his grave countenance with an expression of affectionate inquiry,--she felt that her last words had touched some sensitive point. *Heinrich* passed his hand through his hair as if he wished to banish the obtrusive thoughts that crowded upon him.

"The poetry of Christianity has excited and enchained your fancy. It would be useless to convince you by scientific proofs, since you have formed a religion which is not dependent upon them."

"Certainly," laughed Cornelia.

"You *wish* to believe, and therefore you do. You are fortunate! You have produced a wonderful harmony between your skeptical reason and enthusiastic heart. I admire you; for this theory of spiritual revelation by natural means, which can go hand in hand with science, is the best that a talented woman can appropriate. Who taught you all this?"

"Her own harmonious soul," said Veronica. "She has a keen intellect, and a soft, feeling heart; therefore she does not believe unconditionally, as we are obliged to do, and yet is full of religious devotion. Thus she found that harmony, as you call it, and restored peace to her mind. When you know her better, you will be astonished at the wonderful symmetry of her nature."

"I am already!" exclaimed *Heinrich*; "I never had any intellectual pleasure which could be compared to my intercourse with you. I could listen forever in rapturous delight to the thousand turns her thoughts take. Tell me, Cornelia, from what noble union of wondrous hearts did you spring, to be mentally and bodily so beautiful,--so beautiful?"

Cornelia looked at Veronica. The latter passed *Heinrich* a cup. "Take some tea, and I will tell you the story of my musical urn, which interested you so much just now. You will thereby learn our whole history, if you care to know it."

"Oh. pray tell me whatever I may be permitted to hear. You do not know how eagerly I desire it."

"I have already told you," began Veronica, "that Cornelia is the child of my adopted daughter. This adopted daughter, the wife of the political martyr Erwing, was thrown upon my hands by a singular destiny, and I thank God, that, through her and afterwards through Cornelia, he gave my life a purpose and meaning. I enjoyed a mother's pleasures without being compelled to suffer her pains; for when God took my dear adopted daughter from me, my grief would have been infinitely greater if the lost one had been mine by birth. But Cornelia has, as yet, given me nothing but joy. She was difficult to educate, but even the toil of reducing these chaotic talents to order was a pleasure. That I have succeeded in doing so is a wonder to myself, for I never had an opportunity to study these powerful characters. My mother, to the day of her death, had a childlike heart. She was only sixteen years older than I, and seemed like a friend and playmate rather than a mother. The governess my father procured for me really educated the mamma at the same time with the little daughter! This gay, innocent youth has been the foundation of my character. My grandfather was a Danish nobleman, who became a widower at my mother's birth, and lived a solitary life upon his estates at Soröe, though he opened his house to all the nobility in the neighborhood. It chanced that an acquaintance one day introduced a friend named Albin, a native of Holstein, who was traveling through the country. Herr von Albin, a handsome, attractive man of fifty, was seated at dinner next to my mother, who at that time was not quite fifteen, and she particularly remembered that when some magnificent strawberries were served at dessert, the gentleman assured her that much larger and finer ones grew on his estate. This greatly astonished my mother, for she had always believed the strawberries in her garden the best in the world.

"A few weeks after a servant summoned her to her father's room, and the latter informed her that she would soon be married. She said, 'As you please, dear father,' and went sorrowfully back to her governess. When, however, on the following day Herr von Albin was presented to her as her future bridegroom, she was greatly delighted, for she thought of the wonderful strawberries that grew on the kind gentleman's estate.

"This Herr von Albin was my father. He loved my mother with touching tenderness, and did everything in his power to prevent her from feeling the great difference in their ages. He took journeys with her, and as German society pleased her far better than the formal Danish etiquette of those days, lived by turns upon his Holstein estates in summer, and the North German City of B---- in winter. Thus it happens that my whole nature is thoroughly North German, and I have also inculcated some of it into Cornelia's mind. When I was in my fourteenth year I lost my father, and my mother, then scarcely thirty, was still very girlish in her appearance, and equally so in character. The death of the kind husband whom she had loved with childlike reverence was the first sorrow of her life.

"With the same obedience with which she had formerly married Herr von Albin she now, at her father's command, wedded a second husband; but this time she did not rejoice over beautiful strawberries.

"My stepfather, an attaché of the Danish Embassy in N----, was very rich; and as my father's estates were entailed an male heirs, and my mother had also inherited little or nothing, my grandfather, whose property likewise reverted to the crown at his death, wished by this marriage to secure his daughter a future free from care. But whether my mother was happy with this man I will leave you to decide. He was a cold aristocrat, chose society which was distasteful to us, and left us much alone at a retired country seat, where we led a life devoted to books and belles-lettres.

"Chance made me acquainted with a young officer, who, despite his youth, was already a widower, and the father of a little two-year-old daughter. We loved each other, and he asked for my hand; but my stepfather refused his consent, because the marriage did not suit his plans for me, and perhaps, also, because he had no inclination to give me a dowry. What a nature that young man possessed! Alas! he bore the doom of an early death. During our stay at our country seat my mother sometimes permitted him to visit us. She became constantly sadder and paler, and the only hours that she seemed more animated and joyous were those we all spent together. I sang and played upon the piano passably well, and the choral we have just mentioned, which was peculiarly in harmony with my Edmund's religious feelings, I sang for him again and again. We spent many such evenings as this together, and were never happier than when assembled around the steaming tea-urn in North German fashion. My friend often said it would be charming if its confused humming could be transformed into a distinct melody, for he found all the charm of northern sentimentality in its mysterious music.

"Just at this time my stepfather suddenly died, leaving my mother a large fortune, and there was now no further impediment to our marriage. We wished to have my betrothed husband resign from the army at once; but he would not consent. He wished to take part in the last great campaign against Napoleon before he resigned himself to the happiness of private life. We parted as betrothed lovers; I took his little daughter from her boarding-school to my own home, to be a mother to her, for I loved the child; but my mother clung to the little one with peculiar affection. After the departure of my affianced husband, she was often confined to her bed, but her still youthful and beautiful features beamed with almost superhuman love when she clasped the little girl in her arms. She was then thirty-eight years old, and I two-and-twenty. Alas! it was only later that I first suspected the true cause of my mother's quiet illness. Her poor heart had never known love,--let me be silent." The speaker's bright eyes suddenly grew dim, and tears ran down her pale cheeks.

"Oh, God!" murmured *Heinrich*, involuntarily.

"She was constantly thinking of what we could do to surprise Edmund on his return," continued Veronica. "One day she said she would like to have him find on our table an urn constructed exactly as he had desired, and that the toy, whose idea she suggested to me, should play his favorite choral, 'Schau hin nach Golgotha!' As I saw how greatly she had set her heart upon it, I instantly gave the order to the celebrated mechanician, Gebhardt, and in the course of a few months the work was completed. Alas! it afforded her the last pleasure she ever knew. It played for the first time one dreary autumn evening. She sat up in bed with her arm around the little girl, and listened with childlike devotion. 'May you solemnize a beautiful service of love with this organ!' said she. 'Make his home-life bright and pleasant, that he may always be glad to stay with you; believe me, a solitary wife is a most wretched creature. Make him happy, my Veronica; he deserves it.' 'Grandmamma,' lisped the child, throwing her little arms lovingly around the neck of the fair, youthful 'grandmother.' Her cheeks flushed feverishly, and she concealed her tears upon the neck of the 'little angel.' Do you know, Veronica, that I have begun to write poetry in my old age!' she said, suddenly, with a mournful smile. Yesterday I composed these verses:

"Thank thy God, oh, happy mortal!

Love's thy portion here below,
And, glorified in death by love,
Thy immortal part shall glow.
"Love suffered for thee on the cross,
Upon Golgotha died for thee;
Is ever near, though far away
He whom thou lov'st may be.
"Cheer thee, my heart, though here on earth
Thou seekest love in vain;
Feel that there is no lack with God;
Cry blessings on his name.

"'Oh, mother!' I exclaimed, deeply touched, 'why is this? Do you lack love? Do we not all love you most tenderly?' Weeping bitterly, I pressed her to my heart. Just at that moment a letter was brought in. From him she exclaimed, broke the seal, and sank back senseless upon the pillows. I tore the letter from her rigid hands,--it was the notice of my lover's death. I rushed into the next room to conceal the outbreak of my anguish from my mother, and, throwing myself upon my knees, prayed for strength. Suddenly I heard strange sounds, which made me start up, and, at the same time, the child screamed aloud. In mortal terror I hurried back to find my mother in her death-agony. 'Mother, mother,' I shrieked, despairingly, 'do not leave me alone in my misery!' With a look of inexpressible love, she placed the little one in my arms; I clasped them both in a wild embrace; felt the last breath of her pure lips, and then sank back senseless, dimly hearing, as if from another world, the air 'Schau hin nach Golgotha!' Spare me the description of my sufferings. For a year I struggled with a disease of the lungs, but my strong, youthful constitution obtained the victory. Yet one tiny flower of happiness bloomed for me upon my lover's grave: his little daughter,--his own flesh and blood,--a part of himself. I had not wholly lost him,--was not entirely alone. Nay, the child resembled him so much that with silent delight I saw his living image always before me, but the double blow had so crushed my soul that I needed and sought seclusion. I purchased a small estate in the province of R----, where I devoted myself entirely to the sorrowful pleasure of educating my Antonie and cherishing memories of my lover,--let people say what they chose,--and shut myself up in my little world of feeling. I read everything new that appeared in the kingdom of literature, and in all found myself and my own grief. By degrees I became not only calm but happy; the lonely life I led caused all the pictures of my memory to assume so tangible a form that my lover and my dear mother appeared before me,--I was surrounded by all whom I loved. Thus the dead became alive to me, and the living, with the exception of my child, dead. The happier I felt in these dreams the more anxiously I avoided all contact with reality, that the delicate webs of my fancy might not be torn asunder by its rude touch. Nor was this difficult, for no one troubled themselves about the stranger. Beautiful scenes of nature entranced me with their ever-varying charms; an excellent servant managed my little household; and thus for fourteen years I lived entirely apart from the world with my adopted daughter, my books, and my dead. This is the reason why I seem too young for my age,--I stood still for many years of my life. But when Antonie grew up, I perceived that I ought not to make the bright, blooming young girl a hermit. My parents' house in N---- was empty, and I resolved to move here and introduce my adopted child to society; but how was I astonished to find it so entirely different from what I had left it! Since peace had once more smiled upon the country,--since no universal sorrow impressed its deep seal upon every soul,--men seemed to me more selfish, more material. They doubtless still coquetted with a certain sentimentality, but it seemed to me that with true sorrow true feeling had also vanished. Time had advanced, while during my long seclusion I had remained standing still; I felt that I did not understand this world, and was even allowed to perceive that I no longer suited it. As through my extensive course of reading Antonie and I had obtained knowledge, and also, probably, formed some opinions, several literary people became interested in us, and thus, with Antonie's full consent, I again withdrew from society, to collect around me a circle of men and women who possessed similar tastes. The unfortunate republican, Erwing, then a quiet, much-respected man and a distinguished author, was also introduced to me. He loved and married Antonie; Cornelia was born the following year. At that time Erwing was already developing his dangerous political tendencies. He was a noble man, and sacrificed himself to his principles, and, alas! his wife also, who died of grief for him. God took her from the world; her death broke down all the barriers that had hitherto restrained Erwing, and his sorrow for her increased his political wrath to its height. Soon after, the unhappy man was obliged to fly to America, where he died, leaving the orphan, to whom, since her father's flight, I have filled a mother's place, as I did to her mother. In so doing I have fulfilled a sweet and sacred duty to my dead love, who lives and hovers around me in eternal youth, and blesses my efforts in behalf of his granddaughter!"

The old maid paused, with cheeks crimsoned with blushes; she had folded her hands over her knitting, and seemed wholly absorbed in memories of the past. Cornelia sat lost in thought, with her head resting on her hand.

"What a face, so victorious in its calm pride!" said *Heinrich* to himself; "what hair, what a neck, what an arm! What movements, and lines! What grace! Yes, it is the *soul* that animates this frame, and warm blood that gleams through it so rosily!"

He laid his open palm before her on the table; she placed her hand in it. There was nothing very singular in the action, but her cheeks glowed; it seemed as if he was drawing her head towards him, as if she must bend forward yet he held her hand calmly in his. Veronica, absorbed in her memories, rose to get *Heinrich* a picture of her lover. They were alone! A new expression flashed over Ottmar's face,--*Heinrich* and *Henri* had changed places! the moment had tempted the latter irresistibly. He slowly drew Cornelia's hand towards him, and bent his handsome head to hers; his eyes beamed with inexpressible love, and his voice trembled with fervor as he whispered:

"Poor heart, how much you must have suffered, must still suffer, in the memory of your unhappy father! Oh, if you could but look into the depths of this soul and know how I feel for you!--oh, love!" He pressed his lips gently upon her hand, and let them rest there, without kissing it.

Cornelia scarcely breathed; the touch thrilled through her whole frame like an electric shock. She felt that a new happiness, never known before, was entering her heart, and yielded to it without the slightest movement. Then the organ slowly played the strophe, "Selbst Engel weinen," and died away. *Henri* raised his head, and asked, gently, "What do you think of me now?"

She could not speak, but looked into his eyes with an expression so dreamy and ardent that *Henri* needed no words. His quick ear heard Veronica's approach, and he leaned back in his chair and attracted the attention of Cornelia, who was completely absorbed in her own feelings. The old lady showed *Henri* her lover's miniature, and found it perfectly natural that after these reminiscences Cornelia should burst into tears. Cornelia herself did not know their cause, for she really had no sorrowful memories; the things we hear in early childhood do not make so vivid an impression; and her youth, under Veronica's care, had been a happy one. Far less was it the recollection of her first love, for this now seemed to her like a dream. What was it, then? What had happened? He had told her that he pitied her; that was very natural: she had given him her hand and he had kissed it,--no, not even kissed it, he had only allowed his lips to rest upon it; but it was perhaps that very thing,--how strange!

Henri's accustomed eyes read all these thoughts in Cornelia's face, and with exultant satisfaction saw the net resting upon the wings of her soul. "Cornelia," he said, softly, while Veronica was counting her stitches, "you are reflecting upon the nature of sympathy again, but you will not fathom it yet!"

"You are right," she answered.

She had been playing mechanically with one of her rings, and it now fell from her-hand. *Henri* picked it up, and, with a smile, replaced it on her finger. Again she blushed. "Why?" she asked unconsciously.

"Our child is sad," he said to Veronica, with the winning expression which had always prevailed upon women to devote their lives to him. "What can we do to cheer her?"

Cornelia, as if spell-bound by the magic of these tones, made no reply.

"How kind you are!" said Veronica.

"Are you angry because I call you 'our child'?" asked *Henri*, with admirably assumed simplicity. "I am becoming intimate too rapidly, am I not? Be kind, and attribute it to my warm, truthful nature. Sooner or later we shall meet more familiarly, I am sure; so why delay and so lose the precious moments for the sake of troublesome forms. I would gladly take you to my heart as carefully and protectingly as--a father. Fräulein Veronica will allow me to do so, I am sure. Be our dear child, and let me take some small share in your education."

He arose and stood before her in all his gentlemanly dignity, bent down and kindly took her hands; but the quick pulsations of his heart, which Cornelia heard close beside her ear, accorded strangely with these paternal words. This was the well-calculated charm he had for her: the manly, noble superiority which expressed itself in this fatherly authority, and involuntarily extorted a childlike reverence; and the enthusiastic, almost boyish, tenderness which bowed before her to raise her to giddy heights.

"Teach me, then but permit me to do the same by you," she said, with an embarrassed smile, rising from her chair.

"Certainly," replied *Henri*; "I need it more than you. Oh, I will follow you blindly; the words of those pure lips shall be my oracle!" His eyes-rested upon the young girl's fresh, beautiful mouth with ardent longing. He felt that it would be better to go, and allow the impression he had made to produce its effect upon her in silence. With a violent effort he released Cornelia's hands and hastily took his leave. As he opened the door he heard his name called gently: he turned; Cornelia had followed him a step and asked, with the most lovable frankness,--

"When will you come again?"

"Cornelia!" cried *Henri*, and was about to rush back to her; but *Heinrich*, with a tremendous effort, checked the excited feelings, made her a low bow, said, in a fatherly tone, "I will come as soon as I can; I cannot fix any positive time now," and left the room without looking back.

"What was that?" asked Cornelia, covering her eyes with her hand. "Did it not seem as if another person was speaking from his lips? Did he not call my name so eagerly, and the next moment take leave of me so distantly, so coldly? Can a man's mood change so suddenly? Whims can alter in an instant, I know that by myself; but what we feel, what is deeply and firmly rooted our hearts, we cannot so suddenly deny,--it cannot yield to a caprice. Which is true, his warmth or his coldness?--or is it possible that they can both exist? Ah, do not question, incredulous heart! What he has given you to-day is true: let that satisfy you; and where you cannot understand him, trust him." With a heavy sigh she threw herself on her knees before Veronica and laid her head on her lap. "Ah, Veronica, how could I live without the man you loved!"

"What a submission!" thought *Henri*, as he walked towards home in the proud conviction of a certain victory.

"Take care!" said *Heinrich*: "this submission is no amorous weakness, but the implicit confidence every innocent, loving girl places in the man she adores. If you ever abuse this faith, you will perceive with terror her power of resistance."

XII
THE SEARCH FOR A WIFE

"My dear Herr von Ottmar," said the prince, holding out his hand to *Heinrich*, "you came out of the vexatious affair, which unfortunately I could not spare you, like a hero. Am I to do anything for your *protégé*? Tell me how I can assist the young man."

Heinrich had intended to affect reserve, and to-day was just in the right humor for it. He bowed low with the air of a deeply offended man.

"I thank you most humbly, your Highness. I have already provided for Albert Preheim. I am happy to have proved to your Highness that I have given my protection to no unworthy person, and am always ready to answer for my acts like a man. I have made Albert Preheim the steward of my estates, which have greatly depreciated in value during my long absence. I will also venture to request your Highness to grant me leave of absence for an indefinite time, that I may be able to instruct him in his duties there."

"You wish to leave me now, when I need you most?"

"If I could hope that your Highness still needed me, I should feel happier than is the case at present."

"Do you believe, Ottmar, that a time will ever come when we shall be unnecessary to each other? I rely more upon your friendship for my person, even if, as an independent man, you can do without the prince."

"Your Highness, let me be frank with you. How faithfully I have served you, the sleepless nights during which I have shared your Highness's arduous labors and heavy cares for your country, my deserted home, my ruined estates, may prove. Compelled to leave my own court because I was an adherent of the priesthood, I found with you a sphere of activity in harmony with my political convictions, an only too generous recognition of my humble services, and the highest possible reward in your personal friendship. But now, your Highness, I stand here as a compromised man, a hero of comedy, who played the martyr for his own sins for the amusement of the rabble. This, your Highness, I cannot endure. Society has a morbidly sensitive feeling for indecorum far more than crime; it can ignore a secret sin, but not a public impropriety. It is not for my guilt but its open acknowledgment that men will turn their backs upon me, and I must go into retirement, for I cannot bear to have the finger of scorn pointed at me."

The prince smiled. "Oh, if that is all that drives you away, Ottmar, you can be perfectly at ease: I will become your security. Do you suppose I would have asked my friend to expose himself if I had not possessed the means to make amends for his humiliation at any moment? I am astonished at your simplicity, Ottmar. Should you not have known society better? Why, even if I would allow you to fall, you would still be esteemed; but if I uphold you, people will treat you with the utmost consideration. What advantage would it be to be ruler if I could not even manage the handful of puppets around my throne? You must take a journey, it is true, but on my business; if you wish to visit your estates on the way, I have no objection; but I beg you to remain there, no longer than is absolutely necessary. Do you consent?"

"My time has only the value it possesses for your Highness. If I can be of more use in any other place than here, command me."

"You will be at ease here again when you have forgotten this disagreeable affair. In the first place we will seal people's mouths by a striking proof of my continued favor. This very night I shall present you to my mother as Count von Ottmar."

"Your Highness! I do not know how to thank you for so much kindness."

"As one friend always does another: by honest counsel and assistance when I need them!"

The prince fixed his large, blue eyes upon Ottmar with so kindly an expression that the latter was surprised.

"I am well aware that the title of Count does not make amends for the mortification I imposed upon you; but perhaps the consciousness that, by this act of self-sacrifice, you have won a still larger share of my esteem and confidence, may be some slight recompense. Therefore, my friend, you shall advise me to-day in the most important event of my life. I have summoned you to discuss my marriage."

"Do I know the princesses?" asked *Heinrich*.

"One of them, certainly; and you shall make the acquaintance of the other. One is Princess Ottilie of H----."

"What!" exclaimed *Heinrich*, almost losing his self-command. "Princess Ottilie!"

"Hist! *Pas si haut, mon ami*, the walls have ears. Remember that this is still a profound secret; you are to be the first to mature the affair. I have the privilege of choosing between Princess Ottilie and Princess Marie of D----. The latter is still a mere child; but the former has lost the first bloom of youth. I do not wish to select the lady who will please me best, but the one who will most satisfactorily fill the position of mistress of my realm; it is not permitted me to marry according to the choice of my heart. My love, as you know, is given to the beautiful Hellbach; but I can neither raise her to the rank of my wife, nor degrade her to that of my mistress, and have learned to conquer my wishes. The private happiness my wife can bestow is merely to make no claims upon my love, which has been effaced from my breast with this one image, and not press upon me an affection which is valueless to me. A sincere friendship, and a pure conscience, are all that I shall give and demand."

Heinrich had been reflecting in silence. "What your Highness asks in a wife is little, and yet the most difficult requirement that can be made upon a woman. She is to offer her wedded husband no feeling, desire none from him, save what might be accorded to the merest stranger. She is to give your country the heir to the throne, and yet be permitted to adopt no other manner towards the father of her child than that prescribed by the laws of the coldest etiquette. But she must bestow upon no other the love that her husband disdains; must enjoy through no other the happiness he denies her; and yet is always to feel a calm affection for the man who has thus destroyed the joys of married life. Pardon me, your Highness, I know women well; this is a task which only a princess can perform,--a princess in the true sense of the word; not a young immature creature, who only wears the mask of her position, and in whose mind natural rights far outweigh the claims of her high station. A princess such as your Highness requires, one who has subdued the first eager longings of her heart and resigned herself to consider the duties of her lofty rank as the first necessity, is the Princess Ottilie. Moreover, she is intellectual, lovable as a young girl, truly royal in her bearing, and although no longer in the first bloom of youth, extremely attractive."

"If you, who are so exacting, think her all this, she must really be somewhat remarkable in every respect," said the prince. "You are right in saying I could hardly expect so much self-sacrifice from a young creature like the Princess Marie. Besides, the priests favor the alliance with Ottilie because they rest great hopes upon her influence over her Protestant uncle, the Prince of H----. There is only the consideration that Ottilie is said to be delicate, and thereby the hope of an heir to the throne might be endangered."

"Ob, I do not think so, your Highness. She is nervous, like all lofty, intellectual natures; but such women are usually benefited by marriage. Doctors chatter a great deal of exaggerated nonsense; and besides, it is not for their advantage that the generous princess should be married and leave the country. I have watched her for a long time, and can assure your Highness that she has no more serious illness than all ladies of her rank and age."

The prince paced up and down the room several times, and then paused before Ottmar. "Are you giving me conscientious advice, Ottmar? Remember that the sole object of the heavy sacrifice I am making is to obtain an heir to the throne."

"Egotist!" thought *Heinrich*.

"Your Highness," he replied, "I am no physician. I can only say how I judge of her as an unprofessional person, and that I have never thought her ill."

The prince again walked up and down the room. "Shall I venture?"

"Yes, your Highness."

The prince turned towards his writing-table and showed *Heinrich* a picture. "Is this a good likeness?"

"Yes, your Highness; but she is more beautiful," said the latter, who could not gaze at Ottilie's gentle, noble features without emotion.

"Now look at Marie's portrait."

Heinrich knit his brow as he looked at the picture. "I should not have the courage to choose this Lady. Those eyebrows, that pouting, scornful mouth."

"Yes, Ottilie's pleases me far better," said the prince.

"And besides, I see no object in this marriage. What is an alliance with the little country of D---- to a prince like your Highness? Princess Ottilie, on the contrary, is immensely rich; more friendly relations with the court of H---- would be desirable in every respect, and Ottilie is a Catholic; she might--that is----"

A clock struck ten. The prince started up.

"The council must begin. Ottmar, you are my ambassador; set out on your journey to-morrow morning, and negotiate the matter for me at the court of H----. Consult the physicians, and if you think it advisable, in God's name win Ottilie for my wife! From all you say she will be best suited to me.

The sacrifice must be made at once. Farewell till we meet in the council of state, dear count."

Thus was the weal or woe of a noble, precious life decided, and again *Heinrich's* egotism demanded a victim. Accident had thrown one into his hands in the person of Ottilie. *Heinrich's* resolution was firm. He knew that if Ottilie became his protectress at the court of N---- his power would be unbounded and immovable; for he did not doubt that with her intellect she must succeed in ruling the prince as well as the country. In any case, his influence over her was more assured than it could be over a princess who was a stranger to him; so a marriage with the latter must be prevented at any cost: it might baffle all his hopes. When he passed through the antechamber, his plan was already formed, and around his lips played the triumphant smile which was always visible when he guided men like puppets. Every preparation was immediately made for the journey:

"Anton," said *Heinrich*, during the packing, "didn't you see anything of Princess Ottilie on your way through H----?"

"No, Herr Baron. She seldom drives out, for she is much worse than she used to be."

"Anton, for Heaven's sake, do me the favor not to tell any one that! Do you hear? Finish the packing, and then go this very night to the Hohmeier'sche Restaurant; there you will find the valet of the prince's confessor, Ehrhardt,--they will point him out to you if you ask for him; join him as if by chance. Tell him about H----, and turn the conversation upon the Princess Ottilie. Then say what you know of her beauty, her piety, etc. See that you have as many listeners as possible,--the more the better. Speak of her hair, her eyes, but especially her generosity; in short, make their mouths water, but do not allow any design to be perceived."

"I understand, Herr Baron," said Anton, smiling. "I'll manage as carefully as possible, and to-morrow the whole city shall be full of the princess's praises."

"That is right, my old friend. I don't think you forgot anything in the village," said *Heinrich*, well pleased.

He wanted to see Cornelia again, but the evening was spent in making various preparations for his journey, and his plan of obtaining Ottilie for the prince required thought and time for consideration. He would compensate himself for the sacrifice after his return, and meantime devote himself entirely to his mission. "How am I to appear before her?--how am I to woo her for another without offending her, when I know that she has loved me, perhaps does still?" This question engrossed his mind, and its difficulties had a peculiar charm for him.

In the course of the evening a court official brought a bill of exchange for five thousand florins for "Count Ottmar's steward, Albert Preheim." The prince had given him this sum from his own private purse as a sort of compensation for his sufferings. He would not allow himself to be humbled by *Heinrich's* proud reserve, and thus made amends for the injustice which had thrown Albert entirely upon *Heinrich* for assistance.

Albert's joy knew no bounds, but his gratitude to *Heinrich*, whom he considered the indirect cause of this favor, was even greater. Thus they set out on their journey, Albert and Anton as happy men, while he to whom both owed their good fortune, whom both loved and honored, knew no happiness, no peace, destitute of support in himself, and unsympathizing even towards those to whom he showed kindness. Already the city lay behind him. He looked back towards Cornelia's house, from thence the dawn would crimson the horizon, from thence his sun would rise to pour light and warmth upon him, and with foreboding longing he gazed over the snow-covered fields towards the golden streaks in the east. The morning air blew icily over his brow; here and there under the snow lay dry branches of frozen weeds; not a bird, not an insect, was stirring far or near: frozen nature was silently awaiting the spring. It was even so with him. His mission, his petty intrigues, everything at that moment retreated into the background, and covered itself with the icy mantle of eternal indifference. From that strip of light life must come to rescue him and lure fresh germs from the frozen clods. The rising sun threw its rosy glimmer into his eyes till they filled with tears; it seemed as if they flowed from his own breast, as if his own feelings and not the light had called them forth, and he might shed more. But he was mistaken, for when he turned his eyes from the dazzling rays the treacherous fountain dried. The unfeeling man could not weep: the blessing of tears was denied him; and the vanished spell left the egotist cold and unsatisfied.

XIII
A SACRIFICE

Directly after his arrival, *Heinrich* went to Ottilie's physician to make inquiries about the state of her health. It was of importance to himself to be correctly informed in this respect; for it would have been very useless to base his ambitious plans upon one doomed to an early death. With her, these, and perhaps even the favor of the prince, might sink into the grave; since he had described her as healthy, the responsibility would fall upon him if she died. The physician, it is true, said that she was delicate, but, according to the principles of the old school, declared that her illness was a nervous one; and *Heinrich* boldly requested a private audience with Ottilie to obtain her consent before he presented himself to the Prince of H---- as an ambassador.

As he passed through the antechamber, a fair-haired little waiting-maid issued from Ottilie's room, glided by, starting violently as she caught sight of him, and disappeared through a side door. *Heinrich* perceived with astonishment that it was Röschen. The servant ushered him into the reception-room. The uniform, unvarying stream of hot air from a Russian stove vibrated around him with suffocating sultriness, increased by the fragrance of numberless flowers grouped in hot-house fashion in the lofty windows of stained glass. The heavy carpets and portières exhaled warmth; it seemed to *Heinrich* as if his lungs were bursting with the longing for a breath of fresh air. He dreaded this first meeting, for in Ottilie's presence his insolent frivolity deserted him, and he stood before her as if she were his conscience. The fervent heat and deathlike stillness that surrounded him increased his embarrassment. There is something strange in the official silence of royal apartments, which rouses the greatest excitement and impatience in any one who is anxiously awaiting an important audience. This was the case with *Heinrich*. He wished to repeat what he was to say to Ottilie, but could no longer remember it. "How shall I appear before her?" was his only thought; and the polished courtier feared this great soul whose prophetic vision had penetrated his inmost heart, and which he now approached like a thief, to try to steal it for his own plans.

A clock struck twelve, and was answered from every side by a multitude of larger and smaller ones, whose buzzing and humming lasted several minutes; then all was silent as before. *Heinrich* uttered a deep sigh. Why did she linger so long? Was she, too, obliged to collect her thoughts, and could she not obtain the composure needed to receive him? "Oh, God! if she should love me still!" he thought, wiping the cold perspiration from his brow.

Just then a door opened noiselessly,--he did not notice it,--and Ottilie floated across the room as lightly as if her feet did not touch the carpet.

Heinrich started as if roused from a dream, when, beautiful as a glorified spirit, she stood before him. Both looked at each other a moment in silence neither could find words; their souls were too full for the narrow forms of speech.

At last Ottilie held out her hand to him, and there was deep sadness in her expression as she said, "Is it really you?"

"I understand the reproof in your question, princess," replied *Heinrich*. "I was prepared for it; and yet accompanied with that voice and glance, it now pierces deep into my breast. As the ambassador of my princely master, I had courage to appear before you--as your friend. My heart trembles, for I well know I shall not bear your sublime, angelic judgment."

Ottilie motioned to him to be seated. "Yes," she began, after a pause, "I had wished to see you a different man, and I do not even know whether I still have the right to tell you so."

"Speak! heap upon my head the whole burden of your accusation, princess."

"Do not fear reproaches from me. All that there is to be said I represented to you, if I remember rightly, long ago. You did not obey my warning voice; what was useless then will also be vain now."

Heinrich covered his eyes with his hand, as if obliged to conceal his tears; and yet it was not all hypocrisy, for it really seemed to him as if a pang of remorse shot through his breast.

Ottilie remained silent for a long time.

"Be merciful, princess," pleaded *Heinrich*; "you reproach me with my change of opinions, but you do not know what may exert an influence over a life, how even the most independent man may be forced into a course contrary to his wishes, and where he must be untrue to himself; therefore be charitable, princess; do not give me up!"

"Ah, how could I!" exclaimed Ottilie, in an outburst of feeling. "Do you not see that I grieve for you, pity you, deeply and sincerely? I do not accuse you; but let me lament that you have defrauded yourself of all true happiness. Do not tell me the career you have adopted satisfies you; in it you can neither follow your own convictions nor develop your talents. I speak now as a woman who has done with self, who is bound to life by no wish, no hope. What have you made of yourself, Ottmar? How have you used the gifts God so richly, so abundantly, bestowed? I have carefully watched your political activity; alas that I must say it you have fallen lower in my eyes the higher you rose in the world. Forgive the harshness," she pleaded, extending her hand to him, "it is the most heartfelt anxiety that speaks from my lips. Do you not see the double danger to which you are exposed? You are robbing yourself of your moral freedom as well as the nation of its political rights; you are servilely bending your noble soul to the dominion of principles in which you do not believe, making yourself the slavish supporter of an impotent reaction. Thus you are losing your intrinsic dignity, and sooner or later your influence as a statesman; for a new and invincible spirit, purer than that of the revolution, is pervading the nations,--the spirit of a profound political knowledge. We cannot subdue this with cannon, nor shut it into prisons; where we believe it to be shattered, it unites again above our heads. It is the child of the age, and unceasingly advances, demanding its rights. And you, instead of throwing yourself into the free current and allowing your breast to expand with the universal impulse, prop yourself with narrow-hearted blindness against the crumbling steps of a throne, to withstand the weight of the approaching shock. You will fall, and as an enemy of ideas which you cherish with every drop of your blood, fall a victim to your hypocrisy, not your convictions. Then you will seek to find compensation in yourself, and perceive with despair that by your perpetual untruthfulness you have destroyed yourself."

"It is very possible," murmured *Heinrich*.

"Oh, believe me; through many a sleepless night I have stretched out my hand to you to draw you out of the gulf into which I saw you sinking. Yet I still trust you; what you did could not estrange me. I still hope, still pray for you; I can say no more than I have already done; but I know that although you have not yet listened to me, quiet hours will come, hours of repentance, when my long silent words will unite with the voice of your conscience,--then, perhaps, you will obey me."

Heinrich seized Ottilie's hands and gazed into her sparkling eyes. A deep blush was glowing upon her cheeks. "Ah, the old magic! Ottilie, Ottilie," he cried, "I fear I am too deeply entangled in hypocrisy! If you could read my soul you would reject me."

"This is one of the moments of depression which utterly subdue such natures. To-morrow, in another mood, you will smile at it. But it is true that you think yourself worse than you really are, that you have less faith in yourself than I in you. Every power needs to be used, even that of the soul. Exert your strength in doing right, then you will first ascertain your own capabilities."

"Ah, princess, how am I to help myself? I know not; I have gone astray into this path, and cannot find strength to retrace my steps. I am well aware that my political career is not in accordance with the spirit of the age; when I entered upon it I really had no other thought than to save myself from a momentary humiliation by the Jesuits, and therefore considered my position in N---- a mere episode. But by degrees my success, and the magnificent means at my command for the advancement of my apparent purposes, charmed me. My influence over the prince tempted me irresistibly. The power he placed in my hands roused all the ambition of my nature. Power, Ottilie, has often transformed a hero into a despot. This being the history of my political development, everything else follows as a matter of course. As everything was at the command of the feared and admired favorite, I felt myself justified in enjoying all. That, in so doing, I formed many a sacred tie only to break it again, and profaned many a bond that already existed,--everything was considered allowable, because everything was granted to me,--you will of course suppose. But I will confess to you, to you alone of all human beings, that this haughty, envied Ottmar became a crushed, wearied, joyless man, an egotist,--who does not even love himself. I can no longer distinguish between truth and falsehood; for everything has two sides, and, as no voice within my breast pleads for either, I decide in favor of the one which will bring me the most immediate advantage. There is no philanthropy in my nature, and thus I make men happy or miserable according as it will be profitable or injurious to myself. I perceive that all this is reprehensible; I envy those who act from principle; I would fain be virtuous, yet cannot discover what virtue is; for my blasé feelings make me perceive, in all the dogmas of religion, morality, and philosophy, only arbitrary beliefs without any eternal foundation, which change at every advance of the nations in civilization, are now wrested here, now there, nay, even dependent upon the fashion of the day; and thus I have formed the despairing conclusion, that there is no virtue, believe the loathing of my own deeds which sometimes seizes upon me to be a relic of old school prejudices, and despise myself. Therefore I have no rule of conduct for my acts except advantage; and when this is obtained, it does not make me happy. I scorn it, as well as the men by whose weakness I won it!"

Ottilie had hung upon his words in breathless suspense. This frank self-accusation had borne her along with it, and she was obliged to collect her thoughts before she could reply.

"Then you are even more unhappy, more worthy of commiseration, than I feared. All lofty, independent natures yield unwillingly to the human law of right and wrong; for the same power which instilled the theories of goodness lives also in them and justifies them in giving its law to themselves. But in you, my friend, this power was only sufficient to dissolve existing beliefs, not to make them unnecessary to you, for you are now wandering, unsupported, without any clear standard of measurement, amid the ruins of your shattered world of ideas. You are seeking for a higher divine law, and because it does not reveal itself to you you despair of virtue. It would be useless to refer you to religion, for you do not believe it; but even without religion a man of lofty character feels a moral want, which, without regard to reward or punishment, impels him toward the right. Though such a man is never quite happy, for only faith can give the highest joy, he will yet experience that peace which a pure conscience bestows. But you have destroyed even this. Your heart is desolate, your soul flutters wearily upon the ground. I no longer see deliverance, blessing, or hope for you. So I must behold the fairest work God and nature ever made, the noble image in which I joy with reverent admiration, sink into the dust, and stand powerless, unable to stretch out a hand to save for God a soul which he has favored beyond all others. Alas, Ottmar! By the sorrow in my own heart, I feel how your Creator mourns over you!" She leaned back upon the sofa and wept aloud.

Heinrich could not resist the contagion of her emotion. For the first time the request he was about to make seemed like sacrilege, and yet he could not give up all his carefully matured plans for the sake of a "fit of sentimentality," as he mentally called it. He perceived that she clung to him with unchanging affection, and that no political considerations whatever would induce her to wed with such a nature as that of the prince. If he won her, it would only be by means of his influence over the heart so susceptible to his power. Years before she had taken an oath that she would never become his wife, so she must either part with him or marry his ruler. The more she loved him the greater was his power over her, the more surely he would succeed in convincing her that she could not live without him. Thus he was compelled to throw the whole weight of his own personal attractions into the scale, and there was a strange blending of honesty and hypocrisy in his plan of persuasion. He really felt what he wished to say, but his manner of turning it to account was artfully calculated, and converted truth into falsehood. "Your Highness," he exclaimed, at last, "I have come to bring you a crown; but at this moment I see a halo shining around your head, and can scarcely venture to offer the pitiful diadem of royalty. Princess, it is of great importance to my interests to bind you to the country in which I play a part; I came here to obtain your hand for the prince, to cunningly win your consent, even at the cost of your happiness. But before your noble nature all the arts of diplomacy dissolve into nothing. Therefore, my friend, I will leave you free to choose, will not steal the decision of your destiny, but tell you frankly that it is from selfishness I press my master's offer, for I wish, I long, to have you near me. Your character is formed, your opinions are matured, you will advise me when God is silent in my own breast. You will aid me to give a new direction to our politics, one more in harmony with the spirit of the age; supported by you, I will venture it, without you I cannot. Look, Ottilie, the crafty diplomatist is prostrate in the dust before your victorious truthfulness, and prattles out his whole programme like a school-boy. I do not plead for the country whose salvation you would be, nor in the name of a philanthropy I have never known, but by which I might win your gentle heart; I do not implore you to aid a nation I helped to crush: I renounce all this acting, and plead simply and openly for myself; for in this hour I perceive more clearly than ever what you are to me. If I have hitherto thought I needed you for the attainment of certain advantages, I now know that you will do more for me by teaching me to despise as well as dispense with them."

Ottilie gazed silently into vacancy; her breath came more quickly, and her hands were burning as though with fever.

"I know," continued *Heinrich*, "that it is the sacrifice of your whole life; but you have yourself given me the courage to ask it, for you give me the belief that you will make it."

"Oh, God I what do you ask?" Ottilie began. "You wish me to marry,-- to destroy my life! Is it possible? Have I deserved this from you? You wish to lure me from my home to a desolate career of grandeur, to chain me to a man whom I know to be a cold-hearted weakling, and scorn as a mere tool in the hands of the oppressors of his people. And by the painful act I am to perform I do not even make one person happy."

"Ottilie, how can you say so? Thousands will lavish blessings upon you, the gratitude of thousands will recompense you, if the happiness of one whom your presence can transform into another man does not reward you," cried *Heinrich*, reproachfully.

"Ottmar, if I knew that I should be permitted to exert a good influence over you, no sacrifice would seem too great. But you are deceiving yourself now, as usual. You are easily moved, easily excited: the moment carries you away with it; the present person is in the right with you, and when you turn your back upon this room the emotions you have experienced will be effaced with all their impressions. What influence did I exert over you while you lived in H----? It would be precisely the same thing again, and then I should not even be allowed the one consolation of mourning for you unheeded, in quiet solitude."

"Do you think me so unstable?"

"Confess, my friend, that you have given me proofs of it. Besides, you are mistaken if you hope to obtain goodness from any influence whatever. The true man is everything to himself; what he does not become by his own strength, no other can make him. A character that depends upon influences is unmanly; the acts and developments of such a temperament are decided solely by ever-changing accidents. Prosperity has spoiled you; you have measured your powers only against those weaker than yourself; they have thereby become relaxed; and, if destiny does not compel you to put forth your strength in a contact with more powerful elements, all is vain, you will remain----" She paused.

"Pray go on," said *Heinrich*, bitterly; "I shall remain a characterless weakling, who balances to and fro like a juggler on the narrow line between right and wrong! Is not that what you meant to say?"

Ottilie gazed into his beautiful, restless eyes with an expression of deep sorrow. "Forgive me if I have caused you pain; I only wished to convince you that the use which I might be to you is too little for the sacrifice you demand."

Heinrich felt the moment for persuading her had now arrived; for he knew by experience that a woman can never be more easily won than at the moment she believes she has been too harsh.

"You feel you have caused me pain, Ottilie. Oh, make amends for it, and follow me to my country as my protectress, my guardian angel! You reproach me with being unmanly. Well, if I am so, and depend upon influences, the one you exert over me will be my salvation, and that of all with whom I am connected by any ties. What do I ask of you that is so very terrible? I wish to make you mistress of a beautiful and wealthy land, to give you a position in which alone your superior qualities can make themselves valuable, wed you to a prince whom you greatly undervalue, and who will understand and love you as you deserve."

"I want no love," interrupted Ottilie, "I am weary of suffering; do not grudge my repose; I have, by a violent struggle obtained the peace of the grave. Oh, do not drag me back to life! for life is conflict. Ah, Ottmar, have pity upon me! Your glance sinks into my soul, and the spark that flashes from it kindles anew the vital flame which was buried beneath the ashes of my dead hopes. You seize my hand, and by some magnetic attraction I am compelled to follow you. I know not by what invisible threads you hold me: loose them and I sink peacefully towards the grave; draw them firmly and I am forced to yield to your wishes. Oh, the victory you obtain is an easy one! Renounce it, leave me, Ottmar! You can test your power everywhere; why must you try it an one who has no longer any defense save the resignation of a dying woman?"

"Good heavens, princess, what a strange mood you are in! See, this is the result of your seclusion. Whence come these thoughts of the grave? You are healthy, in the very prime of life, beloved by all, regarded by the nation with the warmest affection. How could you resign yourself to such melancholy fancies? Nay, I will rouse you now. You must learn to use your vital powers, as well as I my moral strength. Why should you wither here, useless and lonely, without having fulfilled the eternal vocation of a woman? Even if you have no feeling for the man to whom I wish to unite you, you do not know that he may not become dear to you."

Ottilie sadly shook her head.

"But granted that you can never love him as a husband, you will some day as the father of your children. Fate has granted no desire of your heart, and with royal dignity you have learned to crush it; but, because the first joy of love was denied you, must you now also renounce the maternal happiness this marriage can bestow,--the only one which is a wellspring of lasting joy to a woman? I cannot believe, Ottilie, that with your pure, womanly feelings, the thought of being a mother would have no charm for you."

"Oh, God! have often dreamed of such bliss; but I am not born for it. I shall perish without object or joy in life."

"Do not believe it," said *Heinrich*, with melting tenderness. "Rise again in the strength of hope; a prosperous future is still before you. You will find the prince a man full of delicacy of feeling and dignity, a man formed to understand you. He, too, bears a secret sorrow in his heart, and needs a wife who will know and pity the wound."

"Alas, poor prince!" murmured Ottilie. "That would rouse my sympathy for him."

Heinrich suppressed a smile. "Do you perceive the true state of the case? You will become attached to him, for he is noble and wishes to do good to all. His despotic principles are rooted in his education; to him despotism is an absolute dogma, like religion. He now depends upon his confessor and upon me,--errors which are the result of his youth. When you are his wife, he will, like all of us, rely on you. But even if you could never produce any change in his maxims of government, you will, perhaps, have the satisfaction of inculcating into the mind of a son what you have vainly tried to obtain from the father, and through the former obtain for your people the fulfillment of their dearest hopes. Then, Ottilie, your name will be blessed by thousands and recorded in history; then you may bend to death your royal brow, armed with the noble words, 'I have not lived in vain!' Oh, I know you will some day smile at the thought of the time when you were consuming away in fruitless dreams, and could find strength neither to live nor die! Then I shall perhaps stand as your most faithful servant at the steps of the throne to which you gave new splendor, and a friendly glance, radiant with the pleasure of ruling and giving happiness, will be my highest reward, my greatest satisfaction. Take courage, Ottilie, and gain new strength to live, to rule, to make others happy."

Ottilie's breath came more and more quickly, as, following *Heinrich's* movements, she rose from her seat. Her sparkling eyes were fixed upon his lips, and a ray of melancholy pride flashed over her face. "Ottmar, you have conquered. Happy I can never be, so let us try whether I can still accomplish some good."

"Then I have your promise, princess? You think me right?"

"You are right; yet it is not that conviction, but a secret necessity, which impels me to obey you, although I feel it will be my death. In you, I am well aware, my destiny is fulfilled; you have made me the prince's wife, you overmaster me by your powerful will, and call from my lips the 'yes' that you ask, and I am forced to utter it, no matter for whom. I must utter it because you ask it."

Heinrich was perplexed by this outburst of long-repressed feeling. The seriousness of his relations with Cornelia had already taken so deep a root in his nature that none of that frivolous delight which overwhelms vain men at the sight of their conquests stirred within him. On the contrary, a holy awe seized upon him at the sight of the frank truthfulness of an omnipotent feeling. But he did not understand that this very feeling no longer needed to disguise itself; because, by self-renunciation, it had become purified and transfigured. He therefore thought himself obliged to lead Ottilie's feelings, as far as possible, back to their former moderation, and yet dared not wound this sore heart by coldness. "Ottilie," he said, at last, after a long pause, with an air of sorrowful resignation, "princess, do not make it too difficult for me to perform my duty as suitor in my princes's place. I might forget that I now stand before you as your subject, who no longer dares desire what belongs to his master!"

Ottilie looked at him earnestly. "Ottmar, that recollection would shame me if I could suppose you did not remember the oath I took in your presence years ago, and doubted the firmness of my resolution. But that you cannot do; you will not inflict upon me the humiliation of seeing myself misunderstood by you. I belong to your prince,--my heart to the past."

"Then let me offer you the first homage as my princess, my saint!" exclaimed *Heinrich*, and sank an one knee to kiss her hand.

"The saints are above," whispered Ottilie, waving him back. "May they take us under their protection!"

Heinrich did not notice that it was difficult for her to stand erect while she dismissed him, and armed with Ottilie's consent, pressed forward as unyielding as fate. With this promise, he held in imagination the portfolio which was to be the price of his years of self-deception. That he would rule where Ottilie reigned was to him a matter of course; to secure her influence over the prince should be his care, and to rule appeared to him the only really valuable gift in life. To assert his power everywhere, to use the terrible will which had divided his own nature according to his pleasure, to let it weigh upon a whole country bending before him, to promise joy or sorrow by his smile or frown,--this alone seemed divine, and could make him resemble God. He confidently expected to be appointed ambassador extraordinary to conduct the affair of the marriage; the prince had no one more suitable, no one with whom his relations were so intimate. He reported Ottilie's consent, and requested further instructions, then arranged his own and Albert's business in regard to the estate, which was very badly managed.

Albert sought Röschen at her father's house, and learned that since the death of Ottilie's head waiting-maid, which had occurred two years before, she had filled her place. *Heinrich* smiled when he heard this; he readily perceived that love for him had induced Ottilie to keep near her person the young girl he had tried to win; for true love embraces not only its object but everything connected with it. He had already often observed how noble womanly natures did not hate those of whom they were jealous, but treated them with sorrowful tenderness, how they kissed them as if seeking on their cheeks and lips traces of their lover's caresses. As we keep a flower or a handkerchief because the absent one has touched it, Ottilie had taken Röschen into her service to inhale from her presence the lingering breath of his love.

Poor Ottilie!

The prince kept him waiting a long time for his instructions, and Ottmar began to grow weary of his incognito. "Albert," said he one day, "you don't seem to have any great desire to see your Röschen. Try to arrange a meeting with her, and let me be a secret witness of it; I should like, for a change, to be present at such a touching scene."

"I have settled it with her father that I am to have an interview next Sunday, Herr Count," replied Albert. "Röschen cannot leave the palace whenever she chooses, so I must wait. But, if you are tired,--excuse the boldness of my question,--why don't you write to the Prison Fairy?"

"To the Prison Fairy? Why, my good fellow, you don't understand such matters. I neglect it because I wish her to love me."

"No, I don't understand it," cried Albert. "If that is what you want, I should think you would be obliged to write to her at once."

Heinrich smilingly shook his head. "Blessed simplicity! Ten letters would not have the success obtained by the weeks of anxiety in which she has brooded over my silence."

Albert looked at *Heinrich* almost sorrowfully. "But you have caused her pain. How can any one wish to grieve a creature he loves?"

"She will be all the happier in my affection afterwards."

Albert was painfully agitated, but kept silence; and in a few moments turned to leave the room, murmuring, "poor Prison Fairy!"

On the same day a letter arrived from the prince, containing instructions to make an official request for the hand of Ottilie, and appointing him ambassador extraordinary. *Heinrich's* duties now began. It was a great satisfaction to him to play a distinguished part at the very court from which he had been so ignominiously dismissed; and when, in a private audience with the Prince of H----, he presented his credentials, and the request for an alliance with Ottilie, written by his master's own hand, he was delighted at the sight of his embarrassment, and felt fully conscious of his own importance. The prince, pleased with the proposal made to his niece, overwhelmed him with marks of honor, which he accepted very condescendingly, almost patronizingly.

"Herr Count," said the old man, "you have shamed us deeply; for I know it is to you we owe this great piece of good fortune, and do not deserve it at your hands."

"Your Highness," replied *Heinrich*, "I joyfully seized upon this opportunity of proving that my loyalty to your royal house is greater than the sense of the mortification I suffered."

"You are a noble man, count," said the prince, pressing his hand; "our political opinions are dissimilar, but I have the highest respect for your character."

Heinrich bowed low and smiled as he thought: "If I do not soon believe myself a noble man, modesty will be my greatest fault."

The solemn betrothal at last took place, and Ottilie remained firm. In the presence of what was now unalterable, and before the eyes of her man, she was every inch a princess. Pale, and almost as inanimate as a marble statue, she went through the usual ceremonies; but not the slightest change of countenance betrayed the conflict within. A weary smile sometimes curved her delicate lips; but even this was conventional; her eyes did not join in it: the same shadow lingered in their depths; and when she had coldly and firmly signed the deed, it seemed to *Heinrich* as if her manner conveyed a gentle reproach. Her glance rested upon him as if to say, "You have conquered, cruel man, and I am your victim." The look haunted him incessantly, and long after the ceremony was over he felt as if there was a weight upon his heart, as if the deed he was to take to his master was stolen property, from which the mute reproach in Ottilie's glance constantly warned him. He had no compassion for the sufferings of this noble nature, deceived by all; but he perceived that there was a fiendish mockery in adorning such misery with the colors of joy. We have pity upon a sick animal, and let it die in peace; but he dragged a writhing, dying heart to a bridal mummery. It was devil's work, he confessed it to himself; and yet--the deed could not now be undone. Why did she allow herself to be so easily persuaded?

Meantime Albert's interview with Röschen had taken place, but led to no union. Röschen declared she would gladly become his wife and atone for the wrong she had done him, if she did not know that the poor princess needed her more than any one else in the world. She was very unhappy, and there was no one to whom she could betray her feelings. Only a short time before, when she found Ottilie half fainting and in tears, the princess said, "You will stay with me, Röschen, if I go to a foreign country, will you not? you will stay with me as long as I live, that I may have one true, faithful soul near me?" Then Röschen had promised never to leave her, and she would keep her word.

Albert asked why the princess was unhappy, but Röschen said she did not know; and even if she did she would never betray what was not her secret. When Albert repeated this to *Heinrich*, the latter exclaimed, with a laugh: "A rare instance of discretion; really Röschen might be a worthy companion of John of Nepomuk. Were you equally prudent, Albert? Did you confide as little of my affairs?"

Albert reddened with embarrassment. "Herr Count, I only spoke of things which I supposed were no secrets: your kindness to me, your friendship for the Prison Fairy--"

"But, for Heaven's sake!" interrupted *Heinrich*, vehemently, "how could you tell her that, of all people?--her!" Albert looked at him in alarm. "If she should tell the pr---- Oh, Albert, it was very imprudent!"

Heinrich now watched Ottilie closely at all the entertainments given by the court, but observed nothing except her immovable calmness and apparent coldness; this, however, might be the result of her royal pride. But when, after the betrothal ceremony, he requested a private audience and was refused, he bit his lips and muttered, "Albert's prating has already produced its effect; she is aware of my relations with Cornelia!"

Yet he had again misjudged Ottilie. At the official farewell audience, in the presence of the ladies of the court, although very dignified and evidently exhausted, she was so gracious, and the prescribed forms of etiquette were pervaded with such an atmosphere of true feeling, that *Heinrich* could not doubt that he still retained her favor. When she dismissed him she whispered, "Take all my future subjects my kind wishes and blessing." The words were simple, but they were accompanied by a significant, tearful glance which told *Heinrich* all.

He again assumed the air of struggling to repress emotion, which he could so skillfully adopt. "Will your Highness deign to accept my heartfelt gratitude for the message, and the assurance that the blessing cannot be fully received until your Highness appears in the home of your subjects in person."

Thus the audience ended, and Ottmar was obliged to confess that Ottilie was a mystery to him. This was because the comprehension of true womanhood was still denied him. The power of virtue, the strength of self-sacrifice, which woman, spite of her many weaknesses, possesses, were unknown to him; fate still reserved this great lesson. He was to buy it dearly enough.

XIV
CHURCHYARD BLOSSOMS

Heinrich departed to take his master the betrothal documents, and Albert cheerfully remained behind as steward of the estates of Ottmarsfeld. He did not make himself unhappy about Röschen's refusal. He had wished to keep his word, and asked her to be his wife, but he could not help secretly acknowledging that, after all that had passed, he now loved her only with a brother's affection. Both were in the same situation, for both had formed ideals of beauty and perfection. They dared not even raise their eyes longingly towards them, but they could not bear their mutual comparisons with them, and in their insignificance no longer satisfied each other. These glittering images must be obliterated by time before the old calm affection could revive in their hearts.

When Ottmar once more saw the steeples of the city where Cornelia lived, his long-repressed desire to see her seized upon him with such power that he thought his impatience must hasten the locomotive. After all these days and weeks of constraint, and of deprivation of all pleasure, he was at last to taste once more rich, infinite joy. *Henri* longed to clasp the beautiful, love-breathing woman in his arms, and in one burning kiss relieve his oppressed heart of its secret. *Heinrich* wished for the fresh, full tide of her intellect, and with astonishment felt a world of new ideas spring to life at the thought of her. When the train arrived he hurried home, changed his dress, and went to the palace to deliver the papers he had brought. While the prince was reading the documents, the ground seemed fairly to burn under his feet; but his alarm was indescribable when the latter informed him that he had a second mission for him. *Heinrich* must set out immediately as envoy extraordinary to the court of R----, ostensibly to announce the betrothal, but at the same time to secretly ascertain how the government of R---- was disposed towards the commercial treaty which had long been a favorite project with the prince.

The journey to R---- would occupy several days, for at that time railways had not yet penetrated the country; so that *Heinrich* foresaw he must spend weeks in settling the business, and be deprived of Cornelia's society still longer. But he was obliged to submit and thank the prince for this new proof of his confidence.

When the audience was over he hurried to Cornelia, but she and Veronica had gone to spend a few days with a friend at her country seat, and thus the hopes he had fixed upon this interview were blasted. In the worst possible humor, he set out upon his journey that very evening. On arriving in R----, he was loaded with honors. As usual, the most distinguished ladies coquetted with him, and displayed all the magnificence and all the charms which the luxury of a great and brilliant court can bestow upon women. Now and then a dazzling beauty or a bold, exuberant intellect surprised, but nothing captivated, him; he had long been familiar with the blending of social qualities in all their shades and variations, and every comparison only served to increase his longing for Cornelia. At last his mission was performed. In return for the announcement of the betrothal he received a diamond cross, and his secret diplomatic commission was rewarded with the best possible success. He induced the government of R---- to favor the ideas of the prince, arranged the preliminaries of the commercial treaty as far as his office permitted, and set out on his return, followed by many angry and many tearful glances, for the ladies of R---- would not believe that a man of so much intellect and personal beauty could reserve his advantages for a "simple German."

After a long and toilsome journey he reached N----. Once more his first visit was to the prince, and he now received instructions to go to H---- to arrange the marriage ceremonies. But this time he was more fortunate, when, after the audience, he hurried to Cornelia. The old servant with the sulky face opened the door, and without waiting to be announced Ottmar entered the salon. It was very silent and lonely; the setting sun shone upon the yellow damask furniture, and the roses in the flower-stands exhaled their fragrance as usual. *Henri's* heart beat almost audibly; he gasped for breath, for the opposite door opened,--and Veronica in her light robes floated into the room. *Henri* stood before her completely disenchanted; he had so confidently expected to have a moment alone with Cornelia that it cost him an effort to maintain his usual winning courtesy.

"My dear count!" cried Veronica, holding out her thin hand in its white net glove. "I am glad you still remember us. You have been traveling about the world so much without giving us any news of you that we supposed ourselves entirely forgotten."

"I do not deserve this reproach, my dear Fräulein," said *Heinrich*, apologetically, for in Veronica's presence he was again *Heinrich*. "I could not suspect that I might venture to give you written news of me; how and upon what pretext could I have done so?"

"My dear count," said Veronica, with her simple frankness, "that is not truthfully and sincerely spoken; for our great interest in you could not have escaped your notice. You would have needed no other pretext for sending a letter than the consciousness that by doing so you would give us pleasure. Yet Heaven forbid that this should seem like a reproach; we have not the smallest right to make one. We must even be grateful that when here you bestow many an hour upon us. I, at least, make no claim to occupy a place in your memory."

"*You* do not? But, Fräulein, Cornelia?" asked *Heinrich*, watchfully.

"Nor does Cornelia; yet she took your silence less calmly than I. In such matters youth is more unreasonable than age."

Heinrich no longer controlled himself. "Tell me, where is she?"

"Who? Cornelia? She has gone out."

"Gone out!" exclaimed *Heinrich*. "Gone out, and I set out again at ten o'clock to-night to remain absent for weeks! For months I have longed for her society, and now shall not see her! I hear she is angry with me, and shall not be able to defend myself! I have caused her pain, and cannot make amends! Oh, tell me where she is, the sweet, lovely creature!"

"Alas, my dear count, I cannot," replied Veronica, while a shadow stole over her face.

"Why not? Do you not know?"

"I know, but----"

"Then tell me, my dear, kind, motherly friend. You are weeping: what is the matter with Cornelia? I must know!"

"You are completely beside yourself," exclaimed Veronica. "Well, I cannot help it; I must tell you. She is in the churchyard."

"In the churchyard?" asked *Heinrich*, in amazement.

"Cornelia goes there every day and mourns over the grave of a friend. Go, my dear count, go to her; I see you feel more affection for her than we supposed. Ah, I hope your presence may exert a favorable influence upon the poor child."

"What is the matter with her?" asked *Heinrich*. "She was once betrothed----"

"I know it," he interrupted.

"But her lover died under very painful circumstances."

"That I know also."

"She seemed to have long since ceased to grieve over the unfortunate affair; but some time ago the old affection and sorrow broke forth afresh. She has become silent and sad; goes to his grave every day, and at night it often seems to me as if she were weeping gently."

Heinrich heard all this with strange emotion.

"You have an influence over Cornelia," continued Veronica, amid her tears; "if you could cheer my child, remove the black shadow from our once sunny life, under what infinite obligations you would place me!"

"I will!" cried *Heinrich*, pressing Veronica's hand to his lips. "Is she in St. Stephen's churchyard, where the revolutionists are buried?"

"Yes," replied Veronica.

"Farewell till we meet again." And he hurried out of the house.

For the first time in many years *Heinrich* entered a churchyard alone; he had formerly only visited them as a part of the throng which attended some aristocratic funeral; and in spite of the haste with which he moved along the paths, the holiness of the spot, the silence of the dead, unconsciously allayed the excitement of his soul, and made his mood grave and gentle. With downcast eyes he wandered through the long rows of graves adorned with headstones and flowers; he was well aware that it was useless to seek Cornelia here, and hastened on by the churchyard wall to where the lonely, simple crosses of the criminals rose above the mounds. In one corner he at last perceived among the neglected graves a group of trees and bushes, surrounded by a hedge of wild roses. The cool breath of the spring evening rustled through the leaves, and amid the branches the nightingales softly trilled their songs. *Heinrich* paused and gazed through the shrubbery. Upon a hillock, overgrown with lilies of the valley and ivy, sat Cornelia her head rested on her hand, and her bosom rose and fell slowly, as if burdened with the weight of sorrowful thought.

Just at that moment *Heinrich* emerged from the shrubbery. She sprang up with a startled cry and gazed at him as if in a dream; then a deep flush overspread her face, her limbs refused to support her, and, without a word, she sank fainting upon the mound.

"Cornelia!" exclaimed *Heinrich*, and there was the promise of inexpressible happiness in the tone, as he threw himself at her feet and laid his clasped hands in her lap. They gazed at each other long and silently. "At last! ah, at last!" he murmured, in delight.

"At last!" repeated Cornelia, with a heavy sigh; then she gently clasped his hands in hers, held them more and more firmly, and asked, with an expression of unspeakable delight, "Ottmar, is it you?" Tears dimmed her eyes, her voice trembled, and she averted her face to conceal her emotion.

"Cornelia, my life, my soul!" exclaimed *Henri*, who, after a violent struggle, supplanted *Heinrich*. "Grieve no more; love has arisen. You wished to conjure up the shade of the dead man to be an ally against my image in your heart, and instead he sends me to you. Your place is not by this grave, but here, here, on my warm breast! here throbs the heart in which your life is rooted; here breathes the love you vainly sought under moss and stones. Rise, come away; do not press your beautiful face upon the damp grass. He who sleeps below does not feel; but I do, and long for you so ardently, so inexpressibly! You do not answer; what is the cause of your struggle? Do you find it so difficult to choose between this tomb and me? Come, come, be truthful. I know you love me; say so, say so, Cornelia!"

She rose and bent towards him; he clasped her in his arms, and the two noble figures clung to each other in an ardent, silent embrace. At that moment it seemed to Ottmar as if his two natures also embraced, as if their opposing qualities were blended by the enthusiasm that pervaded both his intellectual and sensuous existence, and all the powers of the harmonious man expanded to exhaust the intellect and physical delight of the moment. He closed his eyes and clasped Cornelia more and more closely to his heart; he thought and felt nothing except, "She is mine!" And blissful peace descended upon him. Just then a funeral-bell tolled, and roused the lovers to a consciousness of what place they had selected for the cradle of their happiness.

"Come away from this ghostly spot, Cornelia."

"Oh, stay! the scene is a dear and familiar one to me."

"Strange child, who must be sought in dungeons or graveyards! How does it happen that you always choose so gloomy a background for the radiant picture of your life? Does a churchyard suit our mood? have not the flowers which garland our first embrace sprung from corruption? Why think of death when we are just crossing the threshold of a new life?"

"Why not? Death has no terrors for me. Is it not pleasant to see how life rises anew from corruption? Look the bodily form of a friend is springing up around me in spring flowers; his nature was as pure, delicate, and fragrant as a lily of the valley, and perhaps in these evening breezes his gentle spirit hovers around me in benediction. Why should I not rejoice here, where I have so long mourned you? How often the rustling of this shrubbery has deceived me when I thought I had summoned you hither by my ardent longing! how often these birds have sung of hope and consolation when I believed myself lonely and forgotten, and came here to atone to the dead man for having forsaken him for the sake of one who loved me not! I have never left here without being aided, and am I now to carelessly turn away from the spot because I no longer need its modest consolation? Should I avoid the grave of my young friend,--the grave which, in the perfume of these flowers, has so often poured forth blissful promises of love?"

"Cornelia, how happy you are even when grave, and how profoundly earnest! I have never known a nature upon which all the delicate and noble instincts of the soul were so clearly impressed. Come, let me clasp you to my heart again, that I may convince myself you are really flesh and blood, and no glorified spirit, which may some day soar upward from whence it came."

"Even if I were a spirit, I would not fly from you," said Cornelia, gazing up at him with a face radiant with joy. "I would gladly submit to all the sorrows of this earthly life, in order to be able to taste its joys in your heart, you noble man."

"Girl!" cried *Henri*, his eyes blazing with a sudden light, "what a world of love your tender breast conceals! Yes, you will know how to love as I desire,--warmly, nobly, overpoweringly. Come, kiss me once more; it is so lonely here: no one is watching us. You cannot kiss yet, Cornelia. When I return I will teach you."

"When you return? Are you going away again?"

"This very day; but it is for the last time, then I will stay with you."

"Where are you going?"

"To attend the marriage ceremonies between Princess Ottilie and our prince. Only a few weeks more, and I shall be wholly yours."

"But you will write to me now?"

"Every day. My sweet one, did my long silence grieve you?"

"Oh, deeply!" sighed Cornelia, and her eyes filled with tears. "How I have wept for you!"

"Poor angel! If I had known how you love me, I would never have tortured you so; but I will make amends for it. Do you believe I can?"

"A thousandfold!" laughed Cornelia, amid her tears.

"And now come, Cornelia; I will accompany you home, for I must prepare for my journey."

"No, *Heinrich*; I cannot appear before others with you now. Go alone, and leave me here a half-hour longer, until I have collected my thoughts; such sweet sounds must echo through the stillness."

"You are right. Oh, if I could only stay with you! Farewell. Do not look at me with that earnest gaze, or I cannot turn away. I feel as if I were a banished man, let me press you to my heart once more. Now send me away, or I cannot leave you!"

There was a rustling in the branches. "Hark! What was that? Has any one been watching us?"

"It was the evening breeze that warns you to go if you must set out on your journey to-day. Go, my beloved; think of our meeting, not of our farewell. I will shut my eyes, that they may not detain you."

"Then, farewell, until I have discharged my duty to the prince. Do not fly away to heaven, my angel!"

When Cornelia again raised her eyes, *Henri* had departed. She watched him striding rapidly along, then clasped her hands upon her breast, as if to conceal the overwhelming burden of her happiness. A deep stillness surrounded her; the sun had set, the birds were silent. Suddenly a dark figure appeared as if it had started from the earth, a tall, handsome man with a broad scar upon his brow, clad in the long coat of a priest. He fixed his dark eyes upon Cornelia for a moment, and then walked silently on.

"Who was that?" she murmured, in terror. "Why did he look at me so strangely? What had the gloomy apparition to do with this bright hour?" She now felt the chill of the night air for the first time, shivered, and overwhelmed by a haunting dread, hurried swiftly between the graves towards home.

XV
A ROYAL MARRIAGE

"H--, May 15th.

"You ask me, my Cornelia, whether our love is to remain a secret. Yes, I entreat you to keep it so. Let no one, no matter who it may be, touch the tender plant which is budding in our hearts. So young an affection needs concealment until it is strong enough to withstand all storms; and believe me, my angel, they will not be spared you. I am far too well known, have too often had occasion to thrust others aside, not to have obtained the ill-will of persons who will take pleasure in casting poison into your heart merely out of malice towards me. That I have given them sufficient cause, I will frankly confess; for until a character like mine is complete within itself, it must fall into a thousand errors, contradictions, and inconsistencies. No man of real ability escapes this crisis of development. The more variously and richly he is endowed by nature, the more severe a process of purification he must endure; and this cannot be accomplished without expelling, by a violent fermentation, the dross which indelibly sullies his outward life, if, like me, he has been exposed to the eyes of the public. The private citizen experiences such epochs in silence; he is not watched, and therefore his errors are not observed; the false step taken in a position as lofty as mine is visible to the whole world, it is imprinted not only upon the personal *chronique scandaleuse* but upon the history of the times, and receives an official character. Therefore beware, Cornelia, of wishing to become acquainted with my nature through any other person than myself; beware of exposing the chaste secret of your heart to curiosity, malice, perhaps even envy. Do not think that foolish vanity makes me use this word, for the present inordinate thirst for marriage it is only natural that envy should be excited in all circles, when a young girl is loved by so prominent a man. Keep aloof from all these profaning influences. Believe me, I know woman's nature, with its thousand delicate threads of feeling and consequent excitability and sensitiveness, and I warn you to conceal my image in your inmost soul. We do not at first perceive the injury such a tie sustains by a rude touch; but as a fruit beaten by the hail continues to grow and shows the blemish and bitterness only when eaten, so the sore spot our hearts disturbs our happiness, and at last develops a bitterness all our love cannot soften. I make the greatest sacrifice because I can only see you clandestinely; but the time will come when our love will dare to show itself openly before the world, when we can no longer lose each other, and then you will perceive that I was right and thank me for my present self-sacrifice.

"Say nothing, even to Veronica; age is garrulous; I sincerely respect her, but I cannot acquit her of this peculiarity of her years; you have already made her so accustomed to your independent habits, you dear little piece of obstinacy, that she will not think it strange if you keep this letter from her as well as the others. It will be the last I shall write from here, for Prince Edward, who is to marry Ottilie as a proxy, arrived day before yesterday; the ceremony will be performed day after tomorrow, and then we shall set out at once. As the princess's health is somewhat delicate, and a journey by rail exhausts her more than to travel by ship, I shall bring her from B---- by water. We shall arrive on the 21st. Be sure to be at the harbor; the papers will give you all the particulars. Then, Cornelia, I will lay my weary head upon your breast, and rest peacefully after the thousand miserable anxieties of diplomacy and etiquette, which torture a poor ambassador extraordinary. Yes, you may be right when you say I was born for something higher than to be the servant of a prince. When I read such words, something stirs within me like an awakening power, which only needs the impulse to cast off its chains, to shake itself free by one mighty effort. Whether and from whence this will come to me, from without or from within, I know not; but this I do know, that only you can rouse the ideal powers which a misdirected life has lulled to sleep.

"Farewell till we meet, my angel.

"Your own *Heinrich.*"

It was late at night when *Heinrich* finished this letter, and while he went calmly to rest and fell asleep with Cornelia's name upon his lips, the princess was wandering up and down her chamber like a restless ghost. The lamps were burning brightly in their ground-glass shades beside her bed, whose silken curtains waved slowly to and fro as Ottilie passed them.

"It is impossible; I cannot do it," she said, as she leaned for a moment against the window. "If it were only day! The night makes all anxieties rise before us like impassable mountains! Or, if sleep would overpower me! But now it has been wholly put to flight by the thought that I have but one more day of freedom,--freedom to love and suffer; and then--then I must tear my heart from all to which it clings so fondly,--forget, cease to feel: and woe betide me if I do not wholly succeed in doing so! To see him daily, to be obliged to distinguish him from among the nobles of my country as my husband's favorite, and yet force back what my own heart feels; to feign an indifference which makes the forms of courtesy--the true expression of my opinions--a lie! And you could undertake such a task, unhappy one? You could allow yourself to be so confused and persuaded that you did not shrink from the tortures your consent would impose? If it were only suffering!--alas! I am accustomed to that. It is the fear of guilt that terrifies me. It is not only in act that we can sin, but in thought. Each thought that steals back to that time of quiet, patient longing is a robbery of what I owe my husband,--a crime against my vow. Woe betide me if those ardent dark eyes, which beam only with love, even upon those for whom he does not feel it, should ever rest in all their power on mine! Shall I be able to prevent absorbing death from them with ardent longing? And if at such a moment my husband should approach, secure in my affection----"

She threw herself on her knees and hid her blushing face in her hands. "Oh, God! my God! thou who knowest better than I whether I am right in thy sight, have mercy upon me and deliver me from this night of doubt and anguish! Thou hast placed me in this lofty station! Give me the strength, the coldness, the dignity,--not only the outward, but the inward dignity,--which raises the reigning princess above ordinary women. Let me not be compelled to expiate it so terribly, because I willfully cherished an affection for a man whom thou didst not destine for me. Have mercy, have mercy, oh, Father, thou who hast been the only one to extend thine arms lovingly in answer to my search!--thou to whom alone I could fly when, like a lost child, I despaired in this cold world! I have brought thee my tears, complained to thee of the sorrows other children weep out on their mothers' breasts, and to-day--to-day for the first time--thou wilt not permit thyself to be found."

She rose and saw that a bar of light was bordering the horizon. Her glance fell upon the mirror and showed her a face so pale, so tear-stained, that she was almost startled at the sight of her own image. She gasped for breath, and, utterly exhausted, at last threw herself upon her bed and fell asleep. When she awoke the sun was already high in the heavens. The deep slumber had strengthened her, and she rose with a feeling of new life. With the light of day more calmness and clearness of judgment had returned. She collected the last remnant of her strength, and felt ashamed of her weakness.

"Be a princess, be proud, Ottilie! Worthily fill the place for which God has appointed you. Pay the debt you owe him for the gifts he has bestowed, and which you have held at so cheap a rate because they were valueless to one. Perceive that it is the call of God that rouses you from this selfish melancholy. Obey it, fulfill your destiny like all other created beings; and if your strength fails, what can befall you worse than the death for which you are always longing? Life will never be so dear to you that you cannot hail it as a last blessing. My Lord and God, I lay my broken heart, my hopes, my wishes at thy feet, and make but one prayer,--grant that, in return for all my sacrifices, I may not be denied the joy of fulfilling my task and making others truly happy."

She stood erect, as if surrounded by a halo of self-abnegation, when Röschen suddenly begged permission to enter. "I most humbly pray your Highness's pardon for having come without being summoned," said the young girl, "but the chamberlain has just brought your Highness the news that Prince Edward was thrown from his horse this morning and so dangerously injured that he cannot appear at the wedding as proxy."

"What? Oh, God! is it possible?" exclaimed Ottilie.

"Will your Highness deign to receive the chamberlain's news in person?"

"No, no! But ask him whether the marriage will be deferred, or if some one else will take the place of the prince."

Röschen withdrew, and came back with the reply that the wedding would, in all probability, be deferred. Count Ottmar had already sent a telegram to N----, and they were now awaiting an answer.

Ottilie seemed to be animated with new life. A delay,--a respite,-- although only a short one, enabled her to breathe more freely. "Dress me, Röschen, and then send for Countess Carlstein. I will drive for an hour; I need the sun and air. Ah, Röschen," she continued, as the young girl was arranging her toilet, "how will you feel in a foreign country?"

"Oh, I shall be contented anywhere, if I am with your Highness; especially as you have graciously given my father a place in your train. We shall still be able to see each other when I have any spare time."

"Good, contented little one," smiled Ottilie. "Tell me frankly, Röschen, has your heart no need of love? Do you not regret that you have rejected Albert, and must go through life alone?"

"No, your Highness," exclaimed Röschen, cheerily; and two charming little dimples appeared in her plump, rosy cheeks. "Life in your service is so pleasant, and I love you and my father so dearly, that I haven't the slightest wish for the constant restlessness and feverish excitement of a betrothal."

Ottilie stood thoughtfully before her. "Tell me, my child, how did you succeed in forgetting Herr von Ottmar so easily, since you love no one else?"

"Oh, your Highness, I did not forget him easily," said Röschen, raising her large, childlike, blue eyes frankly to Ottilie's face. "I cried a great deal at first, and thought I should die; but by degrees I saw that it is a sin to covet anything we know the dear God does not intend for us; besides, my confessor, Herr Lorenz, represented how hard it would be for my old father if he was compelled to see his daughter waste away thus. Then I felt ashamed of myself, went busily to work again, and broke myself of my useless longing and sighing. Ah, work is good for everything: it leaves one no time to weep, and at night one is so tired that sleep conquers all grief. So I soon began to take pleasure in living again, and thanked God that he had punished my sin so mildly. Anxiety about poor Albert was the only thing that troubled me, and now I am relieved even from this. He is a happy man."

The princess felt the reproof contained in the young girl's artlessly prattled philosophy. Her glance fell upon the mirror, and, as if reflecting the reproach in Röschen's words, it showed cheeks paled by her long-nourished sorrow, in the sharpest contrast to the bright, blooming face of the waiting-maid.

"Yes, yes, you are right," she murmured, at last, gazing at Röschen's image in the mirror. After a long pause she began, in an almost expressionless tone, "Have you learned no particulars from Albert as to whether an acknowledged love exists between the count and the young girl called the Prison Fairy?"

"Albert does not know it positively, your Highness, but he is almost sure of it; for ever since the count came back from N---- he has written to her very often, and seems entirely different from what he used to be,--much more cheerful and happy."

Ottilie compressed her lips, and involuntarily laid her hand upon her heart, as if she felt a sudden pang.

"Does anything hurt you, your Highness? Does the pin I put in there prick you?" asked Röschen, anxiously.

"Yes, take it out; it hurts me," said Ottilie, and thought, "Ah, if you only could!"

"Your Highness, your heart is beating violently! Your Highness is certainly suffering from that pain in the breast again! If you would only tell the doctor about it!"

"My good girl, he can do me no good." A short cough interrupted her, and she glanced smilingly at Röschen's troubled face. "Be calm, my child, people do not die of such things; and if I should, I shall leave you a legacy which will support you all your life."

"Your Highness!" exclaimed Röschen, with a deep blush, while the tears rushed into her eyes. "If your Highness thinks it is only for that,"--she could say no more.

"My dear Röschen, have I hurt your feelings? Indeed, I did not intend to do so. Then there is one heart that loves me for myself. God will reward you for it far better than I. Do not cry: give me my dress."

Röschen smiled through her tears, threw the dress over Ottilie's shoulders, knelt down, and pulled the folds straight. Then she gazed with childish admiration at her mistress's tall, stately figure. "Ah, how beautiful your Highness looks now! I cannot imagine that any one can be handsomer or more noble. Your Highness is so--what shall I call it?--such a holy apparition."

Ottilie smiled involuntarily. "Oh, how delighted your Highness's proud husband will be when he sees he has obtained such a beautiful wife!"

"Do you think so?"

"Of course; he must be pleased. He has chosen your Highness without knowing you. Even if you were ugly, he would still be compelled to keep you; but if you are beautiful, it is a real piece of good fortune,--a true gain to him. He will undoubtedly rejoice."

For the first time in many days, Ottilie felt tempted to laugh. "You are a perfect child," said she. "May God preserve your innocence! You are like a fresh spring day to my soul, and that is of great value to me. But do you know we have spent two hours in curling hair and dressing?"

"Yes, your Highness; but I can't help it," replied Röschen, apologetically.

"No, no; I know it. Tell me, Röschen, how would you feel if you were obliged to meet a stranger and greet him as your husband?" asked Ottilie, with as much apparent unconcern as possible.

"Oh, dear me! It must be strange, I think. No doubt it is very hard for a royal lady that she cannot have her own free choice and take the one she wants; but she must bear something in return for the many advantages over others which she enjoys, or she would have everything quite too pleasant; and every human being must have one sorrow, or he will not deserve heaven."

"Very true; but what would you do if you were in my place?"

"Why, your Highness, if matters had gone so far that I couldn't change anything, then I would in God's name reconcile myself to them, and make every effort to become as fond of my betrothed as I could, that I might have some pleasure in him myself, for it must be terrible to belong to a man whom one doesn't love."

"But if you cannot love him?" asked Ottilie, with interest.

"Why should one not love the husband to whom one is wedded in the sight of God? One can become fond of any worthy man, if one has a kind heart, like your Highness: and the prince is said to be both handsome and good. It is better for any one who can choose freely not to betroth herself to a man whom she doesn't love, or to a stranger; but if one must take him, and can't get rid of it, one ought to meet him trustfully and lovingly, that it may be not only outwardly but inwardly a true Christian marriage."

"Yes, we must question the oracle of a simple heart, if in our over-refinement we wish to find the way to truth and nature," murmured Ottilie. Her toilet was now complete, and she thought that she looked better than usual. "If the Lord so wills, he can speak from the lips of a child!" she thought to herself, for she had received unexpected consolation from the simple girl who was so greatly her inferior.

Just at that moment the chamberlain announced the ambassador extraordinary, Count Ottmar, who requested a private audience to communicate the wishes of his prince.

Ottilie started at the sound of his name, but moved on with a firm step to the reception-room where *Heinrich* awaited her.

"Pardon me, princess, for having ventured to request permission to speak to you once more alone."

"My future husband's messenger must always be welcome to me," said Ottilie, with stately courtesy.

Heinrich looked at her in astonishment. It was difficult for him to find the precise tone that would harmonize with this address. He was unaccustomed to such coldness from Ottilie, and felt confused. This did not escape her delicate feelings, and to fill up the little pause of embarrassment she motioned him to be seated.

Meantime *Heinrich* had regained his composure, and began, in a firm, grave tone: "Your Highness, permit me to speak to you once more in the language in which I formerly had the happiness of making myself understood; for the point in question does not merely concern a commission from the prince, but private relations of a delicate nature with which it is connected, and which I can only discuss with your Highness if you will permit me once more, and for the last time, to approach you as your friend."

"Count Ottmar," replied Ottilie, in a low but firm voice, "you may be assured that I am not contemptible enough to seek to deny the existence of 'relations of a delicate nature' between you and myself, but I must also expect that you will be considerate enough to say no more about them than is absolutely necessary."

"You may be sure of that, princess. I regret that my introduction to this conversation should have given you cause to fear the reverse."

"Tell me my bridegroom's message. What can he ask to which I would not consent in advance?"

"Then I will discharge my duty. The reason I have used so much circumlocution you will perceive without any further explanation. You are aware of the misfortune that has befallen Prince Edward. I telegraphed at once to N----, as my office required, and have just received from the prince the dispatch I now have the honor to deliver to you."

Ottilie took the paper, went to the window, and read: "Impossible to defer the marriage. All the preparations are completed. The whole country in readiness to give a brilliant reception. Unadvisable to disappoint the expectations of the nation. If agreeable to the princess, I appoint Count Ottmar proxy on Prince Edward's place. Count Ottmar will inform the court at once, etc." Ottilie could read no more: the remainder concerned only matters of etiquette; the words lost their meaning, the letters swam before her eyes. She stood motionless as if struck by a thunderbolt. Every tinge of color faded from her cheeks, she seemed frozen into a marble statue. She must exchange rings with Ottmar, be wedded to the man for whom she longed, only to belong to another; she must vow to be faithful to her husband, and she loved his proxy. The forms which would have sealed her life-long happiness, had they been true, now only served to sanction the lie at the thought of which her heart bled. And yet ought she, as the betrothed bride of another, to make the humiliating confession to *Heinrich* that she felt too weak to bear his presence at the altar?--ought she to give way to such weakness herself?

Heinrich read these thoughts reflected upon her brow. "I knew this news must affect you unpleasantly, princess, and therefore preferred to give you the information privately, that you might be able to tell me frankly whether it would be agreeable to you to stand before the altar with me or not. I hope you will understand my 'consideration' now; for if the inquiry had been made officially, you would not have been able to offer before the eyes of the world the insult of refusing to accept me as a substitute. But here, alone, you can tell me if it will be painful to you to have me beside you; and I will not take the acknowledgment as a humiliation, but receive it as a sacred confidence, and find means to delay the progress of affairs without mentioning your name."

Ottilie struggled with her feelings for a moment, and then held out her hand to him. "I thank you, my friend. Your forbearance is kind and noble, but it is unnecessary. How could I meet the prince, my husband, if I had not done with--everything?--if I shrank from this last drop in the bitter cup? What has been begun must be finished. If I have the courage to accomplish the great falsehood of my life, it ought not to fail me in this short, painful comedy. Ought I to rob an expectant country of its festival of joy, leave its garlands to wither, suffer its good-will to be transformed into anger, on account of the cowardice of a sore heart? Ought I not, as the mother of the country, to understand my duties better? No, no, Ottmar; I am stronger than you thought. I will go with you to the marriage ceremony; I will think only of my people, pray for them alone,--my kind people, who are hopefully expecting me: that will give me strength to bear the mockery of fate which places my hand in yours,--to part me from you forever." Here emotion suffocated her voice: she motioned to Ottmar to withdraw, and turned away.

"Oh, princess," he cried, "if you knew what grief I feel at the sight of your silent suffering, at the thought that I am its author, and can now do nothing, nothing to lessen it! I am an unhappy man, who always acts solely from egotism, and yet is not bad enough to be able to witness the result of his deeds coldly and without remorse. No, God is my witness that I am now speaking the truth, and not acting a part!" He threw himself on his knees before her. "Forgive me, princess; I have committed a terrible crime against you!"

She laid her band gently on his head. "I forgive you all, Ottmar. May God bless and guide you in the right path!"

"I thank you!" cried *Heinrich*, springing up. "Then I am to give the court notice that the marriage will take place?"

"I have already said so."

When *Heinrich* had closed the door behind him, Ottilie gave free course to her tears. "Oh, God! oh, God! how much can a heart bear without breaking?"

She had told the truth: hers was not one of those natures in which grief, by a violent assault, swells the veins to bursting, strains the nerves to their utmost tension, and excites a wild conflict in the heart; she belonged to those deep, silent characters, which do not have the strength to offer the resistance which increases it to despair, or conquers it, but patiently suffer it to obtain complete possession of them, and conceal it in the deepest recesses of their souls, where it gently and gradually gnaws away the roots of life. This proceeds from no lack of strength or courage. They use all their moral power in the conscientiousness and capacity for self-sacrifice peculiar to them, in order to accomplish the tasks of superhuman difficulty which fate most frequently imposes upon these very natures.

Ottilie performed such a task when on the following day she went to the altar with *Heinrich*, and succeeded in stifling the thought of his close proximity by fervent prayer. She did not cast a single glance at his face, but stood as pale and calm as a corpse adorned for the grave. All were weeping around her, although they could have given no reason for it, even to themselves. Her manner after the wedding exerted a sorrowful influence: it seemed to each person who offered her his congratulations as if he were uttering a lie, and a thrill of melancholy ran through his whole frame as she bowed her beautiful head in acknowledgment. With the firmness to which all royal personages are trained, she went through all the customary ceremonies; but in saying farewell she could not restrain her tears, and held her uncle's hand closely clasped in hers as she thanked him for all his kindness.

The old prince was deeply moved. "Ah, Ottilie," said he, "I fear that in you my country is losing its good angel. True, I ought not to complain, since it will obtain great advantages by your marriage; but they will be no compensation to my heart for you. Farewell! May God give you happiness!"

The journey was the greatest martyrdom to Ottilie's weakened nerves; for she now had not a moment in which she was unwatched. She must guard every word, every look; she dared not yield to any feelings of exhaustion or depression. Thus passed a day of torture. Fortunately, when night came, her bodily fatigue was so great that sleep relieved her for a few hours from her excitement and anxiety.

The following day they reached the frontiers of Ottilie's second home. Here she received a portion of her new court, and dismissed her former train, with the exception of those who were appointed to a place among the ranks of her future attendants. The exchange between the old and new courtiers was a matter of comparative indifference to her, for she had never expected to find these men anything more than mere conventional machines. She welcomed one party with the same affability that she displayed in bidding farewell to the other, without any special feeling. The cordial reception given her by the country people in the first little town on the frontier was a joyful surprise, and when she at last reached the prince's yacht which lay awaiting her and gave her a royal salute, when she had entered it with her train, and on a most lovely day floated down the broad stream, past shores adorned with tokens of welcome, her heart began to swell with the thought, "You are the mistress of this country. It belongs to you, and its happiness, its freedom, will perhaps be in your hands." And this ray of hope cheered her soul for a moment.

Heinrich watched her with alternate dread and joy, according to the mood expressed upon her features. It was a great source of anxiety to him how Ottilie would bear all these exertions. If her strength failed, if she met the prince as a sickly, feeble woman, all the blame would fall upon him who had made this match. She still seemed outwardly firm; but in spite of her faultless bearing it did not escape him that her breast rose and fell more and more rapidly the nearer she approached her destination. He would gladly have sustained and animated her spirit as one seeks to save and protect en expiring light, but the unapproachable dignity of manner which she had adopted towards him since her marriage made it impossible, and caused him the greatest perplexity. The last stage of the journey was reached: he saw her grow still paler; and she received deputations from the city at which they had arrived, and some of the highest staff-officers who had come out in two yachts to meet her, in a voice so faint that the words were scarcely audible. It was with great anxiety that *Heinrich* saw the moment of the meeting between her and the prince approach. And he was not wrong.

When the three steamers left the last stopping-place and glided, calmly and majestically, side by side down the broad stream, countless boats adorned with gay streamers put off from both shores and accompanied the large vessels; on the right and left, before and behind, they assembled hundreds; as far as the eye could reach there was nothing to be seen but a moving stream of fluttering pennons. The mistress of ceremonies signified to Ottilie that she ought to go on deck and show herself to the people. Scarcely had she done so when a loud cheer rang from thousands of throats: a greeting from the students, the most promising young men in the country. And now music rose from the foremost boats, like an eagle extending its wings above the confused, brilliant throng. The echo repeated the strains majestically from the rocky shores; a fresh breeze ruffled the water, and as if borne along by the sound the boats dashed on.

Ottilie clung dizzily to the railing of the deck. It seemed as if her soul must escape from its tenement and soar into eternity upon those tones, and she gazed with a strange, unearthly expression at the magnificent spectacle and the sunny air thrilling with the notes of the music. The sweet sounds blended into a threatening roar, a volley of artillery! Masts, flags, and steeples appeared in the distance.

"The harbor is close at hand, your Highness," said *Heinrich*. Ottilie turned pale: the shadow of death rested upon her face. "Take courage; compose yourself, or all is lost," he whispered.

She still stood erect, and he watched her in painful suspense. The distant steeples became still more distinct; there was a second roar of artillery from the accompanying yachts,--a third,--the harbor opened before Ottilie's eyes, and now began the thunder of a hundred guns, while the ringing of bells floated athwart them in majestic waves of sound. The boats fell back with a repeated cheer, and the steamers slowly entered the harbor. The rigging of the ships that lay at anchor was filled with sailors, who waved their hats and shouted a wild "hurrah!" A countless throng of people on the edge of the harbor, at the windows, and on the roofs of the houses, which were gayly adorned with flowers and tapestry, sent forth their shouts of welcome to Ottilie, amid the thunder of cannon and the ringing of bells. Everything swam before her eyes. The impression was too powerful; all this produced too violent an emotion in her oppressed heart. Yonder stood a group of gentlemen, the foremost must be the prince just ready to enter the boat which was to bear him to the ship; a mist gathered before her eyes, her heart stopped beating, the blood flowed coldly through her veins: she laid her damp, icy hand upon the shoulder of the mistress of ceremonies, and tottered. *Heinrich* caught her by the arm, and both carried her down into the cabin, where she sank back utterly unconscious.

"I thought so," muttered *Heinrich*, and went up to receive the prince, and if possible detain him.

The mistress of ceremonies knew not what to do, and called the lady's maid. Röschen appeared and applied the usual restoratives. Ottilie breathed faintly, but was unable to raise her head.

"The prince is on board," said a chamberlain.

"Oh, God!" moaned Ottilie; and again she trembled violently.

"Will not your Highness try to rise?" pleaded the mistress of ceremonies, in the greatest anxiety; for the prince might now enter at any moment. Röschen caught her in her arms, the door was thrown open, and "his Highness" was announced. One last violent effort, and Ottilie stood erect. The mistress of ceremonies withdrew with Röschen. The prince entered. Ottilie bowed with her usual stately grace. The prince's eyes rested with surprise and pleasure upon the beautiful, although pallid, face. The aroma of aristocracy which surrounded her was wonderfully pleasing to the man of forms.

"Allow me to express to your Highness my most heartfelt gratitude for the confidence with which you intrust your future to me, a stranger; and receive the assurance that I shall hold so precious a gift as sacred, and know how to guard it."

Twice Ottilie essayed to speak, and twice her voice failed. At last her tongue obeyed her will, and she began: "Your Highness, the confidence for which you compliment me so highly is only a fitting tribute that every noble-minded person must pay to a prince whose political as well as private life lies open and blameless before the gaze of all. It is far different with me. My existence has flowed on in silent seclusion. You know me only from descriptions and from my letters; the latter might be dictated, the former invented. I myself, my own character, can alone win for me your esteem, your friendship. Your Highness will perceive it is only natural that this consciousness should disturb me, and pardon my embarrassment. Moreover, the kind and magnificent reception your Highness and the people of the country have bestowed upon me has moved and confused me deeply. I am not accustomed to such things. I am well aware that it is not given to my person, but my position; but I have so identified myself with my new dignity and its duties that I cannot help taking these festivities to myself, and allowing their overmastering impression to influence me."

The prince had listened admiringly to the melody and grace of her language. "Your Highness is in error if you suppose this reception is given solely to your position. Certain forms of course are indispensable on such occasions; but a rumor has preceded you, which not only secured my esteem, but excited the greatest enthusiasm for you among the people, and this you must have felt. The reception was a sincere one, and if you had been known the tokens would have become still more enthusiastic, for I freely confess that your appearance has surpassed all our expectations, and must win the heart of every one who sees you."

"This praise from your lips, your Highness, makes me very proud; for I believe you far too noble to expect insincere flattery from you in so solemn an hour."

"You are perfectly right, princess; the hour in which two human beings, who are united for life, see each other for the first time, is a very solemn one, for it holds the key of our whole future. I am therefore the more joyfully surprised to find in you a nature which opens to me the hope of a happy marriage. Permit me to believe that at least you do not feel the contrary to be the case?"

Ottilie tried to speak.

"Do not answer me," interrupted the prince. "How could I be so ungallant as to seek to call forth complimentary assurances from a lady? No, you shall not tell me so; you shall only allow me to feel it. I shall eagerly await the moment when your eyes will tell me that your heart has confirmed the choice which destiny imposed."

"Your Highness," replied Ottilie, "receive the assurance that I have no other wish than that of making you and your people happy. I will be an obedient, and faithful wife, and never ask anything of you except indulgence. Be assured that I shall never claim any tokens of love from you. No feeling of affection has united us who are total strangers to each other; we both yielded to the commands of political necessity. It depends upon ourselves to lend value to such a tie, to form a more or less cordial bond of friendship, but not to conjure up emotions which the heart receives only as revelations. I tell you this, your Highness, that in your noble chivalrousness you may not think it necessary to delude yourself and me by the expression of such feelings. I shall have attained the highest goal of my hopes if you will some day bear witness that I have not entered your life as a disturbing element, but to bring a blessing."

"I understand your Highness's delicacy of feeling. Your every word affords me a fresh proof of the treasure I possess in you, and I hope a bond will be developed between us higher and firmer than one founded on mere chance sympathy,--a bond of mutual comprehension and unchanging esteem. Shall it not be so, my Ottilie?"

"May God grant it, your Highness!"

"Etiquette commands that I should now leave your Highness. To-morrow at the cathedral I shall take pride in presenting you to the nation as its princess,--as a true princess. Yes, I am proud of my noble wife," he added, emphasizing the words, while a cold smile gleamed over his smooth features. He pressed his lips lightly to Ottilie's hand and withdrew. She stood motionless and exhausted; tears no longer dimmed her eyes: her destiny was fixed. She now knew the man to whom she belonged, and what she had to expect from him.

The mistress of ceremonies entered, and again she was forced to add another link to the chain of self-denial which already rested so heavily upon her weary shoulders. *Heinrich* breathed more freely when the prince's own lips expressed his satisfaction with his choice; although he regretted his deed, he must still desire it to be crowned with complete success, since his whole destiny depended upon it. Moreover, his remorse was not so sincere as he had made Ottilie believe in their last interview, or even as he had believed himself. It had unconsciously been heightened by the selfish fear that he had sacrificed Ottilie uselessly,--uselessly for himself, for he could no longer doubt that he had been mistaken in her character. She was wholly changed from what she had been in former days; with the same greatness of soul which had led her to show her love for him when free, she concealed it now that she was bound. He perceived that she possessed one of those deep natures which seize upon all that they believe to be their appointed destiny with silent, unassuming tenacity of purpose, and hold it steadfastly to the end. So had she clung to him when she believed herself marked out for no other fate than to love and suffer; and now she seemed to cleave with the same self-denial, if not to her husband, to the duties of her new vocation. Here was the solution of his false reckoning; and he now quickly came to the conclusion that he had nothing more to hope from her for the furtherance of his ambition than any other; that she would even consider it a needful victory over herself not to favor him. Thus he had now accomplished an act which he must despise as one of the most horrible results of his selfishness,--robbed himself of a friend to whom he might have fled in every vicissitude of life; he had solved so many difficult problems in politics and love, ruled the most reserved and haughtiest women, struggled victoriously with the first intellects of his court, but by the simple greatness of her character his plan was baffled,--because he knew only the strength of her love, not the power of her virtue. Ottilie was a complete contrast to himself; with all his intellect he could not understand a character destitute of all, even the most necessary selfishness; and thus he was at last compelled to confess himself vanquished by the power of a goodness in which he had never believed. He pitied Ottilie as the martyr of exaggerated ideas, and felt that across the barriers of this loyal "prejudice" no sympathizing intercourse could ever take place between them. He was now thrown entirely upon himself and Cornelia; he did not possess even one friend, for he lacked the only foundations of friendship,--unselfishness and confidence. Cornelia alone now captivated his sensual as well as his intellectual nature. She was the last and only thing left him, and the secretly lonely and dissatisfied man clung to her with all the strength of his life. The hours during which he was compelled to attend the marriage festivities dragged slowly and painfully.

XVI
THE TWO BETROTHED BRIDES

Meantime Cornelia awaited him in her quiet salon, where the roses always bloomed like eternal lamps of love. She was alone. Veronica's health had become somewhat delicate of late, and she was taking an afternoon nap in her room. Cornelia hoped to receive *Heinrich's* first glance unobserved. She had spent the three days since Ottilie's arrival in idle dreams, longings, and expectations, and had sought solitude that Veronica might not perceive her indolence. It was impossible for her to fix her attention upon anything except the one thought,--"He will soon arrive." She had never believed that any one could spend three whole days in such complete inaction. She did not go out, even to visit the prison, lest she should miss him, and thanked God when any one rang the bell, because she had the pleasure of fancying for a moment that it was he. To-day this satisfaction had fallen to her lot very rarely; the street and house were silent, and she walked impatiently up and down the smooth inlaid floor, played with the roses, made an old mandarin nod his head, incessantly looked into the glass to see whether she would please her lover, threw herself on the yellow sofa, and fancied he was beside her; thought of a thousand things she wanted to tell him, took up one of the faded velvet-covered albums, turned the leaves without reading a word, and at last started up in joyful surprise, for the bell was now really pulled, and so violently, so impatiently,--it must be he. She hurried into the antechamber.

"I'll tell you if any one comes," said the old servant, as sulkily as if he knew whom Cornelia expected, and walked slowly on to open the door.

Cornelia retired in great embarrassment, and waited behind the folding-doors. Yes, it was the well-known step upon the stairs, along the corridor; he was approaching. The blissful certainty overwhelmed her with suffocating violence, and now she could see nothing, for two eager arms had clasped her and pressed her closely to a throbbing heart.

There was a moment of silence, a moment when the world seemed to be hushed, and divinity itself listened in delight to the sweetest language given to the human heart,--the mute language of love. Then *Henri's* lips sought her own, and softly, softly she whispered a thousand sweet names; but every word died in a kiss; and thus words and caresses struggled long in a secret conflict for the mastery.

"Let me look at you," said Cornelia, at last; and drawing back, took his head between her hands and raised it. "You have grown handsomer; you look milder, graver, and yet happier."

"It is my love for you, Cornelia. If the features take the impress of the soul, I must become more and more like you. You are so perfect, Cornelia, that your Creator in his delight over his work wished to make a copy of you; and see, he chose me! My soul is nothing more than the background upon which the finger of God has engraved your image."

"Ob, noble spirit, you always give the fairest expression of every feeling,--earth and heaven are open to your flight! Will you now linger with me? Do I hold this dear head clasped in my hands? Dare I call you mine, and kiss the brow on which you are enthroned?" asked Cornelia, in dreamy delight.

"Yes, yes, Cornelia, the spirit is yours, for you have been the first to awaken it. Lay the head that contains it on your breast, let your hand rest lovingly upon it, and it will disdain heaven and earth, and linger here, here on this one sweet spot forever, forever!"

He stooped and pressed a kiss upon Cornelia's heart. Blushing deeply, she laid her clasped hands upon his dark hair and raised her eyes in an ecstasy of love. "Oh, God, one who had denied thee throughout a whole lifetime must acknowledge thee in such an hour!"

"You pious priestess, priestess of a religion whose blessings I gratefully feel at this moment, shall I tell you how I pray to you,--yes, pray fervently and devoutly? I know that in you I possess the greatest blessing earth can offer, and that I do not deserve it. If I had not found it I should have gone to destruction; but you will lead me back from the exhausted pleasures of the world to pure nature, to truth and simplicity of heart. A new day breaks upon me through you,--an Easter-day,--for in you my better self celebrates its resurrection. Your breath is the fresh air of morning, the dawn glows upon your cheeks, and in your eyes beams the sunrise of a happiness never known before. Come, let me inhale your breath. Ah, youth, purity, and strength emanate from you to revive and cheer!" He again pressed his lips to hers for a moment. "Now," he continued, "the whole man is exclusively and entirely yours, yours forever; do with him whatever you choose, for he has no longer any claim to a life which you alone preserved to him, and which without you would have been lost."

"What shall, what can, I say to you in return for such words? Not I, but you yourself took the new flight which has made you so dear to me. What could I be to you? What influence could the few moments we have spent together exert?"

"And if I should ask you the same question, and inquire how you could love me in so short a time, what would you reply?"

"Why, that love and mutual understanding do not depend upon time."

"The case is precisely the same with me, my child. Years of study and intercourse are not necessary to understand a superior nature. A few traits enable it to be characterized, single extremes allow its full compass to be measured, and as one accord contains the elements of music, so it can easily reveal to the observer the keynotes of its soul; and you did this. Wherever I struck, it echoed. I know the whole scale of your nature, although a thousand sweet harmonies which may be formed from it are still concealed from me."

"Tell me, *Heinrich*, how long have you loved me?"

"Since, since--permit me to answer you with the most common of all forms of speech,--since the first time I saw you."

"Since our meeting in the prison?"

"Yes; I cannot tell you what a powerful impression I received from you. I was astonished! Your boldness, your disregard of my dignity, your philanthropic enthusiasm, so entirely devoid of all affectation and sentimentality, aroused the greatest admiration, and your beauty excited my love. Had you been merely beautiful, I should only have desired you; but since you showed an equal intellect, I love you, and loved you from the beginning as I never did any other."

"As you never loved any other?" asked Cornelia. She had seated herself upon the sofa, and he took a chair beside her. She folded her arms upon the little barrier the broad side of the divan formed between them, and they gazed lovingly into each other's eyes.

"As I never loved any other," repeated *Henri*. "If you fully realized your own value, you would not look at me so incredulously. You would know that you must be loved differently from the commonplace girls with whom people can only trifle, whose insignificance renders all serious conversation impossible. There is nothing which continues to keep a woman interesting to a man except *originality*; and before I knew you I almost despaired of finding it. The female mind cannot reach the perception of things by the established, endlessly long path marked out for it; it has not sufficient perseverance, cannot keep pace with man. Most women pause half-way, with the goal before their eyes, but unable to reach it; they then become weary, disgusted with the world, and consume themselves in idle longings, which they at last permit some friend to heal. Others turn into by-paths of fruitless scholarship, and wonder aimlessly to and fro; such persons become utterly disagreeable, a terror to every man, for they enter into a sort of intellectual competition with him, which is charmless and a mere waste of time, because there is no true honorable victory to be obtained in such an unequal struggle. The true womanly nature knows the extent of her powers; she does not strive for things too far beyond her, for she cheerfully makes out her own object and builds her own path to it. This unthinking exercise of natural instincts, this radiance of free, pure thought, beaming from a youthful brow, is extremely refreshing, and while I am with you I regret every moment that I cannot philosophize with you about everything in earth or heaven. But the mouth which speaks so wisely is far too sweet, and so my senses are constantly battling with my intellect. I cannot kiss you without wishing you were talking, and I cannot hear you speak without wanting to kiss you. Is not this an unfortunate contradiction?"

"Ought it not to be harmonized? Cannot people be both sensible and affectionate?" asked Cornelia.

"No, my angel! In your presence I have not the necessary calmness," said *Henri*, involuntarily casting down his eyes. "Clearness of thought requires cool blood; and when I am so near you, when your sweet breath floats over me, and your warm hand rests in mine, my heart throbs violently, and sends the blood so quickly through my veins, that I can think of nothing but you and my ardent love!"

"Oh, do not look at me so fiercely! Your kindling eyes pierce my soul until I cannot help blushing. You do not know how terribly your glances flash. I do not fear you, but a strange horror overwhelms me when I see you thus. I feel myself a match for the spirit that darts menacing looks from those eyes, and a shudder thrills my soul as the wind rustles gently through the banners before a battle."

"So you are belligerently disposed towards me, Cornelia?"

"No, indeed; except when you are in your present mood then, I know, I shall often be compelled to uphold my standard against you."

"And what standard might that be?"

"That of gentleness, truth: in one word, virtue," she said, simply and firmly.

"Do you think me destitute of them?"

"Yes. Understand me correctly. You have a multitude of great and lovable qualities which distinguish you from the million,--a multitude of *virtues*, but not the *virtue* which we designate by one word, and in an indivisible sense. A person may not possess nearly as many noble traits, and yet be far more virtuous than you. Virtue is the pure, conscious will which unites the scattered capacities for good, and matures them to moral actions; and this quality you lack."

Ottmar had become very grave. *Henri* was present no longer: *Heinrich* had taken his place. Cornelia laid her head upon his hands, and said, in a tone of the fondest affection: "Now you are so quiet and cold, have I vexed you?"

"No, my child; but you have given me something to think about, which makes me grave. You women have a wonderful talent for moralizing. Your conscience wishes to make up for the too great indulgence of your hearts, and therefore you are the sternest censors of the man you love."

"We women? Have you said the same thing to other women?"

"Only one except yourself; but her theories were repellent. She gave me no proof in her own person that she possessed a cheering power in her own nature. She was a sad, pale, melancholy vision, so her influence over me also faded; yet, I shall always hold her memory sacred."

"Who was she? Heinrich, a shadow has fallen upon your mood: who was it you mourn for as a departed spirit?"

"A poor creature, whose suffering constantly pervades all my joys, whose misery always appears greater to me the more my own happiness increases, the more I learn to believe in the might of true feeling. Yes, yes, Cornelia, you are right; I may have virtues, but they principally exist in the fact that I can still regret the virtue I lack. Oh, if I could but cast aside my past with all its errors and reproaches, like the cocoon of a butterfly, and soar forth in freedom as a new, winged, purified creature!"

"I will tell you the name of the unhappy woman about whom remorse is now torturing you," began Cornelia, after a pause of earnest thought,--"it is Princess Ottilie."

Heinrich started up. "Girl! How did such an idea enter your head?"

Cornelia looked at him intently. "It is so."

"Who told you?"

"I thought of it myself. Ottilie imposed inviolable secrecy upon Röschen; what motive induced her to do so if she did not love you? What duty led Princess Ottilie to spare Herr von Ottmar except a tender obligation of the heart? All this, however, might be explained; but I was at the harbor when you arrived, I saw the princess turn pale, saw you approach anxiously and whisper a few words, perceived how, with a glance at you, she composed herself, how earnestly you watched her, and at last sprang to her assistance as if the whole responsibility of caring for her devolved upon you alone. I saw this lady was experiencing some great inward conflict; and your anxiety showed that you were aware of it. I felt there was some silent, mutual bond between you,--in what it exists I know not, but it does exist; and if I make it agree with what you have just said, then, *Heinrich,* I fear you have great cause for self-reproach."

"You have watched me with the eyes of love, and formed a tolerably clear idea of the true state of affairs. It would be useless to deny your guess, you would still believe it. In such matters one can deceive the world, but not the instinct of a clever woman. What shall I say to you?--spare me further particulars concerning things which are not my secret. I will freely confess that, with the exception of yourself, she was my only friend,--that I owe her much and shall always pity her."

"Poor lady!" said Cornelia, softly. "If she loves you, she is greatly to be pitied, for she can never forget you,--never be happy again!"

"Does your own heart tell you that, Cornelia?"

"Yes. Whoever has once felt the magic of your nature can never love another, and is bound to you for life; the whole world contains nothing nobler than yourself."

Heinrich took her hands and pressed them to his breast. "Dearest, you are my happiness and my salvation! Cornelia, I love you. I would fain breathe forth my life in those few words: 'I love you!" Cornelia felt that tears were dimming her eyes, and tried to conceal them. "Oh, do not be ashamed of these tears! Happy is the human being who can weep. Teach me the lesson too, and you will have accomplished what not even God could do!"

"And if I should succeed, *Heinrich,* it would still be only by the help of God, who blessed my efforts. He will let me find means to do so, if he wishes to raise you by my hand. Do not smile. I cannot help calling the power to which you give a thousand titles by the name of God; cannot intentionally fail in my duty to him. I cannot live without this God,--may not deny him. When I was a child he stood beside my bed and I could talk to him. I associated with him all my thoughts of my father; my mother appeared to me beautiful and radiant in his heavenly majesty, I have so often folded my little hands reverently and thought he heard me; and am I now to believe the soulless air wafted my fervent prayer away,--that so much love, so much devotion, was lavished an a phantom? Oh, my childish faith has increased with my growth!--it has somewhere become part of my nature; for if I try to separate from it, a pang passes through my soul, and I feel that some spiritual nerve, the connecting link between God and myself, is wounded."

"You are a woman, Cornelia, and it would be wicked to cast a word of doubt into the sanctuary of your pious heart. We have already spoken of this matter once, and you almost made me an enthusiast."

"Is it really so?" interrupted Cornelia. "Oh, if you confess that, much is gained, and I shall henceforth work upon your 'enthusiasm'! You know, *Heinrich*, that natures like ours are always set apart from the rest of mankind. Life often becomes unendurable; reverses of fortune may occur which even philosophy can no longer help us to bear, and we can nowhere find a home. Then it is fortunate if we can flee from earth to that wonderland of fancy, our inalienable home. There are sorrows, too, *Heinrich*, which cannot endure the classical training of an empty doctrine, and which, destroying everything in their course, dash wildly over us. Then the soul grasps for some support, and in its agony shrieks for a God; and if there were none, it would create him for itself, that its cry for help might not echo back from an empty void. But such a self-created God gives no comfort, but jeers at you mockingly, like the spectre of your own agony, and melts away before your eyes, while the true God cannot approach to comfort you, for you do not believe in him, and only by faith does he work his miracles." Cornelia paused; for *Heinrich* was on his knees before her with his face buried in her lap.

"If in such an hour I still have you, I need no God!" he exclaimed, fairly beside himself.

"Do not blaspheme!" pleaded Cornelia "And suppose you did not have me? Suppose it should be God's will to separate us, and you were alone,-- entirely alone?"

"Cornelia, how can you think of such a thing while you clasp me in your arms? If we should lose each other, what should I become? An embodied negation, separated from all connection with mankind, withered in mind and body,--a living corpse, to which the world is only a grave."

"*Heinrich*, dear, dear *Heinrich*! you inspire me with both compassion and horror! Oh, banish these gloomy spirits from your mind, and become light-hearted and gentle! Fate is not subdued by threats and blasphemies; the ground on which happiness willingly builds its nest must be firm and peaceful, not trembling with volcanic shocks and rumbling with peals of thunder. Come, be gentle; such wicked words suit your delicate mouth.

Smile again; Veronica will soon wake up, and then we can no longer express our love in fond caresses."

"Yes, that is true!" cried *Heinrich*; "let us enjoy the moment while we may." And it was *Henri* who now threw himself upon the sofa beside Cornelia and drew her closely to him.

Cornelia looked at him in astonishment. His eyes were beaming with ardent feeling; a warmer color tinged his cheeks; his mouth, half-pouted for a kiss was irresistibly alluring. "It often seems as if you changed places with some one, and in an instant became an entirely different man. I never saw such sudden alterations of mood."

"Ah, do not speak! kiss me!" pleaded *Henri*. "Darling, how I have longed for those lips! Many a night have I tossed as if in a fever, thirsting, yearning for you. Did you think of me when you went to rest?"

"Yes, a thousand times. I have never fallen asleep without calling 'Good-night, *Heinrich*!' and the words became my nightly prayer. I shall never forget it."

"How beautiful! What time do you say it?"

"At eleven: when I am in bed."

"In future I shall always say, 'Pleasant dreams, Cornelia!' You will remember it, won't you, my darling?"

"Of course I shall," she whispered, pressing her cheek close to his.

Light, scarcely audible footsteps approached. Cornelia started up. "Veronica is coming!"

The door slowly opened, and she entered, kindly as ever, but pale, as if there was not a drop of blood in her sunken features. Her slender figure seemed still more shrunken, and there was not a tinge of color about the ghostly apparition except the light-blue ribbon upon her white cap. The lovely eyes were more hollow, more lustreless, than in former days; the silvery curls drooped more negligently about her face. *Henri* perceived a change in her, and as it soon became evident that there was no alteration in her intellectual powers it must be a bodily one. In such delicate equable natures all secret changes give very faint external tokens of their existence, and it requires a watchful, practiced eye to detect them. Cornelia was too mach preoccupied with her own feelings, the slight, gradual alterations in Veronica's appearance did not attract her attention; but *Henri*, who had not seen her for a long time, noticed them at once.

"My dear count, I did not know you were here, or I should not have yielded to the heavy slumber which always overpowers me now. I must beg you to excuse me, but I have no doubt Cornelia has entertained you so well that you have not missed me. Besides, age no longer harmonizes with youth. It is too dull for the sympathy and susceptibility required to enter into the rapidly changing details of a conversation."

"Oh, do not say that!" pleaded *Henri*. "With your fresh intellect one can accommodate one's self to every form of change; but it would be uncourteous to Fräulein Cornelia, if I did not say that I am indebted to her for a most delightful hour." He smilingly took her hand and pressed it warmly.

Veronica looked earnestly at them both, and *Henri* noticed it.

"Are you satisfied with my influence over your Cornelia? Is she not once more as blooming as a rose?"

"Oh, I am very grateful to you for your friendship, my dear count! But, Cornelia, you are not only blooming, you are fairly glowing to-day. You must have been talking very earnestly."

Cornelia's blushes grew still deeper at this remark. She glanced at *Henri*; he was apparently gazing irresolutely into vacancy.

"What is the matter, my child? Does your head ache? You really make me uneasy."

Cornelia started up and threw herself at Veronica's feet. "No, I cannot bear it; I could keep silent, but I cannot lie. Veronica, forgive my past reserve, it was painful enough to me but now you question me, I will tell you the truth. Veronica, must I speak plainly? Yes, yes, it is as you think."

Henri was in a state of painful embarrassment, and thought to himself, "Who can teach a woman to be silent?"

Veronica sat speechless and clasped her trembling hands. After a pause *Henri* approached and touched Cornelia's head. "Here is all the happiness that earth contains. You will not refuse it to me, my motherly friend?"

"I have wished and thought that this might be, but now it has happened I am so greatly startled that I can scarcely speak!" Overpowered by her emotion, she clasped Cornelia in her arms. "My child, my only one, my all, whom I have so faithfully cherished, I confide you to the protection of this noble man, and am perfectly assured that he will make you happy. Come, my son, and receive my blessing." She laid her clasped hands upon his brow. "May God be merciful unto you and bless you, and show you the light of his countenance and be merciful unto you!"

The last words died upon her lips; the emotion was too great. She sank back, while *Henri* and Cornelia affectionately supported her. The latter was deeply agitated. She now perceived, for the first time, in what a frail shell this beloved life was contained, by what feeble threads it was still bound to earth, and hot tears rolled down her cheeks. *Henri* himself was not wholly destitute of sympathy. He esteemed Veronica, and understood Cornelia's feeling. At last she regained her consciousness, and gazed at them with her loving eyes. "Have I alarmed you? I most sincerely regret it; but my life has long flowed an so calmly and equably that I am unaccustomed to all emotion. But, dear Cornelia, you must remember the possibility of my leaving you. Do not weep; let the consciousness that you have never cost me a single sorrowful hour console you. You have developed a lofty, free, and noble nature, and yet always given me the submissive heart of a child; have spared my weaknesses, and never permitted me to feel how far you had risen above me. God will reward you for it. And now that my last wish is fulfilled, and I know you are safe in the arms of your betrothed, I can cheerfully depart to my sainted lover."

"Oh, do not talk so, Veronica!" pleaded Cornelia. "You are strewing wormwood over this blissful hour."

"Why, my child? You do not grudge me the peace contained in the thought of death, and I feel that the time which separates me from my betrothed is drawing to a close. If you only knew how I rejoice over it! We have been obliged to wait for long years,--he there and I here; but a human life is but a short span compared to eternity. We shall meet again, and our temporary separation will only be an interruption, not the destruction of our intercourse."

Cornelia gazed silently into vacancy. The grave conversation had brought *Heinrich* into *Henri's* place. "It is a beautiful and enviable faith," said he.

"Which you do not share, because you are a man, and still young; but, I assure you, the older we grow the thinner becomes the partition our earthly bodies form between our immortal souls and eternity, and single rays from the other shore often fall through. This gives to us old people the religious trust at which you young philosophers smile."

"I do not laugh at it, Veronica," said *Heinrich*; "but I think you have yet many years to enjoy life and our happiness."

"Well, it is as God wills. I will gladly live and gladly die,--both are welcome to me."

Heinrich looked at her in astonishment. "Fortunate is the person who can say that, and contemplate with equal serenity the day and night of existence."

"Enough of this grave subject; tell me, my son, how soon you wish to take Cornelia away? I shall miss her so terribly that I dread the thought of losing her, and really do not know how I am to live without her."

Heinrich bit his lips. "Calm yourself; unfortunately, I cannot call her mine as soon as I would gladly do, and must even request you to keep our engagement a secret for the present. My position at the court is just now in a very important crisis. This must first be decided before I can establish a home here. There are a thousand things to be considered, a thousand little difficulties to remove, and six months may elapse before my affairs are settled. So you will have Cornelia longer than I like, for if it depended only upon myself I would take her in my arms to-morrow, and show her to the envious world as my dearest possession."

"I understand, dear Ottmar," said Veronica; "but I only wonder that you, who have stood so firmly in your office, should suddenly find yourself in a crisis."

"Unfortunately it is so. The ministry is now engaged upon new laws, which, if unapproved, will lead to a change of ministers, and perhaps I may also fall a victim. This is an important time in my life, which claims all my activity and attention."

"Thank God that I am permitted to keep my angel so long! You are very sensible, my son, to wish to wait until after this epoch. Besides, a marriage made outside the limits of the most aristocratic circles will not be very favorably received at court, and it is, therefore, best to keep the matter secret until your position has been confirmed anew."

The conversation was beginning to be painful to *Heinrich*, and the striking of the great clock afforded him a welcome pretext for rising and pleading the necessity of attending a court soirée. He bade Veronica farewell, and begged Cornelia to accompany him to the door. The young girl was grave and quiet.

"Do not grieve about Veronica, my child," he said, in the antechamber; "it is the way of all old people, to talk continually about dying,--she may live a long time still."

"I think so too," replied Cornelia; "but I feel oppressed. It is like the plants whose leaves droop after being exposed to too much sunlight. I was too happy just now,--there must be a reaction."

"But what troubles you, my angel?"

"Oh, it is nothing that can be changed. The thought of being so much your inferior that such strict secrecy is needful grieves me. To conceal from the world the beautiful emotion that fills my breast, perhaps even often be compelled to profane it by a falsehood, is painful; but do not let it grieve you,--I shall soon conquer this mood."

Heinrich drew her to his breast, and stroked her luxuriant hair. "My own sweet love, I understand you. But consider that this burdensome constraint is only imposed upon us for a *short* time, and that it also has its good side. I can say no more than I wrote in my letter. As regards making the affair public, you see, by what Veronica says, the necessity of the precautions I am compelled to take. Come, love, smile upon me again; do not let me go with the knowledge that you are sorrowful." He took her hand and placed it on his heart. "Do you feel that its every throb is yours?"

Cornelia threw her arm around his neck, and gazed intently into his face; but he closed her eyes with kisses, and left the house. She went to the window and watched her lover's tall figure as he strode away. No one could bear himself more proudly, no one could hold his head more haughtily erect. Now he met an acquaintance, removed his hat slowly and condescendingly, and continued his way without glancing up, for he seemed to have noticed that the gentleman was looking after him. It wounded Cornelia, and when the latter raised his eyes to the window she blushed with a strange feeling of shame and retreated. She would not go to Veronica; something in her mood demanded solitude, so she leaned back on one of the ancient carved chairs and gazed thoughtfully at the dark oak wainscoting on the walls. Twilight spread its shadows over her,--twilight also brooded over her soul, and she knew not whether it would change into night or day. Why should she feel ashamed because that stranger looked after Ottmar and then glanced at her? why should it cause her pain because Ottmar passed on without looking? Secrecy made this caution necessary. It required that he should deny her in the presence of the first chance-comer, that she should steal a glance at her lover like a thief in the night, and blush if surprised in the act, as if she were doing wrong. How painful! how humiliating! But was this secrecy really needful? Were the reasons he alleged sufficient and strong enough not to be vanquished by the strength of a genuine, manly love? Ought he not to sacrifice everything to spare her such a humiliation? How far would his marriage with her, with their mutual fortunes, be dependent upon a crisis in office? What induced the ardent lover to consent to this patient waiting? Could his private relations exert a disturbing influence upon his position as a servant of the government? What made him so timid, if it was not the fear of forfeiting his place at court by a mesalliance with a plebeian, the daughter of a republican? But what would the delay of a few months avail?--would not the marriage be precisely the same at whatever time it occurred? If he feared that, he would *never* dare to wed her. She fell into a deep reverie. Suddenly her eyes flashed, and she held her breath as if the very air was poisoned. Suppose he should be false?--suppose the dread of prejudicing himself should be stronger than his integrity? She could not doubt his love, for his ardor had already made her tremble. Suppose he wished to plunge her into the same abyss that had engulfed so many others? suppose the reports concerning him were true, and he should prove false, terribly, fiendishly false? Yet scarcely was the suspicion born ere her whole nature rose against it in all its strength. What a monster you are to have the thought of such baseness arise in your young brain! Is your imagination so corrupt that the most sacred thing is not too holy to be thus sullied? Her horror was now not of him, but of herself. He was not the traitor, but she,--she who could cherish so disgraceful a doubt, whose love was not strong enough to crush it in the bud; she had betrayed him in her own heart.

She started up, rushed into her room, and lighted a lamp; then in the anguish of her soul threw herself on the floor before his picture,--the same one she had received from Fräulein Hedwig. Her eyes wandered over the sketch and strove to animate the mute features and unravel their mystery; in vain, the solution was concealed in her own breast, and everything there was confused and gloomy. Thus, tortured by doubts of him and of herself, she was at last attracted towards the pure, faithful heart of her foster-mother. She entered the tea-room and found Veronica sitting with her clasped hands resting in her lap, absorbed in sorrowful thought.

"Are you come at last, my darling? You have left your old Veronica alone a long time. But I understand it. In this solemn hour you must first be at peace with yourself. You happy, fortunate child!"

Cornelia threw herself upon a stool at Veronica's feet, and asked, cautiously, for she did not wish this unprejudiced mind to catch a glimpse of her troubled soul, "Do you believe in *Heinrich* as firmly as I do?"

"Certainly," replied Veronica. "I think he has given us sufficient proof that he is a man of honor."

The old servant brought a lamp and the musical urn into the room; Veronica took out her knitting-work, and as they sat so quietly together with the sweet melodies circling round them with the rising steam, the memory of the evening of their first unseen meeting rose gently before Cornelia's mind with all its magic and blessedness. Her excited nerves grew calm, her mood dissolved in tears. She remembered so many lofty words, so many glances full of true nobility of feeling. All those fair moments passed before her. With what joyful affection he had met her that day! Can one who has any evil design be so frank, so confident? Oh, if he should suspect how she had doubted him!

"Do you think it necessary to keep our love a secret?" she asked, at last.

"Oh, yes, my child," said Veronica, calmly.

"To me it is only very painful," murmured Cornelia.

"That may be; but it is something that happens a thousand times. You must be reasonable. We cannot know that he is not in the act of obtaining a higher position, and in that case his engagement with you would be an obstacle in his way. Therefore he must deny it until the expected promotion is secured; then only he can venture to defy all the prejudices of his circle and take you for his wife."

"I do not see what his private relations should have to do with it."

"Why, Cornelia, you speak as if you knew nothing of the world! Are you not yet aware how much personal matters are taken into consideration in these circles? Besides, we cannot conceal from ourselves that you bear a name with which the most unfortunate political associations are connected. Perhaps he also hopes that in the course of time our noble princess may exert a softening influence upon our strict aristocracy, and wishes to await this favorable opportunity. There are a thousand things to be considered, and it is very delicate in him to conceal them from us. You are a young, enthusiastic hot-head, and always want to fight your way through to your ideal; he a steady, experienced man who takes things as they are, and yields to them with prudent self-control. I would far rather trust you to such a character than a fanatical reformer, like your unhappy father."

Cornelia listened with delight to this argument in favor of what she herself most ardently desired. Veronica was so calm, so confident, and she was not blinded by love; should not this restore all the peace of confidence? Oh, if her deeply injured lover were only here, that she might implore his pardon for the wrong she had done him! How she would embrace him if he came to-morrow! how happy she would be with him!

Veronica's voice roused her from these thoughts and dreams. "Let us take tea, Cornelia; I am very tired and would like to get up early to-morrow morning to go to church. I long to raise my heart to God."

Cornelia silently obeyed. When tea was over Veronica went to bed, and Cornelia, who had helped her undress, knelt before her. "I thank you, dear Veronica, for having been so kind to me and *Heinrich*; I thank you also, at this turning-point of my life, for all the love with which you have treated me as a daughter, and made me a good and happy creature. I can never repay you for it, but your clear eyes look into my heart and see what no words can express." Overpowered by her emotion, she pressed Veronica's hand to her lips.

"Oh, my child! my dear, dear child! God knows how fully, how richly, this hour repays me for all I have done! What better things can one purchase than a hand to close one's eyes, and a warm tear to fall upon one's grave? This is a happiness which comprehends the joys of a whole life,--and for this I thank you. Good-night, my child."

Cornelia embraced her and went to her own room with tearful eyes. As she reached it she heard Veronica call, and went back. The latter held out her arms. "Let me press you to my heart once more. God bless you, joy of my old age! Good-night. Wake me to-morrow."

Cornelia remained awake for a long time. Veronica's manner had roused a feeling of subdued melancholy. Besides, the wonderful day must be lived over anew, its discords harmonized, its joys and sorrows interwoven with her inner nature, ere dreams could be permitted to lead her into another kingdom.

It was broad daylight when, after a short slumber, she rose and went to wake Veronica.

The little dusky sleeping-room was cosy and silent. Single shafts of sunlight stole through the closely-drawn green curtains and flickered over the hangings of Veronica's bed. No sound of breathing, no motion, disturbed the stillness of this sanctuary of slumber. Cornelia softly entered and stood for a long time before the bed; she was loth to disturb the peaceful silence in which Veronica reposed. But she had requested it, and it must be done. She drew the curtains slowly aside. There she lay, apparently lost in pleasant dreams, but--was it the green light?--pallid as a corpse! Cornelia took her hand. Oh, God, how chill! "Veronica, dear Veronica, wake!" In vain; in her slumber she had passed into another life. The pale face seemed in death to wear a smile, to greet the loved one for whom she had always lived and so confidently expected to meet again. Her death was as peaceful as her life.

"Wake me to-morrow," were her last words. "Oh, if I could only do so!" sobbed Cornelia, sinking upon her knees as if utterly crushed.

XVII
INSNARED

Anton was fastening a new order upon Ottmar's court dress, when the latter violently pulled his bell.

"It's unbearable!" grumbled the old servant as he took the last stitch and hurried in with the uniform.

Heinrich was striding impatiently up and down the room. "Are you ready at last? Give it to me; make haste, and let me get off. I have no time to lose."

The dressing was quickly finished. "The new star is magnificent," said Anton.

Heinrich looked at his image in the mirror with the satisfaction of a man who knows he is handsome, and reckons his beauty among his own merits, as if he had compelled nature to give him the form he desired.

"I must go to Cornelia after dinner and show myself to her. She understands and values my beauty better than any one else," he thought, pushing the order straight. "Besides, it will do no harm to let her see some of my importance as a courtier; old Veronica takes the matter too easily. It is not I, but she, who lulls the dear creature into dreams for which I am not responsible. It is not I who deceive her, but Veronica, when she assumes as a matter of course assurances I never gave; and yet I cannot, by a premature contradiction, destroy my whole happiness. I would far rather resolve to verify them, if there could be no other arrangement." A ray of sunlight fell upon the diamonds in his order and made them glitter. "Do you wish to warn me, you star of honor, that you sparkle so? No, I will not forget you. Let others yearn for the stars of you unattainable distance; my earthly wishes depend upon you, that you may not pale before the sun, but with your rays make your chosen one shine forth from the darkness of obscurity, and distinguish him from the masses. With you on my heart, and Cornelia's love within it, what do I need more?"

A servant announced that the carriage was waiting.

Heinrich took his gold-embroidered hat, and smiling, threw himself upon the soft cushions. The beautiful white horses tossed their heads, and dashed away through sunlit avenues and crowds of gayly-dressed foot-passengers.

The dinner, the first which had been given since the marriage, was magnificent. The court displayed its greatest splendor. Ottilie herself was one of the most stately personages who ever graced a throne. Although no smile rested upon her lips, she did the honors in a most winning manner, and was gracious even to *Heinrich*, although no more so than to all others. The prince, however, treated him with marked distinction, and once whispered, casting a well-pleased glance at Ottilie, "You were right; she is a real princess." The princes, princesses, and courtiers who were present followed their master's example and loaded Ottmar with civilities; had never been so attractive or so much admired. He stood at the zenith of his favor at court; and when, after the dinner was over, he drove to Cornelia, he scarcely saw that it was already dusk, so brightly did the lights, the white necks, the sparkling glances, the diamonds, and the gold-embroidered uniforms still gleam before his eyes; glittering silken robes rustled around him; smiling faces looked forth longingly from behind costly bouquets. The material comfort of the moment was too great not to rouse the other half of his nature. *Henri* alighted when the carriage stopped. He pulled the bell, and the door of the silent house slowly opened. The staircase was dark. The black form of a servant glided by and ushered him into the anteroom. The salon stood open; he entered. It, too, was dark and empty; everything was in disorder: the furniture was pushed back, and there were no roses blooming on the flower-stand. *Henri* felt strangely oppressed. The gloomy silence ill suited his mood. A glimmer of light and a dull murmur of voices penetrated through a door which was partly ajar. He opened it, and stood as if rooted to the spot. Several women were engaged in dressing a corpse. *Henri* pressed his hand to his brow; was he awake, or did some dream torture him with its sudden changes, in order to show him in a single hour the splendor of the world and the end of all lives? Just at that moment Cornelia, who had been completely absorbed in her mournful occupation, suddenly perceived him, came forward in her mourning robes, looking very pale and languid, and drew him aside.

"My dear Cornelia," said *Henri*, kissing her tearful eyes, "what has happened since yesterday? I can scarcely trust my senses. What a contrast!"

"Ah, *Heinrich* thank God, you have come at last! Ever since early this morning I have borne this terrible sorrow alone, longing in vain for your warm heart. Alas, how heavily such an unexpected blow falls!"

"My poor, sweet love, you are trembling as if in an ague-fit! Who would have thought of this? Kind Veronica dead!"

She nestled timidly in his arms. "*Heinrich*, my heart aches terribly, and besides I feel this horror of death. You do not know what it is to dress a cold body which is no longer the dear one it personates."

"Then leave the others to finish the task, and stay with me, my angel."

"We have finished it, and they want to bring her in here. You must go into the tea-room, or they will see you."

"Willingly. But now leave everything to these women and come with me. You are completely worn out."

"Yes, I will stay with you. I can no longer be a witness," said Cornelia; then gave the necessary orders to the servants, and went into the tea-room with *Henri*. They had scarcely entered it when they heard pieces of furniture pushed aside, and the creaking of the coffin, which, when once heard, is never forgotten. Cornelia trembled violently, sank down beside *Henri*, and bursting into tears, hid her face upon his breast until the noise was over. Then she looked up. "You think me very weak, do you not? I have kept up all day, but now my strength is exhausted; terror has overpowered me."

Henri gently raised her and drew her on his knee. She made no resistance, but threw her arms around his neck; her head sank wearily upon his shoulder, and joy and sorrow, deadly horror and sweet content, began to mingle strangely.

"Oh, do not give way!" said *Henri* to himself, while his throbbing heart seemed ready to burst. He cradled her in his arms as if she had been a child, and breathed upon her cold hands.

Gradually her tears ceased, and warmth returned to her cheeks and hands. Never is a woman more grateful or more susceptible to love than when a great sorrow has broken her strength, and she gropes helplessly for some support. At this moment Cornelia could have worshiped her lover as some superior being; all suspicion was forgotten, she clung to him as if he were some consoling angel.

"Cornelia, are you happy now that you are clasped to my heart?" whispered *Henri*.

"Oh, infinitely happy!" she murmured. "What should I be without you, my life? Now I am cast wholly upon you, you will never forsake your orphaned love?"

Henri strained her to his breast with almost suffocating violence, and exclaimed from his inmost heart, with the utmost sincerity, "If I ever forsake you, accursed be the hour when I was born, the couch on which I rest, the air I breathe, the lips with which I kiss! I raise my hand and call upon all the powers of evil to witness against me if I break my oath."

Cornelia laid her finger on his lips. "Do not be so violent; that is no oath, but a curse."

"Is it not equally binding?"

"Certainly; but it makes me anxious: as if there would be no blessing upon it; as if you felt the possibility of becoming faithless, and your better self was threatening you with punishment."

"You angel! Look me in the eyes; do you no longer believe in your *Heinrich*, and yet love him still?"

"Ah, *Heinrich*, forgive my distrust! I feared to lose you, because you are the dearest thing in the would to me. I cannot think clearly to-day, I am so bewildered and worn out by grief. How contemptible I must seem to you!"

"If you knew how lovely you are in your weakness! You are not contemptible, you are only a true, tender woman, and therein lies your charm. Do you suppose firm muscles, large bones, and nerves of steel are attractive to men? It is your very helplessness that rouses our magnanimity; your delicacy demands our indulgence. To support a beautiful, trembling woman on his strong arm, and defend her from real or fancied terrors, is a sweet joy to a man,--sweeter than admiration of an abnormal strength, which woman attains only at the cost of her charms."

Cornelia listened to his words with increasing delight.

"Do you suppose," he continued, "that you were ever dearer to me than at this hour, when I am permitted to cradle your weary form upon my knees and fondly caress you? when your strong mind succumbs to the laws of womanly nature and you fly to me in your horror of death? You have trusted yourself to me more than ever before, and in your sorrow are sacred. You have nestled confidingly to this heart, and it shall never deceive you."

"*Heinrich*! *Heinrich* What a magic you exert! You banish all griefs with a single glance of love, and your words fill my soul with peace. Ah, it is beautiful to love in happiness! But we only know what we are to each other when we need each other. No language can express what you have been to me in this hour. A dark, starry sky arches over me in your eyes and invites me to repose; it extends over my whole soul and seems as if it enthroned the God to whom I bewail my sorrows, in whom I trust, to whom I shall send up my nightly prayer, and then rest--sleep!" She closed her eyes as if exhausted, and laid her head upon his breast.

Henri clasped her closely in his arms. "Oh, bear this happiness! bear it firmly!" he murmured to himself.

She sat upright again. "I cannot lean upon you; your hard orders hurt me."

"Then rest on the other side," he pleaded.

She pushed her hair back from her brow, looked sadly at the flashing decorations, and rose. "It is late, Heinrich; you must leave me now."

Henri cursed the diamond stars with sincere vexation. What had they availed him? They had destroyed the happiest moment of his life; and the magic night of love, with all its sweet dreams and illusions, which Cornelia's weary soul had spread around herself and him, had melted in their rays.

He rose and extended his hands imploringly to Cornelia. "My darling, you shall never again be parted from the place where you belong. I promise you. I shall never wear them in your presence."

"Ah, yes, put them away; they have hurt my cheek, but wounded my heart still more."

"Cornelia, are you angry with me?"

"I angry with you? Ah, Heinrich, I love you only too well! Tell me, where is this to end? If I am away from your side a moment, I feel as if the cold breath of the grave floated over me, and a throb of pain thrills my frame as if I had torn away a part of my own nature. Heinrich,--beloved, terrible Heinrich,--where is this to end?"

"In a happy, ardent love," cried *Henri*, radiant with joy. "You shall not miss me often. I will spend every leisure hour with you. But say, my angel, shall you still be accessible to me? Does Veronica's death make no change in your situation?"

"Oh, I had entirely forgotten that. Old Herr Linderer is my guardian, and the executor of Veronica's will. He proposed that I should reside in his family for the future."

"What! would you do that?" cried *Henri*.

"It would be very painful to me, and I might remain, for through Veronica's generosity the house and everything she possessed is mine; but a young girl ought not to live so entirely alone, without protection."

"And have you not a moral protection in yourself, and a personal one in your servants?"

"Certainly."

"That I cannot visit you when you are living with Herr Linderer is a matter of course. Our intercourse must be broken off, for it cannot exist under the watchful eyes of that family; so you have but one choice, my darling,--either to remain here and be the happiest of betrothed brides, or dispense with my society for the sake of a world that will not thank you for the sacrifice."

Cornelia clung closely to him. "Do without you? Oh, *Heinrich*, how could I?"

"Well, promise me you will take courage and refuse Linderer's proposal; then, Cornelia, I shall first believe in the strength of your love."

"But the world,--how would it judge of such a plan?"

"Cornelia, I should have thought you philosopher enough to despise the world and its judgments."

"Perhaps,--but custom--"

"You may offend against custom, but not morality. Our love bears the highest consecration in itself. If you are thoroughly pervaded with its influence, you may trust yourself to it without fear. But what am I talking about? Ask your own heart whether you will make me of less importance than consideration for the opinion of the world,--whether you can inflict this sorrow upon yourself and your *Heinrich*."

"And do you not take the same precautions, *Heinrich*? Do you not deny me before society for the sake of 'its despicable prejudices'?"

Henri was embarrassed for a moment; then he said, calmly, "If I now make confessions to the influential circles which have the decision of my fate, it will be done while I am not compelled to be deprived of you. If I had only the choice of leaving you or giving up my plans, I should not hesitate a moment to do the latter. If you go to Herr Linderer's, you will place me in this alternative. I must either give you up for a long time, or prematurely acknowledge our relations and destroy my hopes for the future. Speak, my angel! If you demand the latter, be proud to prove that I love you better than you do me, and can make greater sacrifices."

"No, no, my dearest! You shall not think me so selfish; I should be ashamed to accept such an one from you. I will stay in this house and refuse Herr Linderer's offer. People may say what they please; better they should suspect me than that you should doubt my love."

"Those words were worthy of you, Cornelia!" cried *Henri*. "What gratitude can reward you as you deserve?"

Cornelia gazed into his eyes long and earnestly. "Justify my confidence, *Heinrich*, and you will give me the highest, the only reward I ask. And now farewell for to-day."

"Must I leave you? Ah, one moment more!"

Cornelia shook her head sadly. "No, it cannot be; it is late, and I must rest; but you can go through the room with me,--will you?"

"Yes, my angel, I will go with you to the threshold of your room; and then turn away from the door of heaven like a condemned spirit."

"Come," said Cornelia; and slowly entered the room leaning on his arm.

There lay the corpse in the coffin, a wreath of blossoming myrtle on the head, and Cornelia's red roses on the heart. Her tears flowed again, her grief burst forth anew, as she looked down on the silent, pale, old bride.

"Oh, faithful guardian of my childhood!" she sobbed, "will you leave your Cornelia alone? Open your lips once more and tell me, oh! tell whether I am doing right in what I have just promised my beloved one! Ah, speak to me once, only once more, true, pure heart, which has been my refuge in joy and sorrow!"

"Have you forgotten that I am by your side, Cornelia?" said *Henri*, reproachfully.

She turned from the body, pressed a fervent kiss upon his lips, and allowed him to lead her through the apartment to her own room. Here she paused. "Thanks, dearest Heinrich! farewell!"

"Must I leave you alone with your tears?"

"Oh, the would gush forth again whenever you went, no matter how long you might remain!"

"Do you not fear your own thoughts while you are in this excited mood?"

"Not in this cheerful chamber. It is protected by all the thousand dreams of love I have had here. There is your picture; where that is the icy breath of death cannot enter. Farewell!"

"Ah, if I might only sleep on the threshold before your door, I would never seek soft pillows!" Again he clasped her in his arms; then, with an effort, tore himself away. "Good-night!"

"Good-night, Heinrich!" she cried in a tone which revealed all the wealth of ardent feeling she had repressed with so much difficulty; then disappeared in her own room and locked the door.

Henri averted his face as he passed the corpse. He had once more received a solemn lesson, and it was only when his agitated feelings began to grow calm that he was able to justly comprehend the importance of the last hour.

He returned home absorbed in thought, and the first thing he did was to cast aside the star-bedecked uniform. Then he paced up and down his room, while the most conflicting thoughts whirled through his brain. Cornelia's sacrifice had shamed him deeply. Was he to misuse it, and abuse her confidence? Must he not reward her better?

Again he paced up and down the room.

But he would requite her with a thousand joys. Free love was spared the heavy cares of the married state. He could easily teach her to despise the social "prejudices of morality," and as soon as she disregarded them, of what would she be deprived if their relations lacked the legal stamp? He would never desert her,--he had sworn it; so their union would contain the fundamental principle of marriage. He would never wed another. What did she want more? He believed her unconventional enough to regard the claims of custom lightly. She had already done so to a certain extent by the promise she had given that day. The first--most difficult--step was taken. But if he misjudged her, if his plan failed, and she could not endure the disgrace. If he should lose her! He was obliged to confess that he could no longer live without her. Did she not outweigh his triumphs and his prospects at the court? But suppose the new law did not pass? could not fall a victim to it, as he had made Veronica suppose, for he was one of its opponents. To whom could the prince turn, in forming a new ministry, except himself? Suppose, by his marriage with Cornelia, he should lose the prince's favor, and with it the portfolio? This turned the scale. This period must be awaited.

The magnanimity of love! How many an innocent, womanly heart has already been led astray by this will-o'-the-wisp of tender sophistry! Deeds like Cornelia's sacrifice of a public betrothal, and her promise to live alone, veil themselves beneath a semblance of such nobility that an unsuspecting nature does not hesitate to perform them, believing itself to be yielding to an impulse of generosity, and not suspecting that it is merely following the guidance of its own passion. Cornelia was too innocent and inexperienced to penetrate *Henri's* unprincipled tactics. If doubts again arose they could not give sufficient proofs of their justice, and were always crushed as "idle fancies" by the power of her love.

Veronica's funeral took place, and it touched Cornelia deeply that Heinrich was present; she considered it a fresh proof of his uprightness.

Old Archivrath Linderer heard with actual tears her refusal to become one of his family. He ventured a few timid remonstrances, but was far too courteous to use his right as guardian and compel her to yield to his views. He could not force himself to be uncivil to any one, and according to his ideas he would have been so had he attempted to impose any restraint upon Cornelia. Therefore, when he saw that his timidly uttered, kindly meant representations were wholly disregarded, he could only wipe the sweat of anxiety from his brow and take leave of her with a deeply saddened heart. Even the sulky servant took his leave, to live upon the legacy Veronica had left him, as soon as he learned that Cornelia intended to keep up an independent establishment.

Several weeks now quietly elapsed in a gentle alternation of joy and sorrow, until the image of the beloved dead receded into the background more and more, and love took exclusive possession of Cornelia's whole existence. At first she did not notice that the number of her acquaintances lessened; and when she at last became aware of it, *Henri's* influence had already taught her to disregard it. She despised the pitiful souls which only judged from appearances, and clung to the few faithful friends that remained to her. But it was unavoidable that one or another of them should meet Ottmar during his frequent visits. It would not do,--people must not always find him with her; so, if he was present, other visitors were refused. When this happened too frequently, and Cornelia perceived that it must lead to misunderstandings with her best friends, she at last consented that Ottmar should spend the evening hours with her. Thus the meetings with others were prevented; but as his presence had been noticed, his absence was now the cause of comment. Had their interviews ceased, or been deferred until another hour? This must be ascertained. A few zealous friends watched her, and saw him come and go. They sorrowfully confided this incredible thing to each other under the seal of silence, warned her, half openly and half by hints, that her fair fame was endangered, and mourned for her as one dead. Yet she still stood erect and stainless, her girlish brow loftily upraised against the humiliations she endured, and pitied the world for being too corrupt to believe in the purity of anything; her last consolation was her good conscience. She trusted to herself and to her lover, and awaited the day which would solve the mystery before the eyes of men and restore her their lost esteem. This gave her strength to endure the "trial."

Ottmar did everything in his power to employ her time and occupy her thoughts. He was well aware that he could only win this noble woman gradually, and by noble means. He read with her, gave her the most beautiful classical works, explained the thoughts of the ancient and modern philosophers, and perused with her the best of modern literature. Thus she learned to associate with him the impressions made by the noblest productions of the intellect, from which he obtained a certain halo that made him worthy of worship in her eyes. He understood all these grand works, and made them comprehensible to her,--it seemed as great a deed as if he had created them himself. She looked up to him as a superior being, and at last could really neither think, feel, nor live without him. He, in his turn, was delighted with her susceptibility and active mind, and became accustomed to impart everything good and beautiful which came in his way to Cornelia, and enjoy it doubly with her. Thus he unconsciously entangled himself in the net he was weaving for the young girl; she became as great a necessity to him as he to her, and he had never been so happy before. Yet this life was not wholly without discord. His twofold nature often wounded Cornelia; he was either passionately excited, or brilliant and cold. She could not be at ease; one she was forced to repel, the other repelled her. Both prevented the calm happiness of loving intercourse which woman's platonic nature so fully understands and needs. She often took for want of love what was merely lack of sensuous feeling, and the glowing ardor which alternated with the coldness could not supply the place of the uniform warmth of deep affection. Ottmar at last understood what she lacked. He perceived that there was a middle path, that he must be at once less cold and less warm, to obtain entire control over her. During the time that his intellect was in the ascendant, he endeavored to assume a more affectionate tone, and the oftener this happened the better it pleased *Heinrich* to press his lips to the brow which contained the thoughts that delighted him, and stroke the hair that veiled it, while it afforded him still higher enjoyment to study in her classic form and features the idea of the beautiful. She became a living work of art to him, and as art is the first mediator between mind and matter, he began to rejoice in her physical charms from an artistic stand-point. *Henri*, on the contrary, ennobled the expression of his love and appropriated more and more of the impulses of Cornelia's soul. Thus intellect began to grow warmer, sensuality to be spiritualized. The separation between them had been lessened by struggling for a common object; if his moral consciousness had ripened in the same proportion as the two extremes approached a normal union, he would have adopted a different course of action. But the individual conflict was not yet entirely settled, and the moral one could not be decided. His mistakes and transgressions had proceeded solely from the gulf in his nature; only when the parts were united in one harmonious whole could they be expelled, for right and truth can only thrive in a soul at peace with itself.

Months elapsed, and the political event which was to decide his own fate and Cornelia's drew near. Ottmar awaited it with eager suspense. He longed to have this uncertain condition of affairs ended. He perceived more and more clearly that to possess Cornelia would outweigh his present position, and made himself familiar with the thought of sacrificing it, if driven to extremities. But the appointment of minister cast a weight into the scale of his ambition which outbalanced the feeble efforts of his conscience; as minister he could not inflict upon himself and the court the disgrace of a politically suspicious mesalliance,--then he would induce Cornelia to make the sacrifice, and he did not doubt that she would do so.

XVIII
CORNELIA AND OTTILIE

Cornelia did not suspect what a sword was hanging over her head, did not question the near or distant future, but lived wholly in the present moment. One thing alone she did not forget,--her visits to the prisoners. She devoted the usual time to them; the place where she first saw Ottmar had become sacred to her, and by her mournful labors for the unfortunate men, her patience with their sufferings and obstinacy, she believed that she was paying fate a tribute for the happiness enjoyed in her love. She rarely appeared in public, for she could not bear the glances that accused her of guilt of which she knew herself to be innocent. She therefore no longer entered a church or theatre; her church was her love, her God in Heinrich's breast, and her studies with him conjured up a world of beauty. She wanted nothing, needed nothing, but him. She made no subtle inquiries and no longer doubted him; he was everything to her, and she knew that with him she should lose all.

Thus it sounded like a voice from another world when one day a "stranger lady" was announced. Who could visit her still? The lady entered, and fixed a half-timid, half-questioning, glance upon Cornelia.

"You are Fräulein Erwing?"

"That is my name. With whom have I the honor of speaking?"

"I have come on an errand from her Highness the princess."

Cornelia gazed dreamily into eyes whose blue vied with the ribbons on the stranger's hat.

"Her Highness wishes to make your acquaintance, and begs you to pay her a visit to-morrow afternoon at four o'clock."

The young girl's voice trembled slightly, and she looked expectantly at Cornelia. The latter stood motionless with amazement, almost terror. What did Ottilie want of her? Röschen--for she alone could execute this confidential commission--was unable to turn her eyes from the noble figure its sweeping black robes.

"Can you not at least tell what has procured me the great happiness of being permitted to wait upon the princess?" asked Cornelia.

"No, Fräulein; I only know you will be received with the greatest kindness, and that only sincere interest induced the princess to see you."

"Say to her Highness that I am truly grateful to her, and that I will wait upon her to-morrow at the time appointed."

"Her Highness will be very glad. Farewell."

"Excuse me, Fräulein; one question more: is your name Röschen?"

A deep blush suffused the lovely face. "Yes."

Cornelia, deeply moved, went up to her, took her hands, and pressed a kiss upon her fresh lips. "We have known each other a long time, have we not?"

Röschen was surprised and greatly agitated. "Yes, yes!" she exclaimed, pressing Cornelia's hand to her lips. "Let me thank you for all you have done for Albert. We can never repay you for it; but the dear God will know how to reward you."

Cornelia gazed into her eyes for a long time with ever-increasing interest. "You ought to have become Albert's wife: the poor fellow has suffered so much for your sake."

"I cannot leave the princess, and besides,"--Röschen hesitated a little,-- "besides, he did not wish it so very much. Ah, I understand it now: he who has once seen you can never love another."

"Oh, my dear girl, what are you saying? You will be reconciled to each other again, or I shall regret what I did for Albert." She glanced anxiously at the clock; for it was almost the hour when Ottmar might be expected.

This did not escape Röschen's natural delicacy of feeling. "I am detaining you, dear Fräulein, and the princess is waiting. Farewell! your kindness has made me very happy."

"Will you not come again, that we may continue our talk?"

"With the greatest pleasure. But there is one thing more I had almost forgotten: the princess begs you to tell no one that you have been requested to come to her. She will refuse all visitors to-morrow on the plea of indisposition, and fears people might take it amiss if she----"

"I understand," interrupted Cornelia, "and will say nothing."

After Röschen had gone she stood for a long time absorbed in thought. The solution of this enigma could not be guessed. She rejoiced over the strange event, for she had loved Ottilie ever since she knew her relations with Ottmar; yet it grieved her to think that she would perceive at every breath a happiness denied the princess. Suppose her eyes should rest upon Cornelia with sorrowful jealousy as her fortunate rival.

The following day and the appointed hour came. In great agitation, and not without a little timidity at the idea of the grandeur that surrounded Ottilie, Cornelia entered the magnificent apartments of the princess. The groom of the chambers conducted her through a long succession of rooms. At last he paused, pointed to a half-open glass door, and disappeared. The silken portières were drawn aside, and Ottilie stood before Cornelia!

A long pause followed. Both looked at each other in breathless suspense. Ottilie was paler than ever; Cornelia deeply flushed. At last Ottilie gently took her hand and murmured almost inaudibly, with a sort of sorrowful satisfaction, "Yes; so my fancy pictured you! So you must be."

"Your Highness bestows upon me so great a favor that I seek in vain for words to express my joyful surprise and gratitude."

"There can be no question of gratitude here; but no doubt you were surprised that I should request you to visit me." Ottilie seated herself, and drew Cornelia down upon the sofa beside her. "I have a great and important matter to intrust to you, Fräulein, and believe I can read in your eyes, an your lofty brow, the certainty that I have applied to the right person." Cornelia looked at Ottilie in eager expectation. After a short pause, the latter continued: "Accident, Fräulein, or rather destiny, made me acquainted with your labors among the prisoners. I perceived with admiration how you had aimed at results which the wisest provisions of the law could not attain; how you were the first to strew over the lifeless forms of punishment the living germs from which sprang new life, remorse, and amendment. You will believe me when I say that no mere idle curiosity, but heartfelt sympathy, impelled me to make the acquaintance of so remarkable a character. I will even confess that I trembled lest I should find your person did not harmonize with the ideal I had formed." She paused, and once more gazed long and earnestly into Cornelia's eyes; then bent towards her and pressed a kiss upon her brow. "Thank God that I now dare love you in reality, as I have already done in fancy!"

"Your Highness," began Cornelia, deeply moved as she sought for words, while her bosom rose and fell more rapidly, "I know I do not deserve what you say; and yet a blissful content, for which I can find no expression, overflows my whole nature. You see me in the light that streams from yourself; but its rays fall upon my soul also, and wake their concealed powers of good, which fill me with pride,--not for what I have done, but for what I shall accomplish. God knows I performed these works of mercy without any desire or hope of recognition. I have long supposed I labored wholly unobserved; but there is so great a recompense in this moment that it would crown the toil of a whole life; and I will struggle all my life to deserve it."

"You are enthusiastic, my child; but this very enthusiasm makes you what you are; so I will accept the flattery contained in your words as the tribute every noble soul offers to the ideal towards which we all strive."

"Oh, not as that alone, your Highness! Deign to accept the childlike, humble reverence of a heart which has long looked up to you as the noblest of women. I know not whether I ought to express in words what has been hovering upon my lips ever since the first moment of our meeting. It might, perhaps, be a great offense against etiquette, but I hope your Highness will regard the essence rather than the form."

"I hope you will do me the honor to be assured of it," interposed Ottilie, with a smile.

"Well, then, permit me to tell your Highness that I have long loved you with my whole heart."

"If that is true, my child, I rejoice to hear it. Love is a voluntary gift, which, whether deserved or not, we are always permitted to receive. I thank you for it; yes, I thank you from the inmost depths of a lonely heart."

"Ah, if you were not a princess!" murmured Cornelia, involuntarily.

"My dear child, how often I have said that myself! God has placed me in this position only to test my strength; for that which compensates others in a similar station for their secret lack of happiness--delight in splendor and grandeur, sovereignty and renown--is denied me. Nothing has any charm for me; my joys are rooted solely in the heart; and even these are sparingly meted out. The gulf which severs the princess from her subjects does not exist in my soul, and cannot separate my affection from them. I love men, respect their rights, admire their works, and thus stand ever alone upon my lofty height, consumed with vain longings, and stretching out my arms across the abyss which yawns between me and the warm hearts of humanity."

"Poor princess!" said Cornelia, earnestly.

"Yes, poor princess," replied Ottilie, her eyes resting dreamily upon Cornelia's beautiful features.

"But your Highness can taste great joys, and satisfy your benevolence by your power of benefiting so many thousands."

"Do you think so, my dear child?" asked Ottilie, with a sorrowful smile.

"That was the one thing for which I always envied princes," continued Cornelia, "which always made sovereignty appear so beautiful, so alluring."

"And the thought tempted me, too," said Ottilie, lowering her voice to a scarcely audible whisper, "when I allowed myself to be wedded to the prince; but I was disappointed, as I have been in so many other things. Believe me, my child, it is sad to be compelled to look an helplessly, while the right way of making a nation happy is earnestly sought, but always missed. The prince's views are so immovable, and so entirely opposed to my own, that I have given up the effort to exert any influence whatever for the welfare of my country, although my heart bleeds for it. I know that no good can come for either party; I see a time approaching when the dissension will increase to such a degree that one or the other must fall a victim. I shall not live to see it; if I am anxious, it is only for my subjects, my husband, and-- perhaps my children," she paused. "God grant that I may not be denied the opportunity of teaching them a better understanding of their times!"

"But cannot the joyful blessings of the many to whom your Highness gives special aid offer you some compensation?"

"Even this is limited. Every one who makes his narrow circle happy in his own way receives more pleasure from his efforts than I: the princess lacks the power of immediate bestowal and reception; but this directness is the source of all the joys of the soul. If you, my child, do good according to your circumstances, you will be rewarded a thousandfold more than I, though I should give a thousand times more. The poor man, whose sufferings you instantly relieve, can show you his joy; it is not only the alms, but your manner of bestowing them, that console him, and the tears sparkling in his eyes certainly reward you far more than I am recompensed by the official addresses of thanks and humble bows of delegates from whole parishes I have saved from misery. I am well aware that we should not perform charitable works for the sake of gratitude, nor do I; but it is so natural to be cheered by the success of a good deed, the same sympathy which induces us to alleviate the sorrows of others makes us long to spare the joys we have prepared. This is denied me; etiquette always stands between me and the hearts of my subjects, and with its icy breath transforms every voluntary show of feeling into the unvarying mien of reverence. You see, my child, the halo your imagination spread around sovereignty is vanishing more and more." She paused, and her large, tearful eyes gazed sorrowfully at Cornelia. "I shall depend upon your well-known greatness of soul to communicate the purport of this conversation to no one."

"I thank you for your confidence, your Highness, and will justify it."

"I believe you," said Ottilie. "And now let me proceed to the principal matter. I do so with a heavy heart, for fondly as I have become attached to you, I must now make a proposal whose acceptance will deprive me of your society, because it depends upon your leaving the city. But I have learned to sacrifice my own wishes for the welfare of others, and will not be so selfish as to claim your presence here when it may prove the salvation of so many unfortunates."

Cornelia gazed at Ottilie in speechless expectation. She felt afraid, for she had gathered nothing from the princess's words except an intention to send her out of the city.

Ottilie clasped Cornelia's hand with evident emotion, and continued: "I have founded in T----, whose lovely scenery seemed peculiarly adapted for it, an institution for the reformation of female criminals, who, on being discharged from the custody of the law, perhaps wholly destitute of means, and alone in the world, would be led to enter the path of wrong anew in order to escape hunger and despair. The idea is not new; it has already been attempted in Germany many times, usually with very indifferent success. All such undertakings require not only money, skillful and conscientious management, and carefully watched exercises, but a genial spirit and loving heart to breathe life into the empty forms, and rouse in the penitents themselves an impulse of repentance, for whose development the peace prevailing in the institution, the pious exercises, and useful occupations will afford a suitable soil. But how many women are there who unite to the highest qualities of the heart a sound understanding, and are noble enough to devote them to such a purpose? You, Cornelia, are such a being; you possess the requisite grandeur of soul and self-denial, and your heart beats warmly for the moral sufferings and infirmities of mankind: you have already proved it. Do you now understand what I wish to ask of you? You shall secure blessings and prosperity for my subjects, you shall receive the position of directress of the institution at T----, and I am sure that this sphere of influence among the poor wanderers of your own sex will suit you far better than to associate with the rude, degraded men in the prison."

Cornelia looked down. "I see with painful confusion," she began, at last, "how greatly your Highness has over-rated me, and how little I deserve the favor you have permitted to fall to my lot in consequence of these expectations. Will your Highness most graciously permit me to correct the last opinion you expressed, that I must prefer to associate with female criminals rather than with men. I feel far less sympathy and interest for a guilty woman; for she has much less excuse than a man. He is created stronger and more ungovernable by nature, therefore his passions must be more violent, his desires fiercer, his acts and thoughts ruder, more energetic, while the moral support given him is not proportionally greater than that of the woman. On the contrary, the moral instincts are more vivid in the latter, and her moral horizon more contracted. How much worse, then, must she be, to sink into crimes which often have no foundation in her nature! No doubt, woman is also the cause of many crimes,--or rather womanly weaknesses; yet these are as repulsive to me as the crimes committed at the expense of all womanly feeling."

"That is a very harsh judgment," Ottilie interposed.

"I am not harsh, your Highness; I condemn such feeble creatures less, but I have not sufficient sympathy, even for them, to be able to devote myself to them with the necessary self-sacrifice. Besides, I should be unable to believe that my efforts in their behalf would be attended with sufficient success, for the same weakness that permitted them to fall into sin would, it true, make them easily susceptible to repentance, but expose them just as readily to any evil influence as soon as they were left to themselves."

"That may unfortunately be true in many cases. But are you not attracted towards the poor creatures who have fallen victims to the highest earthly power,--who have erred through love?"

Cornelia started, and a deep blush suffused her face; she knew not why. Her conscience was pure, and yet she could not bear the clear, penetrating glance of the princess. Why did she feel so startled by that word? Why did the look that accompanied it weigh upon her brow like a secret sentence? Surely she had not erred through love, but she had not been heedful of appearances. Suppose Ottilie judged by appearances, and had spoken with a meaning? Oh, that she could banish this treacherous blush! Must it not seem to Ottilie the token of a bad conscience? She could not bear that. She raised her head and looked the princess steadily in the face.

"Your Highness, the law does not punish the errors of love; but if a woman falls so low that she commits from love crimes which make her amenable to the law, she becomes as detestable to me as all others. You see I lack the first requisite for the vocation your Highness did me the honor to propose,--the true Christian charity which does not judge but pardons."

"But which has already been so touchingly proved by your care for the prisoners of state," replied Ottilie. "I will not be indiscreet, but I cannot help remarking that the reason you have just given cannot be the only one which withholds you from a vocation of Christian charity you have hitherto voluntarily chosen, under circumstances far more favorable to you; for your labors in my institution would not only secure you every pecuniary advantage you could ask,--not only win gratifying success with those intrusted to your care,--but make you famous in the eyes of the would.

Your ambition, if you possess any, would also obtain the most brilliant satisfaction abroad the name and spirit of Cornelia Erwing could soar away from the pleasant work- and prayer-rooms of the institution far more easily than through the gloomy, impenetrable dungeon-walls of the prison."

"Oh, your Highness, pardon the freedom of my words!" said Cornelia, with noble pride; "but you now undervalue as much as you lately overrated me. Does your Highness really suppose that these prospects could induce me to prefer laboring in the institution at T---- to my present sphere of influence in the prison? Do you imagine a pecuniary advantage I do not even need, or ambition for the cheaply-bought fame of being a Good Samaritan, which every hypocrite can obtain, would induce me to do anything to which my own feelings did not urge me? No, your Highness, you cannot think so meanly of one to whom, a few moments ago, you condescended to show the greatest favor. I have no other motive for my actions than my heart. In this alone is rooted my strength or my weakness, as you may choose to term it,-- perhaps my selfishness. But all selfishness that arises solely from calculating reason is foreign to my nature; therefore, when I tell you that my heart does not draw me to the Christian work in T----, your Highness may be assured that no worldly advantage would lead me to it; yet, if the contrary were the case, I would joyfully renounce every material reward."

"I believe you," said Ottilie; "but may I ask what has so strongly attracted you towards the prisoners?"

"Here, also, I only followed the impulse of my own feelings. Love for one of them led me accidentally to the scene of his misery. Love for the individual taught me to understand and pity the sorrows of his companions. Ordinary crimes would have terrified me and filled me with horror. I should have been as little inclined to aid in reforming a debased man as a base woman, but at that time the prisoners were principally political criminals. The idea for which most of them had struggled and erred, to which my father and my dead lover were martyrs, was necessarily sacred to my heart; and although I admit that it may have been erroneous,--even pernicious in the extremes and manner in which they strove to establish it,--I could neither condemn nor abhor those who had suffered for the same conviction to which my father had sacrificed himself. At first I employed my efforts only in behalf of the political prisoners. An accident, however, made me acquainted with a--as people usually say--'common murderer'; and I found in him a weak-minded, but thoroughly noble man, who had been driven by the force of circumstances to do what is recognized among all nations, not only as a right, but a duty; he punished the tempter of his betrothed bride!" She paused a moment, while again a deep blush suffused her face.

Ottilie, too, blushed slightly, and murmured, "I know the particulars of the occurrence."

"That convinced me," continued Cornelia, "how many good and evil powers can exist in the broad breast of a man at the same time,--how mighty the impulses often are to commit crimes which arise in his life; and from that moment I went into the cells of all who justified this view."

"And were there many of them?" asked Ottilie.

"No, your Highness. With the exception of the political prisoners, at the utmost only or five among a hundred and twelve; but these few were sufficient to confirm my assertion."

"And among a hundred female convicts, would you not perhaps find four or five deserving of your sympathy?"

"Very possibly, your Highness; but I could not devote myself only to these: I should be compelled to care for the many wicked creatures who could only arouse my loathing and abhorrence. I have always considered my labors in the prison as an episode, and only employed a few hours of the day in them; but here I should be compelled to devote my whole time--nay, my life--to a vocation which could not satisfy me. I am not one of those persons who do anything systematically, who make the work of mercy a trade,--a mechanical, daily occupation,--in which, through habit, they become so dull that they scarcely feel the blessing of their labors. I wish to perform it freely and earnestly, whenever and wherever I find an opportunity: and whose destiny does not afford one? I do not even want you to be obliged to make it for me,--it must come as a revelation from the inmost heart of life; and when I seize upon it, it must be a quick, joyful deed, gushing full and warm from the depths of a loving breast. Thus alone can it make me and others happy; thus alone can I practice charity."

Ottilie clasped Cornelia's hand, and gazed into her eyes with increasing delight.

"This may be selfish," the latter continued, "but it is natural, and I cannot make myself different from what I am. I want events, emotions, and--love. I want art pleasures. I feel the pulsations of an ever-advancing civilization throbbing within me, and am ennobled by my enthusiasm for everything beautiful which it has created. With this tide of life swelling in my breast, I cannot bury myself behind the walls of an institution for penitents,--cannot turn my delighted eyes from the loftiest model of human greatness to fix them forever upon the lowest caricatures of depravity. In the monotony of such a life I should die of longing for the warm human love which has hitherto streamed forth from the noble hearts that surrounded me. I see no moral obligation to do so, for I am proud enough, your Highness, to believe that God has destined me to make a good and noble being happy. Does it not seem to your Highness far more beautiful to devote a life to this purpose, rather than allow it to wither away in an institution for the reformation of degraded creatures?"

Cornelia had scarcely ended when she found herself clasped in Ottilie's arms.

"Forgive me," said the princess, with deep emotion. "I have esteemed you highly, but not known you; now I understand you. You shall hear no more from me of an expectation so ill suited to your character. You are born for higher things; you belong to the great band of those who are appointed to restore the ideal balance of the world. You are right. Fate allots to each his sphere of labor, and you are to make the happiness of an equally gifted nature. To seek to withdraw you from this object would be committing a wrong against him for whom God created you; and, in truth, he must love the man to whom he has given you for a companion." Again a short pause followed. "Let those for whom life has no longer any hopes, whom it has robbed of all the heart of woman needs, devote themselves to the vocation I have mentioned. For you many great joys and duties are still reserved,--but do not deceive yourself, perhaps many sorrows also."

"Oh, I have never blinded myself to that!" replied Cornelia. "I do not fear them. No one is spared, and what all suffer will not be too heavy for me."

"It is easy for us to say so. God grant you may be spared the hours when we doubt our own strength! Shall I be frank?" she asked, with sudden resolution; and then continued, without waiting for a reply, "I thought I could guard you from such sorrows when I selected you for the position at T----. I believed you to be under dangerous influences, and as I had become deeply interested in you from the descriptions I had heard, thought it any duty to constitute myself your protectress. But I now feel ashamed in your presence, for I am convinced that you are too noble to need my protection; you have the best support in yourself. It depends upon you to make the power that will be exerted over you beneficial or otherwise, and I know now it will be the former."

"Oh, your Highness," cried Cornelia, her eyes dim with tears, "I thank you for those words! But I beseech you not to overvalue me at the expense of another whose influence I have thus far felt as one rich in blessing. I should despise myself if I did not gratefully remember all the beauty and goodness I have received through the very intercourse you feared for me. Least of all, your Highness, could I bear to see the heart which is the dearest thing on earth to me misunderstood by you." She was silent in alarm. Ottilie coughed and pressed her handkerchief to her lips, then removed it and looked at Cornelia with a smile. Cornelia could not speak: she was gasping for breath; she had seen blood on the transparent folds.

"Do you suppose," Ottilie began, as quietly as if nothing had happened,--"do you really suppose I misunderstand this heart? Ah, no! But I see its faults, and wished to warn you of them. God knows whether he has a truer friend than I. As long as he lived at my court in H---- I devoted the most kindly care to him; but my influence was too weak. Perhaps the blissful task of ennobling him is assigned to her whom he loves. May God bless and strengthen you for this work! And of whatever nature the faults you will discover in the course of time may be, beware of them; but do not let yourself be discouraged, they are only the goblin shapes of his twofold nature, which will melt into nothing as soon as your pure, noble spirit is united to his better self. Bear with him faithfully, for he will love you as he never did any one, and must be utterly wretched without you!"

She rose. Her cheeks glowed, and her eyes again beamed with the unearthly expression of a spirit about to take its flight from the earth.

Cornelia kissed her hand with deep emotion. "Your Highness, I stand before you as if in the presence of the guardian angel of my betrothed, and take a solemn vow that nothing shall part me from him except himself! I knew his faults before his good qualities, and they were so great they made me forget the latter. I began by despising, and ended by loving him; and if I should lose faith in him again I should die!"

"Oh, my child, we outlive a great deal! May God protect you and him! Farewell. Remember me kindly until I can see you again." She dismissed Cornelia with a warm embrace. "He will not corrupt her; she will save him," she murmured. "My God, I thank thee!"

"Are you come at last?" cried a well-known voice, as Cornelia entered the room. "Where have you been? I have been waiting for you an hour."

"And you are so much accustomed to have me devote myself entirely to you," said Cornelia, as she laid her hat and shawl aside, "that you are angry because I have given even a few hours to some one else." She sat down beside him, drew back his head, and gazed with winning tenderness into his clouded face. "Must I ask whether you have come to-day as a schoolmaster or a lover? The book lying beside you, and your stern manner, predict the former; but I must confess that I have no mind to give to anything except the wonderful event of this day."

"Well, what has happened to you?" asked *Heinrich*, resting his head upon her shoulder. "Tell me."

"I have just come from the princess."

Heinrich started up in astonishment.

"She offered me the position of directress at T----."

"Ah, she wanted to get you out of the City! She is jealous," he murmured.

"Oh, how meanly you think of that noble soul! She had other reasons which I cannot discuss more particularly and indeed, Heinrich, she is an angel!"

"What answer did you make to her proposal?"

"I rejected it."

"There I see my own Cornelia."

"Oh, is this the first time you understand me? I think you ought to have done so before."

"You are right; you have already made greater sacrifices,--if it is a sacrifice you are making for me."

"Of course it is. I do not know whether I might not have accepted Ottilie's proposal if, after Veronica's death, I had been left alone with my heart full of philanthropic enthusiasm and without your love."

"In any case, you would have been committing a great piece of folly."

"According to your ideas, but not mine. You will never believe how much happiness the good we do to others can bestow; and yet you are not happy, although all your life you have lived only for yourself."

Heinrich sat with his eyes fixed upon the floor.

"Believe me, dearest, the benefits we confer upon others recoil upon ourselves, as well as the wrongs we inflict upon them; and as often as, mindful only of our own advantage, we are compelled to injure others, so often we shall reap a curse instead of a blessing."

Heinrich's eyes were still more gloomy.

"He who wishes to grasp and keep happiness solely for himself will find it quickly fade, as we cannot make a flower our own by plucking it and placing it in the breast; it will only gladden us a few minutes, and then wither uselessly. Only when you plant happiness in the soil of other hearts, and share their joys, will it bear flowers and fruits for you. The law of multiplication does not merely extend through the material, but the spiritual world. All the elements of our being are united in us, and in this unity they collect their strength, but are intended to be scattered abroad when they develop, so luxuriantly that we can no longer seek the limits of our being within the narrow bounds of our own hearts, but in the wide sphere of our beneficent influence. The egotist never knows the satisfaction found in the execution of every great or insignificant law of the universe, for he shuts himself mentally within himself, and draws the juices from the soil which he is rooted without ever enriching it. He believes it well to receive without giving, and yet feels withered within. He does not understand himself, bitterly accuses the world and destiny which have thus insulated and placed him in a false position, and does not perceive that the blessing he vainly expected from others ought to have emanated from himself!"

Heinrich started up. "Yes, my Cornelia, in many instances you have hit the mark wonderfully. But, believe me, my child, the sphere in which I live is not adapted to that beneficent expansion of self. It is, in reality, a sphere of egotism, in which one must greedily cling to his own advantage if he would not have it torn from him. There is no individual connection between us diplomats, we are only united by our functions as constituent parts of the great mechanism which drives the machinery of the government; and neither can the heart develop warm benevolence when one has accustomed himself to look upon nations merely as the material to be manufactured by this machinery into a well-regulated whole. Imagine the feelings of a man, a statesman. You speak of diffusing his own character abroad: I know what you understand by it; it is all very noble and beautiful for the philanthropic members of the masses, but it is the duty of statesmen to guide and govern the populace, and we must not mingle among those we rule. We, too, devote our strength to them, but we associate a more abstract idea with the word than you sanguine philanthropists. You understand it to mean only the people, but we the government, the law, the extension of the interests of trade, the protection of the highest interests in foreign countries,--in short, everything upon which the prosperity of a country depends. To you the nation has a personal, to us only a political, individuality; you are incessantly caring for its position towards the throne, but we for its position towards the world!" He looked at Cornelia, who was hanging upon his words in breathless expectation. "Well, my Cornelia, do we not both live for the whole,--each in our own way?"

"There are your sophisms again, against which my natural intuition strives with so much difficulty. I confess that none of your words have made any other impression than the sorrowful one of self-deception. Heinrich! Heinrich! what will become of you if you accustom yourself to make sport of truth? You have described how a statesman thinks and feels, but not how you think and feel. Of course, there are statesmen who have the welfare of the people at heart; but such men cannot live in a country like this, or they must be short-sighted enough to see happiness in despotism. But you are not so blind. Heinrich, you understand the conditions of a higher national development, and know you are working against it; you are sinning against the most sacred rights of humanity, yet say you are laboring for the whole. What do you understand by this word? To you it is merely an empty sound; for that which gives it life and meaning to us, anxiety for the common welfare, is unknown to you. Do not say you live for the state, if not for the people! Is there a state without a nation? Establish one with ideas instead of men; govern these, and you will have the same reason to boast of your labors for 'the whole.'"

"You are becoming violent and unjust, my Cornelia."

"It always makes me indignant when I see you palliating such faults as these. I can forgive the worst offense if frankly confessed and recognized, but to a palliated error I am unrelenting. Forgive me, if I was violent," she pleaded, clinging fondly to him. "Come, kiss me; you are so cold to-day." She drew him nearer her as they sat on the sofa. "Let us talk quietly; I feel more anxious to discuss this subject fully to-day than ever before. You love power. The impulse of asserting itself is associated with every important endowment; it is a stimulus for it to develop and become of value to the world. Nothing is more just and natural than that you should feel it also. But in you it has taken a false direction; you perceive power only in your present position. But what power? It was voluntarily placed in your hands from above, and arbitrarily endured by the nation; so it is a purely external one, without change of action or spiritual echo. You are conscious of it yourself only by the possibility of having your will executed by means of a few strokes of the pen on a sheet of paper, and extending it further than is permitted to the private citizen. Accident has given you this power, accident may deprive you of it again; therefore it neither makes you happy nor satisfies you. There is only one real pleasure of that nature,--mastery over minds; this can neither be given to us nor taken away, we must win and retain it by our own strength. And what pride can be more noble than that we take in the result of our own merits? Cease to be a machine among machines, and become conscious of the privileges of independent effort; be at least a man among men. Leave your present residence and return to your former home; go into the Chambers, there your intellect and personal magnetism will produce a great effect upon the multitude; there you will first learn to know the manifold charms to be found in such a direct subjugation of minds! Descend from your false height, and let yourself be borne by the hands of the people to the summit of a powerfully increasing development of civilization. You have hitherto served a prince, while you gave laws to the nation; you can henceforth give orders to a prince, while you are a king in the hearts of the people." She rested her cheek against his, and asked, with loving emotion, "Does not this prospect charm you?"

"If all this could be done in reality as easily as in your vivid fancy, my glorious Cornelia, it might well charm me. But I am a practical man; I shall not resign a secure and brilliant position to, perhaps, obtain nothing except the favor of miserable proletarians, or cast aside the moral and political credit I possess, with the probability of losing, by another change of opinion, all trust here and elsewhere! You cannot ask that of me. Let him who has nothing at stake make the desperate venture, but I have not only the advantage but the honor of an established career to lose."

"Honor and advantage,--but happiness? Oh, Heinrich! you have no happiness to lose, for you have never possessed any; and you will only save your honor before yourself and God when you begin a new life. So what do you risk? I do not ask you to proclaim your change of opinion at once to all the world. Leave the service of the government, withdraw to your estates, and live there as a private citizen; win the sympathies of the whole neighborhood, and come forth from your seclusion as a deputy. How can you be threatened with any loss of honor? Be assured the world is not so degenerate as to refuse its esteem for an honest action. You will not fall here, you will voluntarily resign your brilliant position for the sake of your convictions: a manly deed which demands and will receive recognition. Your former party will hail you with joy, and trust you on account of the sacrifice you made to return to it; and in a short time you will have obtained all you now think one of my fantastic ideas. Oh, believe me, I see clearly the path you must choose,--the only one that will lead to happiness!"

Heinrich released himself from Cornelia's encircling arms, and, starting up, went to the window and leaned his brow thoughtfully against the panes. Cornelia watched him in silence. She left him entirely to himself, for she knew he was inaccessible to tenderness when anything occupied his mind. This was the mood to which she had found it so difficult to accustom herself, and now it appeared especially harsh. Suddenly he turned, took up his hat, and kissed Cornelia on the forehead. "Farewell!"

"Heinrich!" she exclaimed, "are you going already? Have I offended you so deeply?"

"Not offended, but you have given me much food for thought; roused a new conflict within me. Leave me to myself to-day."

"Why especially to-day? What does that mean?"

"You will learn when the time comes."

"Another secret! Oh, Heinrich! You never share anything with me except your tenderness and the poetic effusions of your vivid imagination. I am shut out from your intellectual life, and know nothing of it except what my own penetration enables me to guess."

"Do not be angry, my child; sooner or later a time will come when there will no longer be anything between us, when you will obtain possession of my whole existence." With these words he kissed her again, and left the room without looking back.

"Sooner or later a time must come, when--" Cornelia repeated the words. A roseate flush of joy suffused the grave face. Was not the end of her humiliation approaching? Was--she scarcely ventured to confess what sweet, proud hopes these words aroused. Why had her conversation made so strange an impression upon him? Her heart throbbed expectantly: would her fate perhaps be decided that day?

It was decided. *Heinrich's* inmost soul had been stirred by Cornelia's ideas. The thought of playing a great part in the Chamber, of joining the new and undeniably strong movement, charmed him. He could find more change, more excitement, in this path than in the worn-out interests of his court life, and possibly even attain the object of his ambition,--the portfolio. He could marry Cornelia, noble, beautiful girl, without injury to his plans; nay, she would even be necessary to him in this career. Perhaps he might yet be a happy man. If the prince did not take him into the ministry, there was nothing better for him to do than to exchange the worn-out old life for a new one; and by the time he reached home he almost wished it. As he entered his room, absorbed in thought, Anton handed him a paper. He started as he read it,--it was his nomination as minister of foreign affairs. The die was cast.

XIX
THE CATASTROPHE

The following day Cornelia awoke with the first glimmer of dawn. The vague expectation excited by *Heinrich's* ambiguous words had kept her long awake, and now drove her from her couch earlier than usual. She made a hasty toilet and hurried out into the autumn morning. It was damp and gloomy; a thick fog made earth and sky vanish in a gray cloud; the withered leaves fell from the wet bushes with a low rustle as her garments brushed against them. She did not heed it. Spring was in her heart, and the warm life in her breast seemed to glow through the chilling scene around her. Mechanically she entered the path she was most accustomed to follow. It led to the churchyard. She walked through the long rows of graves, apparently the only living creature in the broad place of death; but as she approached the well she suddenly saw, at a few paces' distance, two grave-diggers lowering a little coffin into the earth. She approached and asked, "Whose child is this you are burying so entirely alone?"

"It is illegitimate," said one of the men, dryly.

Cornelia shuddered. "Oh, how terrible!"

"Yes, it's a pity for silly girls to allow themselves to be so blinded. If they thought more of their honor, they wouldn't meet with misfortune. And the poor children always have to suffer for it. This one was put out to board with strangers, who neglected it so that it fell sick and died. The girl to whom it belonged was obliged to go out to service again because her lover deserted her before the child was born, so she couldn't trouble herself about it, and was obliged to leave it to die."

"Poor, poor child!" thought Cornelia, looking at the grave with tearful eyes. "Usually when a child is born it is received with joy and love; but shame stood beside your cradle, shame hovers over your lonely grave. No happy father took you in his arms, no gladsome mother's eyes answered your first trusting smile; nobody wanted you, and the only one who loved you was obliged to deny you until God had compassion upon you and took you to himself. Now your forsaken mother may perhaps be stretching out her arms despairingly to grasp the empty air, and must conceal her anguish as deeply as her darling has just been buried in the earth. Terrible fate! May God protect every loving woman from it!" Tears flowed more and more quickly down her cheeks; she turned away and wept out the emotion that had seized upon her on the graves of Veronica and Reinhold. As she went home she noticed for the first time that it was misty and dreary, and entered the house in a graver mood than she had left it.

"Marie," she said to her chambermaid, "while I was at the churchyard it occurred to me that this is Veronica's birthday. Order some wreaths for her grave; I wish to have it adorned on such anniversaries."

The hours dragged slowly away. Ottmar did not appear at the usual time; but instead the evening paper announced his appointment as minister. That was why he had been so absent-minded yesterday, why his words had contained a vague promise of a speedy decision of her fate; so this was the secret. Surely the turning-point in her life must now be reached; he had obtained what he desired, and might dare to marry. Her heart beat more and more violently. Quarter of an hour after quarter of an hour passed away. He could not come today: he probably had too much to do; and yet she longed so anxiously to see him.

Her servants asked whether they should carry the wreaths the gardener had just skillfully arranged to the grave. "Yes, go," said Cornelia, absently; "no one will come to-day now." But scarcely had the maids left the house when the bell was impatiently pulled. Cornelia opened the door with trembling expectation, and sank upon Ottmar's breast.

Henri had just met the two servants in the street. Had Cornelia ventured to send them away when she knew he was coming? or was she preparing to leave the house? He could form no conclusion, but explained the incident in his own favor; knew himself to be alone with Cornelia, and gave himself up entirely to his own excited feelings.

"You are a minister," she began. "You have now obtained that for which you struggled. It will afford you no greater happiness than your present position; but I perceive this throws too heavy a weight into the scale not to outbalance my counsels."

"Come here, my Cornelia do not let us discuss such matters now," said *Henri*, drawing her upon his knee. "I can do nothing to-day but look at and caress you. Do not grudge me the sweet refreshment after long hours of burdensome ceremonies and fatiguing business. My mind is so wearied that

I can no longer think of anything, only feel that I clasp you to my heart, that you are mine, wholly mine! Is it not so?"

Cornelia leant silently upon his breast. "At last, at last he will utter the word I have so longed to hear!" she thought, clinging to him in a fond embrace. He pressed his lips to her ear, and whispered so low that she could not understand him, but felt he must be making promises of eternal love and tenderness, while his hot breath bewildered her like the fumes of opium. Then a word fell upon her ear more distinctly, causing a thrill never felt before. He had called her his "wife." Overwhelmed with happiness she closed her eyes, her head sank upon his shoulder, and tears of unspeakable delight stole from beneath her long lashes. In this name, for which she knew but one meaning, he had expressed the fulfillment of her fairest hopes. She remained in this blissful confidence a moment longer. *Henri's* voice grew still more persuasive, fell still more distinctly upon Cornelia's ear. Suddenly the veil which had surrounded her soul was torn away; she was forced to hear, forced to understand, what she had never been willing to believe. Springing up, she stood before *Henri* as if frozen into a statue; there was neither life nor color in the face blanched to the pallor of marble, save in the eyes, which rested with increasing firmness and brilliancy upon his startled countenance.

Henri had prepared himself for an outburst of indignation or grief; this speechless amazement, this frozen horror, first revealed to him how deep her trust had been, and how he had ascribed many things to levity, or believed them a triumph of love, which had been rooted wholly in the security of this unshaken confidence. He perceived he had prepared Cornelia badly for his plans; but it was too late: he could not unsay what had been said. At last her lips moved, and word after word began to struggle through them.

"So this is the meaning you give to the sacred words 'my wife,'--in this way I shall not be denied the privilege of becoming yours? This relation does not dishonor--the--minister!"

"Cornelia," cried *Henri*, with a slight shudder, "not this scorn! I cannot bear it. Do you not understand that I have inviolable duties towards my position and the dignity with which my prince trustfully invested me? that there are barriers far more difficult for a man to overleap than for a woman to pass the bounds prescribed by what we call morality? Speak, Cornelia: could you expect me, the representative of the highest aristocracy in the country, the supporter of the most rigid despotic principles of government, to suddenly present to the astonished world as my wife the daughter of a fugitive traitor, who has herself hitherto moved exclusively in plebeian and democratic circles? Would not your pure brow flush beneath the contemptuous glances which would see only your origin, not yourself? I could not present you at court; and would it not be far more humiliating if, as my lawful wife, you were excluded from the circles to which I belong, if you were always compelled to conceal yourself in the darkness of obscurity, like one proscribed, while feeling that the lofty name you bore was a burning-glass to draw upon you the fiery rays of public curiosity?"

Cornelia pressed her hand upon her heart as if she felt the stroke of a dagger.

"Could you bear this ignominy?--could you suffer your husband to bear it with you? You know that to me you are a queen; but the world in which I live would never weary of preparing humiliations for you that even I, as your husband, could not always prevent, and which would perhaps lower my proud, noble love in my own eyes. All this you can avoid if you will remain outside the sphere into which our marriage would bring you, if you will live in seclusion as the sweet wife of my heart, unknown and unnoticed, but surrounded by the glory with which a great self-sacrificing love invests a woman. That I would be a faithful husband to you, my Cornelia, I swear by every solemn oath. No other shall ever stand at my side; no one shall bear the name which, before God, belongs to you, and which I dare not give you before the world. I will open a heaven of bliss to you, and at the end of our days you shall tell me whether, in the true, real sense of the word, you have not been my wife, whether I have not deserved the sublime confidence with which, without the customary guarantees, you placed the happiness of your life in my hands. Come, Cornelia, come to my heart." And, as he uttered the words, he threw himself on his knees before her, extending his arms imploringly.

Cornelia still stood motionless. She saw him at her feet, looking so noble with that mute entreaty on his lips, gazed at him for a second, then, like a despairing cry of agony, the words burst forth,--

"Oh, Heinrich, why, why must it come to this?"

"Why? How can it be otherwise?" cried *Henri*, starting up. "Cornelia, be more merciful than the fate that denies you to me. Could I reject my prince's call to the aid of the throne, withdraw my powers from the service of the state at the moment they were most needed? Ought I to have made such a sacrifice to my love when I was sure you would joyfully offer the lesser one, which is necessary to our happiness? What have you to fear? You are living in exceptional circumstances, have no one's permission to ask, have told me a hundred times that you despised the judgment of the world, that you felt within your own heart a higher power, which justified you in taking your own course. If I had believed any woman capable of a love which had sufficient morality in self to be able to cast aside all laws without degenerating, it would have been yourself; and you are such a woman, you alone. In your lofty breast human nature has developed free and unfettered, as it came from the hand of the Creator; it does not judge according to the ordinances of the church-police, or so-called moral tradition, but, pure and undefiled, unquestioningly follows the guidance of the love which pervades all creation, and which mankind first disfigured and chained by arbitrary laws."

"Indeed!" said Cornelia. "And our ideas of virtue, of the sacredness of marriage, they would lack all firm foundation had not God placed a guard upon our passions in our own breasts."

"Cornelia, can *you* ask such questions? They are a protection to the weak, of course. Marriage, as a sacrament, is a great institution, which the infirmities of human nature rendered necessary; but for those strong exceptional natures that feel themselves nearer the deity it is an empty form."

"So would be morality, honor, family happiness,--all would be mere illusions, and our most immediate aim nothing more than to become thinking animals. This would bring us nearest to our divine origin."

"Do not scorn me thus, Cornelia; I do not deserve it, for I am in solemn earnest. Is marriage, then, merely a civil union formed under the eyes of the church-police? Is it not rooted in those who truly love each other? Cannot they, without marriage-certificate or altar, found a true, peaceful family life apart from society, and therefore the more untroubled? If they have become truly one in spirit, do they need the compulsion of the world and the church to remain faithful to each other? Is not marriage a mere superfluous ceremony to such beings? and is not a relation that depends upon the most profound mental and physical sympathy, and endures through its own power, more moral than a so-called legal marriage, which exists only in form where two persons are united that are repulsive to each other,--two souls that do not understand each other,--where people seek refuge from despair in crime, and, after committing infidelities, play the old falsehood to themselves and the world until loathing and constraint stupefy their souls and the individual sinks into a mere animal? Is this more moral, Cornelia? Could the church consecrate what was commonplace, disunited, separated?

Is not such an alliance a greater blasphemy than if two beings, with the loftiest feelings, give themselves to each other for a life of free love and voluntary faithfulness?"

"And would it be blasphemy if two such beings sanctioned their alliance before the world by a marriage, if they made that which is hallowed in itself saved in the eyes of society?" asked Cornelia.

Henri's eyes fell before her glance. "It would not be blasphemy; and any one whom circumstances permitted to do so would be very wrong not to avail himself of the beautiful form, with its many benefits. But where it would disturb a whole life, natures like ours have a right to dispense with it."

"And wherein does this disturbance of the whole life consist? In the possible loss of the portfolio! This is the lofty object to which everything else must yield, even the feeling whose 'divine power,' according to your views, might dispense with the sanction of the law."

"Oh, no, my angel! Shall I love you less if you are mine of your own free choice? On the contrary, I shall but hold you the more tenderly in my heart. You are too noble, too unselfish, to compel me to sacrifice either the proud goal of my efforts, or the happiness of my love, when it is in your power to afford me both."

"But if I do not possess this unselfishness,--if I asked your hand as a proof of your integrity,--then I must yield to the interests of your ambition, and the statesman would conquer the lover."

"Cornelia, I no longer know you. Is this the self-sacrificing woman who has always cared only for others, never for herself? and could you now suddenly transform yourself into a calculating egotist, who bargains and higgles for a price, and demands the sacrifice of a whole career in return for her love? Cornelia, an unconditional sacrifice, a complete forgetfulness of self, might have won me to anything, but this is not the way to obtain my hand."

He looked up and recoiled a step in horror, for before him stood the gorgon he had once imagined in those eyes. The disheveled hair seemed to move; her gaze rested upon *Henri* with petrifying power. At last the tension of the nerves relaxed, the blood surged into her face, and her noble indignation flushed her cheek with as deep a crimson as it had before been pale. "Heinrich!" she cried, "I have borne your fiendish dialectics long enough! I wished to know you thoroughly, and therefore forced myself to be calm. Now this must cease; the measure is full! Do you really believe I would so far humiliate myself as to bargain and beg for your hand? Do you really suppose the sacrifice you ask would be too great for me, if I could justify it before God and my own conscience,--if you were worthy of it? That you are not you have now shown me. I was obliged to hear the answer you gave me with my own ears, or I should not have believed it; therefore I asked the question. I was forced to learn your falsehood from your own lips, to be able to offer you the only thing you deserve, my scorn. Yes, my nature is so healthful that I have strength to thrust evil from me, though my very life should cleave to it. Oh, Heinrich, that it must come to this! You have stripped the bloom from my existence, stolen the most sacred emotions of a young, trusting heart, wished to take from me honor, faith, all that affords support and protection to a woman, torn the wings from my soul to chain me, and then, when you wished to disown me, to say 'fly away.' Oh, treacherous soul-murderer, beautiful and winning as no other can ever be, for whose creation an angel must have mated with a fiend, I love and hate you with equal fervor! I would gladly ennoble you, yet feel already how you have corrupted me. Yes, I understand that no one resisted you,--that you conquered wherever you went; but here, proud man, is the limit of your victory. The shame you destined for me does not humiliate me, for I am conscious I have not deserved it. See, it rouses every hostile power within me. I feel, with a shudder, how they are taking possession of my heart, calling mockingly in my ears, 'Count Ottmar's mistress,' and painting scenes,--scenes which might well drive me to madness. And there stands the man who loves me, and from pure affection dooms me to such tortures; who will not suffer me to stand by his side before the world; will not give me his name in return for the life he demands: and all this is from pure love; and I,--why do I not from pure love thrust a knife into his false breast to avenge the law he derides?"

"So that is it? Because I will not make you Countess Ottmar! That is what causes you such bitter grief? Oh, Cornelia, you are far more haughty than virtuous!"

"Oh, my God, how have I deserved this?" cried Cornelia. "Heinrich, Heinrich, vengeance will come upon you! You will some day be compelled to answer before God for the heart you have crushed! You wish by your sophisms to drive me to sacrifice my virtue, merely to prove that I am noble and unselfish, that I love the man and not the count. Oh, it is a clever calculation, and may already have led many a gentle heart astray! But it recoils from my firm reason, for the supposition is false, Heinrich. If your love and esteem are only to be obtained by sin, you are so evil that you are not worth the trouble of winning. Believe that I am more haughty than virtuous; believe that my anger is only roused because I am not to become Countess Ottmar; I cannot convince you to the contrary, for God and his commands are higher than you, and God sees my heart and knows how it bleeds and quivers!"

"Do not be so violent, Cornelia; you cannot leave me. You are mine; own that you are. You have inhaled the sweet poison from my lips, and your soul absorbed in full draughts the fiery language of my passion. You have foreseen all the joys of love; womanhood has unfolded its perfect flower. You cannot go back. Come, my dove, you are fluttering timidly, and yet feel that you are bound. Come, my angel, demand my vows; I will give them all to you as if before the altar. Does not Christ himself, to whom you pray, say, 'Where two are gathered together in my name, there am I in the midst of them'?"

"Hold, blasphemer, to whom nothing is sacred!" cried Cornelia, releasing herself from his arms in mortal terror; and with sudden resolution she rushed to the door, along the passage, down the staircase,--heard him following her, and hurried through the dark streets. She did not know herself what she wanted, or where she was going; "away, away from him" was her only thought. A door stood ajar, and a faint light streamed through the opening. It was the church of the Jesuits. She fled into it. The house of God was empty, only a priest was praying at the altar beneath the red glow of the ever-burning lamp. *Henri's* steps echoed behind her. She rushed up to the dark figure, and sank senseless before him.

"Heaven has apparently chosen me to be your good spirit, Count Ottmar, since I always stand in your way when you are in the act of doing things you might afterwards regret," said the Jesuit, bending over Cornelia.

In the haste of the pursuit *Henri* had recognized Father Severinus too late. Now he stood before him in amazement, and beheld his precious treasure lying senseless in the arms of his mortal enemy. *Henri* was painfully embarrassed. "Severinus," said he, "I assure you this whole scene is the result of the folly of an innocent, enthusiastic girl, and that you may safely trust me to escort her home."

Severinus gazed with increasing admiration at Cornelia's pure, pale features, as he aided her to rise. "It depends on the decision of the lady herself whether she will go with you, or place herself under my protection."

"Cornelia!" cried *Henri*, in tones so loud, so full of agony, that she opened her heavy eyes. "Cornelia, angel of my life, do not abandon me!

Come with me, and forgive me for having alarmed you. Give me your dear hand, and let me take you home. Cornelia, have you no longer a single glance for your Heinrich?"

She stood trembling before him with downcast eyes, and did not move. "If this reverend gentleman will take me, I will ask him to accompany me. With you, Heinrich, I shall go no more."

"Come, my daughter," said Severinus, with inexpressible gentleness.

Deep grief, such as he had never felt before, overmastered *Henri*. He tried to kiss her hand, but she withdrew it. "Will you act in opposition to the dictates of your own heart, Cornelia?" he exclaimed. "My love, do not cause yourself so much pain. See, you are pitying me almost more than I pity myself. Be more womanly, Cornelia; you cannot treat the man in whom your life is rooted thus. This is not the place for such discussions. I will forgive your want of confidence and your having exposed me to this gentleman in such a manner. To-morrow, my Cornelia, I shall hope to find you more reasonable."

"More reasonable? You will never find me again."

"Cornelia!"

"I think you will feel yourself that between us no reconciliation is possible. We are parted!"

"Cornelia! and you have loved me!"

"Because I have loved, still love--I fear you," she breathed almost inaudibly. "Should I need to fly from you if I hated you as I ought?"

She fixed her eyes once more on the wondrously beautiful features, now ennobled by pain; tear after tear rolled slowly down her cheeks; she shivered violently, and sank sobbing at the feet of a life-size figure of Christ, resting her burning head against the cold stone.

"Oh, Cornelia," whispered *Henri*, his voice trembling with emotion; "unhappy child, why do you lacerate your own heart and mine so cruelly? Tell me, wherefore do you now suffer all this? wherefore do you renounce me, do you bear this anguish?"

"Wherefore?" she said, looking up to the Christ to which she still clung. "Ask Him. He will teach you."

Severinus had stood a little apart, watching Cornelia as if in a dream; he was deeply moved. With a manner more tender than *Henri* had ever seen in him, he now approached and offered her his arm. She obeyed him almost unconsciously, and passed slowly by Ottmar. The latter threw himself before her, and pressed her dress to his lips.

"Girl, girl, I will not leave you! It is not possible that you can cast me off,--it is unnatural! Cornelia, am I to lose you? can it be? will you take all the joy and happiness from my life?"

Cornelia stood with her hands pressed upon her bosom, struggling for breath.

"Have you no longer a word, a glance, for me? can you see the head you have so often cradled an your bosom at your feet, and not bend and raise it forgivingly to your heart? will you not look smilingly into my eyes, and say, 'Enough of punishment, I am appeased'? Draw your arm from that stranger's and place it around my neck, and I will bear you through the world as lovingly, as watchfully, as a god. See, I kiss the spot where your heart is beating, and it does not burst; its blood does not gush forth upon my breast with infinite sorrow at the thought of a separation. You do not stir; you let me plead, let me extend my arms despairingly to you, and will not throw yourself into them,--say no word of compassion to the man whom you have called a thousand times by every fond name love could utter."

"Heinrich! Heinrich!" cried Cornelia, throwing her arms around him and pressing her lips to his, "this is more than human nature can bear!"

"Oh, my Cornelia! Do you then feel you are mine?--that all your purposes are false?--that nothing is true and eternal except our love?"

"My daughter," said Severinus, gently, "be steadfast as you were just now."

Cornelia looked up and brushed the tears from her face. "I thank you; I am steadfast," she replied, with firm resolution. "Good-night, Heinrich, *for the last time*."

She turned to leave the church with Severinus.

Henri started up like a wounded tiger; all tenderness was transformed into fury. "Go, then!" he shouted, trembling with rage; "you are no woman,--you are a fiend! You have deserted *me*, not I *you*; now we are quits."

The young girl tottered out of the church with Severinus without casting another glance behind.

Both reached Cornelia's house in silence. Severinus paused. "Command me, Fräulein. Shall I leave you alone, or can I be of any further service to you? A young girl doubtless needs protection against such a man as Ottmar."

"Do you know him?" asked Cornelia.

"I do."

"May I ask you to come in with me?"

"Most joyfully."

The servants, on their return, had found the house open, and were in the greatest anxiety about Cornelia. Her maid came to meet her, crying, "Oh, heavens, how you look!"

They entered the drawing-room, the apartment so short a time ago the scene of peace and joy; whose atmosphere was still pervaded with *Henri's* glowing breath. There lay the gloves he had forgotten in his haste. Her tears burst forth afresh. It seemed as if she had just come from his funeral, and could not part from these last sad tokens of his life. She mutely motioned Severinus to be seated; she could not speak,--could not express her emotions in words. Severinus understood her thoroughly, and watched her in silence. She sat with bowed bead, speechless and pale; her hands resting on her lap; her loosened tresses falling around her, wet with tears. She still saw the impression made on the soft carpet where he had knelt before her; there lay a velvet ribbon he had torn from her arm; with a deep blush she looked up at the priest, as if he could read her thoughts. Now, for the first time, she noticed his delicate features, the melancholy expression of his large dark eyes, and gazed at him more earnestly. With an involuntary motion he pushed the hair from his brow, and a broad scar became visible.

"You are Severinus!" she exclaimed, starting up and seizing both his hands.

"Did you not know it?" he asked, in astonishment.

"No, I did not hear your name just now; but I think I once saw you in a brighter hour than this."

"In the churchyard a few months ago."

"Yes. Ah, it was a fleeting happiness!" she murmured. "It is strange that we should meet. Oh, I salute you: the only person of whom Heinrich always spoke with reverence, whom God has sent to be my preserver!"

"May the Almighty grant that I shall prove so! But what can I do for you? Will you raise me to the rank of your friend, that as such I may console you, since I am not permitted to bestow the blessings of my ecclesiastical office upon a Protestant?"

"How do you know I am of the Lutheran faith?"

"Because I have long known you, long watched your quiet labors in the prison; and of late, since the report of your relations with Ottmar went abroad, prayed that the Almighty might save the honor of a being whom he had created or his glory, if at any time she was in danger."

"A report? Oh, God! had matters already gone so far with me? Ah, this despicable world!"

"Calm yourself, my daughter. Do not accuse the world: you yourself are not wholly blameless. Had you submitted more to the laws of womanly custom, everything might now be very different."

Cornelia covered her face. "Alas, I believed all men as pure as myself!"

"You are right. If you had been less innocent, you would have paid more attention to appearances. Yet you now see yourself where it leads when a woman breaks down the barriers that protect her. If you had belonged to our church, and had a confessor whom you trusted, he would have called your attention betimes to the dangers that threatened you, and spared you many a bitter pang."

"Alas, many faithful friends warned me, but I would not listen: I had no thought for anything except this man. I was bound by a magic spell, which permitted me only to breathe with his breath, live in his life. I had forgotten God and the world for him; and therefore I am now punished."

"You recognize the hand of God, my child. Ah, yes! I know it rests heavily upon those he loves. You had suffered yourself to become absorbed too thoughtlessly in the passions of earth, and therefore he tore you away to the purer sphere of self-sacrifice and sorrow. Many an earthly happiness can still bloom for you, but you will be purified and enjoy it with grateful consciousness. This is the blessing of your sorrow."

"Oh, how nobly you speak! Go on," pleaded Cornelia, clasping her hands and kneeling like a little child beside the arm-chair which Severinus was seated.

"You have conquered, my daughter, and your heart bleeds from honorable wounds; yet do not imagine that the contest is ended with this one victory: it will not save you. In the languor into which the soul falls after great moral efforts, it is all the more defenseless against a fresh assault. You must leave here, must withdraw into solitude, where, as your days form the links of a continuous chain of self-sacrifice, you will obtain a quiet, unassuming victory over your passions. In the stillness of a magnificent, lonely region, you will once more hear the gentle voices in which God speaks to mankind. Beneath shady trees, and beside cool brooks, the tumult of the blood will be allayed, the life and labors of millions of innocent creatures will employ your fancy, lead you back to simplicity and childlike faith, and with devout reverence you will receive the duty that takes up its abode in every purified soul."

"Yes, reverend sir, you are right: I need repentance and rest; and balm for all sorrows can be found only in beautiful nature. I must leave here; but where shall I go? I have traveled very little; know not whither to turn; and since my engagement to Ottmar have become so much estranged from all my friends that I could not now ask any one to accompany me; besides, I know of no one whom I would suffer to look into my heart. You are the only person whom a strange accident has made my confidant, you understand, and in these few moments have become so necessary to me that it would be very difficult for me to part with you. Help, counsel me."

"You still have a faithful maid?"

"Certainly."

"Well, then, promote her to be a 'companion,' and take me for your fatherly guide, if you believe I know how to judge and treat you in the present state of your soul."

"What! would you devote your precious time to me?"

"If you need me, yes."

"If I need you? Oh, reverend sir, how can I thank you, how can I reward you for a sympathy of which I am so unworthy?"

"To save your immortal soul, to reconcile you with God, is the only reward and gratitude I ask. I am only doing my duty if I aid your erring spirit to find its home again."

"Oh, my friend, you arouse an emotion never felt before! I never knew my parents. Let me find in you that of which I have so long been deprived: a father on whose heart I can weep out my sorrows. Alas, I have never enjoyed this blessing I know not what it is when a child, overwhelmed with remorse, falls at its father's feet, and the latter, kindly absolving it from its guilt, says, 'Come, you are forgiven!' I have sinned deeply; yet if I had had my parents, everything would have been different. Father Severinus, can you enter into an orphan's feelings? Ah, one who, clasped in the arms of his family, has never lacked love, cannot know what it is to grow up alone, without that warm affection, that blissful interchange of parental and filial love, and, with an overflowing heart, which in its ardor could contain a world, find only sober friendship and partial understanding! My dear Veronica was an angel! I owe her all the good qualities I possess: she reared me lovingly, and treated me like a mother; but she had not a mother's affection, that rich, gushing tenderness which a warm, childish heart demands. I did not need an angel, but a noble, mature human being, and strict discipline. My powers soon carried me beyond her narrow intellectual sphere; she became more and more beneath me mentally, and indulged me wonderfully. I remained an obedient child, and loved her devotedly; but she could not give me what I required. An unfortunate youthful fancy passed over me like a dream. My aspiring mind knew no bounds; my thirst for love vainly sought satisfaction, in society, in toiling for the poor and miserable. Then I met Heinrich, with his ardor, his winning charm; and all the affection a child has for its father and mother, all the passion a woman can feel, I had for him. Now came the result of my education. Always habituated to do as I pleased, I despised the commands of custom, the warnings of friends. After being so long deprived of love, it burst over me like a flood: I gave myself up to it blindly. Perhaps I thereby forfeited my lover's respect, and apparently justified him in inflicting upon me the humiliation from which I fled to your protection, sir." She sighed heavily. "Ah, thank God that I could pour out my heart to you! For the first time in my life I feel the happiness of confessing a fault with remorseful sorrow, divesting my soul of its pride, and placing myself in the hands of a merciful judge! Impose the punishment, and I will bear it; tell me the penance, and I will perform it; but then, then bend down to me and tell me as my father would have done, 'Come; you are forgiven'!"

She laid her clasped hands upon the arm of the chair, and looked at Severinus imploringly. The latter sat absorbed in thought, gazing into her face.

"My dear child, you give me the right to punish and pardon; I can only make use of the latter privilege. Your intellectual development, as you have described it to me, excuses your relations with Ottmar, and your pathetic submission to this unprincipled man. I, too, was orphaned; I, too, have wandered through the world with a loving heart, and never found what I sought. To me also men have seemed cold and empty; they did not respond either to my ideas or feelings. But what drew you down raised me; the overmastering impulse led me to a purer sphere. In our church, Cornelia, reigns the man-born God. I could seize upon him, throw myself into his arms, and there find the love, the condescension, I needed. Our church alone is the bridge which unites the Deity with the earth. The symbols, Cornelia, are the steps by which the clumsy human mind, so long as it is fettered by temporal ideas, climbs upward to the supernatural. Even the most sinful man can reach God, if he makes the symbols his own. While your church requires a purified spiritual stand-point in order to give consolation and edification, ours bends down to the man imprisoned in sensuality and leads him upward, step by step, gradually removing him from his sinful condition." He paused and looked at Cornelia, then continued: "These blessings fell to my lot. My heart also bled when it tore itself away from all the human ties entwined about it; I, too, Cornelia, have struggled until I resisted the false allurements, and so spiritualized myself that the world became dead, and the kingdom of God a living thing to me."

"Oh," exclaimed Cornelia, "I shall never bring myself to that! The world dead! No longer love this beautiful earth, the master-piece of God! No, I cannot; it would be ungrateful to him who created it."

"I do not ask that, my child; I am not one of those bigoted priests who believe that men were made only to pray, that the pious and chaste alone are the elect, and the others the mere wretched laborers of creation, destined to propagate the race. Such a thought is far from me. Whomsoever. God destines to be his servant he calls; and let those whom he does not rejoice in the world for which they were born, and serve God by doing good in their own sphere. I will only warn you not to forget the Giver in the gifts; to remember the Dispenser while you enjoy his alms, is a duty you children of the world so easily neglect. This I will teach you to fulfill, and show you that it does not detract from happiness, but hallows and strengthens it. If you had thought more of God when he gave you Ottmar's love, you would have been more discreet, and perhaps matters would never have gone so far."

"Ah, that is terribly true!" sobbed Cornelia.

"Calm yourself, my child; I do not wish to burden your poor heart still more heavily. You were innocent, and Ottmar's influence was injurious to you. No mortal has a right to decide whether you would have been able to avoid this; I least of all, for I know Ottmar's personal power. I, too, trusted him, and was betrayed, for he is no man's friend, not even his own!"

"Unhappy man! Created in the image of God, so handsome, so noble, so capable of giving happiness, and yet a living lie, a deceitful phantom, which irresistibly allures us, and, as soon as we wish to hold it; melts into thin air. Do you understand, Severinus, that one may love him with all the strength of one's life, and when parted from him be but a broken bough which can do nothing but wither?"

"I understand it, for no other was ever so dear to me. I hoped to make him an instrument for the advancement of the good cause, thought God had given me in him a being to whom the heart might still be permitted to pay the tribute of human feelings, aided with admiration in the development of his great talents, and nursed him with tender anxiety. I listened to his breathing while he slept, watched him like a brother, and saw with delight that his health gradually improved. When he came up to me with beaming eyes, and said, 'My dear Severinus, how shall I thank you?' my heart swelled with proud delight, and I clasped him in my arms." He paused, covered his eyes with his hand, and continued, in a trembling voice: "And when I was compelled to lose him, such sorrow seized upon me that I struggled as if the foul fiend had possession of him and I must wrest Heinrich's soul from his grasp. It was the punishment that befell me because my love did not still belong exclusively to Heaven, as it ought. I endeavored to disarm his malice against the order as much as possible; I had nurtured the serpent, so it was my duty to deprive it of its venom, and thus I was forced to pursue as an enemy one who had been the dearest person on earth to me. Believe me, my daughter, your tears are not the only ones which have been shed for him."

Cornelia seized Severinus's hand with deep emotion; he rose. "I will now leave you alone: you need rest. Compose yourself, and pray. I hope to find you ready to travel early to-morrow morning, and will consider tonight whither I will guide you."

As Severinus went out into the street he met a brother-priest, who was just coming from the Jesuit church.

"Father Severinus!" he said, in astonishment. "How did you come here? what are you doing in Fräulein Erwing's house?"

"I am gaining a soul for the church!" he answered, proudly, and passed on.

XX
THITHER

The minister of foreign affairs sat in his office alone. Stray, feeble rays from the winter sun fell through the window and gleamed upon a heap of documents and papers with huge seals; but the minister's eyes did not rest upon them, they were fixed absently on vacancy. From time to time he dipped his pen in the ink, only to let it fall again unused, upon a diplomatic dispatch which had just been commenced. At last he started up and went to the door. His figure was not so elegant, nor his bearing so haughty, as in former days: his hair and beard were neglected, his eyes and cheeks sunken. Was it work or sorrow that had thus shaken this noble frame? He seemed aged, even ill. Anton brought in some letters, which he hastily seized, then threw them all but one upon the table.

"God grant it may be some good news!" said Anton, casting a troubled glance at his master's haggard features as he left the room.

"God grant it!" repeated *Heinrich*; and his breath came quickly and anxiously as he read:

"Your Excellency,--In reply to your highly esteemed favor of the 15th, I have the honor to say that I must positively reject the denunciation it contains against our reverend brother in Christ, Father Severinus: namely, that without my knowledge he had secretly fled with a young and beautiful lady, and kept her concealed for several months against her will. Father Severinus is a pattern to the whole order for humble obedience and the strictest devotion to all. No false appearances can render his blameless and immovable purity suspicions in our eyes. His relation to that lady is one well pleasing to God and the order, and his course has my entire approval. This I must permit myself to say in correction of your Excellency's erroneous suspicion.

"I have no right to inform your Excellency of the residence of Father Severinus and the lady in question until your Excellency has given us the most satisfactory proofs of your right to the possession of the young lady's person.

"With all due respect to your Excellency, etc.,

"Father R----

"*General of the Holy Congregation of the Fathers of Jesus.*

"Rome, -- 20, 18--."

Heinrich sank upon the sofa with the paper in his hand. "This failed too! All, all in vain!" he murmured, crushing the letter convulsively in his clinched fingers. "What is to be done now? Shall I give notice to the embassies of every country? Shall I add to this consuming anguish the disgrace that I am pursuing an adventuress, who is rambling about with a Jesuit? Cornelia! Cornelia! Have these pious fathers or have you obtained so much mastery over yourself that you can inflict this upon me? It is not possible that they have subdued your free will. You are not one of these natures which allow themselves to be ruled. You have done the most difficult, the most unprecedented thing,--conquered me and yourself in a moment when passion was most aroused. You would not suffer the arts of these men to obtain dominion over you! Noble, wonderful woman! By what cords do you hold me that I will go to utter ruin rather than forget you?"

He rested his head wearily upon his hand. His whole life passed before him. He thought of all the unhappy creatures who had clung to him with the same ardor he now felt for Cornelia, and been repulsed as he was now by her. Again Ottilie's image rose before him. The sorrow gnawing at his heart made him for the first time understand the tortures she so silently, so patiently, bore for him, and for the first time he experienced the true human sympathy he had never felt while grief was unknown to him. "Poor Ottilie! We are now companions in suffering!"

A low knocking roused him from his gloomy thoughts. It was his private secretary, to ask whether Ottmar had prepared the dispatch for the court of R----. "Oh! good heavens, no!" he exclaimed, in great impatience, and sat down to finish it. Thrice he began, erased the words, and then flung the pen aside with a sigh of the bitterest despondency. "I am not in the mood," he said, at last. "My head aches too violently. I cannot give myself up to work now."

"Allow me to remind your Excellency that you will be expected at the council of ministers at twelve o'clock," said the young man, timidly.

"You are right: thanks! Remind me of it again at eleven."

With the most painful effort of self-control he applied himself to the preparation of the document, and then hurried away to dress.

"Your Excellency ought to get a long leave of absence," said Anton, as he assisted him to make his toilet. "You cannot live on so."

"Very likely, Anton. It is an existence which is becoming more and more unendurable to me. But I cannot take a leave now. I must either disappear from the scene entirely or remain at my post."

He left the room with a slow step and drooping head. Anton looked after him sadly. "Poor master! It must have been bad news again. No doubt the young lady has good cause for her acts; but I pity him, for he never loved so before."

A few hours afterward the prince entered his wife's apartments. "My dear Ottilie, I must entreat you to grant me a favor. You did not wish to see any one on account of your indisposition, but I beseech you to make one exception."

"It shall be as you wish, Alfred," said Ottilie, in a faint voice.

She was reclining upon a couch under an arbor of dense exotic plants, which made one forget the cold, wintry landscape without. The prince took a chair and sat down beside her. "The matter concerns Ottmar," he began, breaking a withered leaf from a gum-tree, and thus not observing how Ottilie started. "I do not know what I am to do with the man. Something is wrong with him; I cannot discover what. He seems entirely changed. The youngest attaché could not make so many diplomatic blunders as he. He brought to the council to-day the rough sketch of a dispatch to R----, which was totally useless. He, our most talented statesman! It is incomprehensible! He is apathetic and reserved; nay, he even permits himself to fail in the personal respect which, as his prince, I am entitled to demand, and whose punctilious observance has hitherto endeared him to me. I do not think this proceeds from any diminution in his loyalty,--he has so often assured me that I was his only friend,--but is the result of some secret disturbance, some physical or mental suffering. All my efforts to obtain his confidence are fruitless, so I thought of applying to my charming wife and calling her to my aid in this, to me, very important affair."

"But how can I be of any assistance?" asked Ottilie, in astonishment.

"You shall speak to him, my dear. You are mistress of the art of assuming a condescending manner which induces people to give their confidence freely without forgetting in whose presence they stand. I confess that in this respect you far surpass me. You remove my subjects' awe of the grandeur of your position, and substitute reverence for your person. Thus you succeed in being affable without forfeiting any portion of your dignity, and people, open their hearts to you without overstepping the bounds prescribed by etiquette. It is a great art, for which not only intellect and heart, but the unusual queenliness of air that distinguishes you, are requisite."

"But it is an 'art' which, at all events, I practice very unconsciously," interposed Ottilie, smiling. "Yet I thank you, Alfred, for this praise; it makes me very proud. And now I shall try to earn it by attempting to prove my skill upon Ottmar."

"There is no praise you have not already fully earned. But I will beg you to subdue this reserved diplomat with your--if I may so call it--diplomacy of the heart, and discover what is really the matter with him."

"But have we a right to interfere, my prince?"

"It is not only a right, but a duty. If he merely neglected me, I would ignore it; but he neglects the obligations of his high position, and thereby injures the interests he ought to defend. This cannot continue, so we must discover the cause of Ottmar's trouble and try to remove it. If this does not succeed, then----" The prince rose with the shrug of the shoulders he always used to express what was not yet sufficiently decided to put into words. "At the present critical moment, when everything is crowding upon us, we need men who are thoroughly in earnest, and will hold the reins with a firm hand," said he, continuing his interrupted chain of ideas. "It is no time for personal considerations and indulgent delays. Every moment brings and demands important decisions, which should not be permitted to suffer from the absence of mind of any individual. There must be a change soon. I cannot lecture him like a school-boy, but you can say many things as a proof of friendly sympathy, which, from my lips, would sound like an implied reproach."

"I will try; although I do not expect much from the interview. I can scarcely flatter myself that I shall be able to win from him what he withholds from you, and perhaps the secret may be of such a nature that he cannot confide it to us. Perhaps--he has some love-sorrow."

"Oh, my dear! Would a polished man of the world, a thorough diplomat, give himself up to such sentimentality?"

The glance that Ottilie cast at the prince had a shade of compassionate contempt. "You call it sentimentality because you have never felt the power of a passionate emotion. You must consider that the moderation inculcated into the minds of royal personages, that they may be able to rule themselves and others, is an almost exclusive prerogative of their rank, which no one else shares----"

"Except the priests," interposed the prince.

"You are right. But Ottmar does not belong to that class, but to one of great privileges and few duties, who are accustomed to drop the reins of self-control; and these men often lack all support against their passions. I have already told you that I do not consider Ottmar a genuine diplomat. He has talent, and will therefore for a time skillfully accomplish whatever he undertakes, but he is far too great an enthusiast to be a good statesman. For this he lacks calmness, firmness of conviction, perseverance in labor, and sooner or later the contradiction between his nature and his profession must appear."

"Lord C---- made the same remark about him several years ago. Your knowledge of human nature shows itself more and more, and I daily perceive with gratitude what wise counsels I am always sure of receiving from you. Then you will make the sacrifice for me, and speak to Ottmar?"

"I should be deserving of great blame if I refused my husband's request. Under what pretext do you wish the interview to take place?"

"I think we will give a family dinner to-morrow, and invite him to it. Do you feel well enough for such an effort? In my opinion, it would be the most fitting opportunity."

"I agree with you, and think my strength will enable me to do the honors."

"I thank you in advance, my dearest, and hope I have not imposed any very disagreeable task upon you."

"On the contrary, I so rarely have the happiness of being permitted to do you a favor, that I----"

"Oh, do not say so; your whole life is a succession of kindnesses and self-sacrificing amiability towards me. How ignoble it would be for me to require more than you voluntarily bestow! Pray take care of yourself; the anxiety you feel is felt for me. Au revoir." He pressed a hasty kiss upon Ottilie's small white hand and left the room.

Ottilie looked after him quietly. Not a feature in her pale face altered. She gratefully perceived that the prince tried to give her at least civility, even deference; instead of love. She had never asked more; and now it was easier than ever to resign it. She was no longer solitary, the life that stirred under her heart filled her with blissful promises of an infinite love never known before. This new and cheering emotion aided her to bear more resolutely than before even the thought of being again thrown into Ottmar's society. The outward world passed by her like a dream: there was but one reality to her,--the approaching fulfillment of her mission as a woman; all her powers were exerted for this great end, and peace brooded over her soul.

Thus, on the following day, she met Ottmar. The strength of her soul conquered her physical weakness; and when the dinner was over and the prince was conversing with the other guests, she calmly approached Ottmar with an air of quiet dignity.

"The prince has commissioned me to speak to you, count," she whispered, almost inaudibly.

"His Highness?" asked *Heinrich*, in astonishment.

"Yes; but I do not do so in his name, but my own. We are anxious about you, for we both see that you are suffering. Your manner reveals it to me, while he notices the change by the decreasing interest you take in your business."

"I know it!" exclaimed *Heinrich*.

"He now wishes to obtain some explanation through me; he hopes you will be more open than with him; but fear nothing, I shall not degrade myself to become a spy upon you; nor should I need to do so, for I know the cause of your anguish, and shall guard it as a sacred secret. Yet I consented to the conversation the prince desired because I believed the wish to be a sign from God. Besides, I wanted to speak to you once more about some of the last events in your life; perhaps I may finally produce some good result."

Heinrich gazed at her in the greatest astonishment.

"Will you permit a friend of many years' standing to meddle with your secrets? Will you trust me?" she asked, with all her former winning grace.

"Oh, my princess!" cried *Heinrich*, in delight. "How long it is since you have bestowed any such words upon me! how your returning favor soothes and cheers me!"

"God is my witness that my favor was never withdrawn from you, count." She raised her sparkling blue eyes, and her lips parted to say more; then she recollected herself: her lids drooped again, and she was silent. After a pause she began, in an altered tone, "The prince wishes through me to learn the cause of the change in you, that he may help you; but I can aid you without telling him your secret, and thus save both, and betray no one. Is that right?"

"Perfectly! But, my beloved, noble princess, how can you help me?"

"You have been deserted by the young girl you loved. Is it not so?"

"Yes, yes; but how do you know?"

"The unhappy fate that has come between you is a secret to me, and one I do not wish to fathom. The fault, my friend,--pardon my usual frankness,-- must be with you; for I know her, and will answer for it that you were loved with a rare, pure, and fervent affection."

"Oh, your Highness, you cut me to the heart!"

"I must do so, count, if I am to be of use to you; and this is the only occasion upon which I can. That you love Cornelia Erwing with the first real passion of your life I see by the deep sorrow expressed in your outward appearance, as well as your acts and conduct; and I hail this mood with joy, count, as the gloomy twilight which precedes the dawn of a new day."

"Princess, you do not know what I suffer. If I ever sinned against a noble heart, I am now making bitter atonement. Pity me; do not triumph in my anguish."

"Oh, how greatly you misunderstand me, count I triumph in your anguish! May God keep me from such a thought! I rejoice because your sorrows are a proof of a salutary change in your heart! I rejoice that you love deeply, truly, sadly; because I hope to be able to restore that to which your heart clings so loyally!"

"Could you do so, your Highness?" whispered *Heinrich*, his eyes sparkling with new life.

"Cornelia Erwing conceals her residence from you. Have you searched for her?"

"I have summoned the police of the whole country to my aid, left no means untried, but all in vain."

"Why did you do that?"

"Why?" asked Ottmar, in astonishment. "Because I wished to win her, to have her again."

"And will you permit me to ask one more bold question? If you did succeed in winning her again, what would be her fate?"

Ottmar drew back a step in astonishment and looked doubtfully at Ottilie. Should he tell her? was she strong enough to hear it? should he confess the resolution which, during months of agony and exhausting struggle, had obtained such a powerful influence over him that it governed his whole character and conduct?

"Would you make Cornelia Erwing your wife?"

"Your Highness!"

"If this is the case, I am ready, on my own responsibility, to tell you her present residence."

"Noble, royal soul!" murmured Ottmar, involuntarily. "Well, then, yes. Learn what no one else respects, that I, whom you have so often reproached for my heartlessness, am subdued by a passion stronger than my selfishness, stronger than everything, for I feel I could give up my life rather than this girl, who has become so great a necessity to my mind and heart. For weeks a letter imploring her hand has been lying in my portfolio, but I can find no means of sending it to her, and am almost in despair. Have compassion upon me. If you--ever"--he hesitated--"ever felt for any one what I now feel for this cruel girl, you will know how heavily I am punished."

Ottilie would gladly have extended her hand to him; but etiquette must not be offended in the prince's presence. She turned, so that the rest of the company could not see her face, and looked at Heinrich with an inexpressibly loving expression. The old melancholy, yet happy, smile played around her lips, while tear after tear rolled down her pale cheeks.

"You see, my dear, dear friend, I can really do something for you. Cornelia is now living Rome, and as soon as the company have been dismissed I will send you her address."

"Oh, God, how do I deserve the favor of such a woman? Your Highness, how shall I thank you?"

"Make Cornelia Erwing happy; this is the best gratitude I can ask, for it will be the warrant of your own welfare."

"Ah, if I might fall at your feet and kiss the hem of your garments! No, you are no creature of earth!"

Ottilie involuntarily pressed her hand upon her heart, and thought, "Who knows how soon he may be right!"

"Do you believe I can succeed in moving the heart of this wonderful, resolute girl?" asked *Heinrich*.

"Certainly, for I am sure Cornelia still loves you."

"Did she tell you so in her letter?"

"No; but I know how you were beloved, and therefore cannot be forgotten. Besides, she only wrote to me once that I might know what had become of her, if I should send for her and hear she had gone away. She lamented that an unfortunate misunderstanding compelled her to part from you, and begged me to preserve the strictest silence in regard to her residence that you might not be able to take any steps to shake this resolution, which was necessary for the sake of both. I gave the promise and said nothing; but now I should think it wrong if I did not contribute, as far as I am able, to reunite two such hearts. I had long doubted whether any such woman as you need existed; but I recognized Cornelia as the person whom, in imagination, I had destined for you; therefore she must belong to you. Do you remember the evening I predicted that you would feel a new, great love? It has now entered your heart, and, by the goodness of God, I am permitted to show you the way to the woman in whom the happiness of your life will bloom. My prophecy is fulfilled, my mission to watch over your salvation completed." Tears again glittered in her eyes as she uttered the words, "May blessing and peace be with you both! Farewell."

As soon as the prince saw Ottilie's farewell bow, he approached *Heinrich*, and, after doing the honors to the company a short time longer, the noble pair withdrew. The prince supported his wife with a strong arm, for she tottered as she left the room.

Ottmar had scarcely reached home when Ottilie's groom of the chambers brought him a sealed envelope. It contained Cornelia's address, written with an unsteady hand.

Heinrich immediately sent a proposal of marriage to Cornelia, overflowing with the ardor of unrestrained passion and the most sincere, humble repentance. Great as was his sense of what he had lost in her, it was equaled by his self-accusation, his impetuous pleading for her pardon, her hand; and the whole letter bore the impress of spiritual purification and bitter, heart-felt remorse. A few days after Cornelia's answer arrived.

"Rome, February, 18--.

"You ask for my hand, Heinrich. I have read the words with tears of grateful surprise. You bear a beautiful and noble testimony, both to yourself and me; and in spirit I fall upon my knees before you, and implore your pardon for the reproaches and upbraidings hurled at your dear head on that terrible evening of our parting. Your letter reveals all the wealth of your deep heart, and shows me that you undervalued yourself when you wished to commit a deed so unworthy of you. Forgive me that I too then believed you worse than you are. I thank God for the merciful kindness with which he restored my only treasure, esteem for you; for nothing humiliates a woman more deeply than to feel affection for a man she must despise. I frankly confess, Heinrich, that I could not cease to love you, even for a moment, that I was torn by the most torturing struggle between heart and my consciousness of right. Now, since I have, received your letter and know you deserve my love, I am once more at peace with myself. I write this that you may not think me prompted by anger or bitterness when I refuse your hand. My eyes grow dim at the sight of these cruel words, the fingers that guide the pen are paralyzed; I must pause a moment and collect my thoughts.

"I cannot become your wife after what has passed between us,--I dare not. You have wounded my womanly honor too deeply, shown with too little consideration what a great sacrifice you would make if you raised me to the position of your wife, for me to be able to reconcile my conscience or my pride to its acceptance. I cannot belong to a man who found me in a station so far below him that he thought he could degrade me to the lowest ignominy; although a nobler emotion or an unconquerable affection afterwards leads him to atone for the wrong. I should always fear that, according to the opinions you have often declared, you would consider your marriage with me a mesalliance. Besides, you have described my position as the plebeian wife of Count Ottmar too clearly and distinctly for me not to shrink from the picture with dread and horror; while even if I could myself suffer the humiliations the pride of your aristocratic circle would prepare, I could not bear that you, as my husband, should be compelled to share them with me; for even if your love at first helped you to endure them, they would only too soon stifle it. There would be a perpetual conflict between your heart and the prejudices the world in which you live has stamped upon you. This must banish peace from your breast, and sooner or later make you as miserable as before. Love would yield, and prejudice conquer, for society would neglect no opportunity of bringing new and painful proofs of the justice of its views before your eyes, and then what would be left me in return for all the humiliations I had suffered? Your scorn! Oh, I was foolish ever to permit myself to be so blinded as to believe that happiness for yourself or me could ever be expected to result from a marriage with Count Ottmar! The extent of my folly you first taught me to know in that hour of agony. Do not rebuke the application I have made of your lessons as exaggerated. It might, perhaps, be so in regard to a man who stood further above the views and demands of a narrow-minded circle than you. But with you, Heinrich, it is the direct result of your whole character. You are far too much fettered by the ideas of those who surround you, cling too closely to the false lustre of brilliant positions, accidental aristocratic prerogatives, and personal distinction, to long retain your love for a woman who would constantly inflict the most painful wounds upon your aristocratic vanity. Believe me, love has no worse enemy than doubt of the equality of its chosen object; and even if you thought me worthy of you in intellect, the inferiority of my birth, and the want of esteem shown by society, would weigh heavily against me. You must become another man for me to accept your hand; and--forgive me if I am harsh--your letter gave me no proof of this, although it revealed a depth of feeling for which, since our separation, I had not given you credit. But you are and will remain the minister, Count Ottmar, the court favorite; I can only make him unhappy, as he would me. If you were once more yourself, Heinrich von Ottmar, my Heinrich, who has nothing in common with that unprincipled aristocracy,--if you openly acknowledged what I taught you, what I believe requisite to true manly dignity and greatness,--then, then you should learn how I love you. Count Ottmar, who wished to inflict such disgrace upon me, I do not love, and have sworn never to marry. Farewell! For your happiness and my own I must avoid you, and leave it to God whether and how he dispose your heart towards me. If your love is more than the obstinacy of a passion irritated by resistance, it will unite with your better self and make you a new man, will remove from our path the obstacles that separate us, and upon the open way will find me once more; of that you may be assured. But if it has not the strength to do all this, it would in the end only make both you and myself miserable,--thrice as miserable as we are now.

"When you receive this letter, I shall have left Rome for another place of residence. Do not try to seek me: you will not find me. Do not call me 'cruel'; in these lines you see only the victory I have obtained over myself, but not my anguish, my tears. Beloved, I extend my arms to you, and would fain press you to my aching heart, but only the cold phantom of womanly duty and honor bends toward me, and breathes an icy kiss on my burning lips. Oh, it is hard to be cast off by one you love, and compelled to renounce your most ardent desire! But, Heinrich, it is still harder to reject him yourself, and voluntarily resign that for which you long. These, Heinrich, are superhuman victories, and they strip all blossoms of youth from the heart; but it is better to lose them than reap the envenomed fruit of eternal remorse. May God keep his gentle, fatherly hand over you! He can still lead you to happiness, and he alone.

"Cornelia Erwing."

It was morning when *Heinrich* read and re-read this letter, until a sorrow never imagined before made the words swim before his eyes, and lay like a weight upon his chest, until, with a half-stifled cry of agony, he bent his head upon the sheet lying before him. He started as if bewildered, when Anton suddenly appeared, and informed him that a message had come, summoning him to go to the palace as soon as possible.

A few hours after, the bells rang, the cannon thundered, and the populace shouted with joy, for in the palace a new-born child, a prince, lay in a golden cradle. The hope of the country, whose fulfillment slumbered in that little heart, stood by its side uttering a benediction, and the promise of a great future encircled the baby brow with an invisible crown.

But beside him a precious life was struggling silently and uncomplainingly with death. Ottilie had fulfilled her last and highest task, but it had exhausted the remnant of her strength. She felt that her pulse had but a few more throbs, her breast would rise and fall only a few more times, and, gazing gently and submissively around the circle, Said, "Give me my son,"--took him from the arms of the prince and pressed him closely to her heart. "Oh, God! what do I need more than the happiness of this moment?" Yet a tear fell from her glazing eyes as she kissed the little one and softly whispered, "You are so sweet, so dear! Oh, it must be an immeasurable delight to cradle such a child in one's arms, protect, foster, and watch the awakening of its slumbering powers! It is not allotted to me. I must leave you and give you up to your father. May his soul open itself to *you*! may you become the innocent mediator between him and his poor people!" She pressed the boy more and more feebly to her breast. "Farewell! it grieves me to leave you,--grieves me deeply. Yours was the only heart an which I relied. But I will not complain. I have *borne* you,--this, too, is a mercy from God, and with a kiss upon your rosy lips it is sweet to die." The child fell from her arm, and her head sank back.

"She is asleep," said the prince, dismissing the bystanders, that he might not be compelled to show any grief.

That evening the bells rang out another peal, and thousands wept aloud under the brilliantly-lighted windows of the palace, for behind them, on a black-draped bed of state, lay the beautiful corpse of the princess, and her people's love stretched its arms towards her in vain. With her the last bond that bound the sympathies of the masses to the throne was sundered, and in the child-like ideas of the nation, Ottilie's glorified spirit rose from her death-bed as that of a saint, a martyr, who had vainly struggled and suffered to the end. She hovered above the mourning country in a halo of glory and grief, and despair transformed the angel of peace into a goddess of freedom, who with a mighty power revealed to their oppressed hearts the consciousness of their crushed rights.

XXI
SPRING STORM

The political atmosphere constantly grew darker and more threatening. Throngs of people had streamed from all the provinces to attend Ottilie's funeral, all with the same sorrow, the same rancor; and, after the obsequies were over, they assembled for consultations of the most serious nature, and these consultations resulted in resolutions. Unions were formed and dissolved, deputations sent and dismissed, the press rose and was suppressed. The evidences of the advancing movement became more and more decided, the measures of the government yet more stringent.

Suddenly a shout rang through the whole country.

"Count Ottmar has formed an opposition in the ministry! Count Ottmar has declared for the constitution!" The news ran like wildfire. Ottmar, who had been so long hated as the enemy of all progress, the powerful favorite of the prince, suddenly threw influence, position, and authority into the wavering scale, and acknowledged before the world the cause against which he had so long battled. No one took time to question the motive of this sudden change; enough that it was so, it was help in the hour of the utmost need; and new courage animated the elastic minds of the people. Ottmar was now the centre of universal attention; the last hope was bound up in him. This consciousness gave him a dignity which pervaded his whole character. He was once more the old Ottmar, who strode on haughtily erect, in triumph; but another and a nobler triumph was now depicted in his sparkling eyes, his lofty bearing; it was not the victory of subtle arts over the hearts of feeble women, credulous princes, and less gifted diplomats; but the conquest of a manly action upon minds, and the pride of an honest purpose in lieu of treacherous fascinations.

He was animated with new life. The conflict between his principles and his course of action, as well as that between his love and his career, which Cornelia so greatly feared, had arisen; and although the first impulse to his new deeds, as in the case of Albert's liberation, had been merely the selfish desire to enter the path upon which he might hope to find Cornelia, he again felt with great satisfaction the blessing of his good action.

There is scarcely any soil more favorable for the efforts of man than to represent a nation, be it in whatever form it may, none in which the noblest and purest philanthropy can be better developed; but there is also none from which personal vanity reaps a more abundant harvest. Cornelia knew this, and therefore had sought to lead Ottmar into this career. Vanity was the tie by which she endeavored to unite the egotist to a great cause, until its own nature could enter into him and raise him above himself. The moment had now arrived when her expectation began to prove itself correct. *Heinrich* found himself obtaining an importance in the eyes of the whole country, which he had hitherto possessed only within the narrow circle of the court; saw himself beloved where he had formerly been hated; surrounded with shouts of joy, instead of having men shrink from him in fear, and he would have been unnatural if it had not both flattered him and stirred the silent chords of benevolence within him. Thus the way was opened which he must follow if his opposition in the ministry succumbed, and he sacrificed the portfolio to his new confession of faith.

"Cornelia, wonderful woman, what have you made me?" he said to himself a hundred times, while his breast heaved with a sigh of longing. He pressed his hand upon his heart, which he felt more and more to be the centre of gravity of his nature; where the head whose lofty ideas had given him new life had so often rested and thought. "When shall I hide you here again? When, after all these tumultuous conflicts, shall I hold quiet, blissful intercourse with you? When will your sparkling eyes rest lovingly upon me, and say, I am satisfied with you, Heinrich'?"

Weeks elapsed, and the people still hoped, while Ottmar saw the catastrophe he expected approach nearer and nearer,--for he knew the situation of affairs too well to believe for a moment that his opposition would effect anything more than to give him the confidence he needed for his new career, and make his change of opinion easier. He was not mistaken. From the moment he acknowledged his real views he was excluded from all personal intercourse with the prince, and the majority in the ministry was against him. The prince, calm and immovable in his convictions, did not suspect that in Ottmar alone lay the pledge of his security; his eyes, which were constantly gazing into the obscurity of a long-buried past, did not perceive the feeling of the nation which had assembled menacingly about the liberal minister. But Ottmar felt this invisible power hovering around his brow with whispers of promise, and knew that he was the real ruler of the moment; for with him fell the last barrier that withheld the rising flood from the steps of the throne, and with a proud smile he at last hailed his overthrow in the ministry as the first real triumph of his life.

"May you never be compelled by force, your Highness, to acknowledge the spirit you now deny!" were his last words, as he left the council of ministers. He did not suspect how soon, for the first time, he was to know and estimate at its full power the spirit that, with scornful menace, he had held up as a ghost before the eyes of the prince.

On the evening of the same day the rumor that Ottmar had sent in his resignation spread through the city, so that undoubtedly the question of the constitution had been unfavorably decided. The streets were deserted, but the public-houses were filled to overflowing; conversations were carried on a low tone, and several arrests were made.

The next morning the newspapers confirmed the report that Count Ottmar's resignation had been sent in and accepted; and further remarked that the government, spite of its eagerness to accede to all just and reasonable demands, could not suffer itself to be borne on by the extreme views of this man, etc.

This was too hard a blow for the newly-excited hopes of the nation.

Ottmar himself, by his previous conduct, had unconsciously increased its expectations to such an extent that they could only be crushed by a terrible rebuff, but not subside peacefully.

A nation which has long pleaded and had its most reasonable demands rejected, its highest expectations disappointed, is a terrible power when, with its last hope, its last fear is cast aside. Scarcely had the news of Ottmar's withdrawal from the ministry spread abroad, when all the machines stood still, all the looms stopped. A strange bustle began to make itself heard in the streets. Workmen ran busily to and fro, groups formed and separated. Crowds of men, engaged in earnest conversation, surged up and down. Towards evening the strange mysterious rabble, the vermin which always crawl forth when the soil of popular order is disturbed, began to mingle with the throng. The questions and interference of the police were answered with contempt or a slap in the face. At last, with the gathering darkness, the aimless tumult assumed purpose and direction; Ottmar's house was the point towards which the pulsing life of the whole City streamed. A cheer was raised for the discharged minister, the fallen representative of the people. A few hasty charges from the patrol dispersed the scarcely organized, defenceless crowd; but the result was that the following day it assembled again, and the scene was repeated; this time with a cheer for Ottmar and a hiss for the government. The advancing soldiers found a part of the crowd armed, and a struggle ensued. When the first wounded man fell a furious yell burst forth, and the resistance became desperate, until a second detachment of mounted gendarmes dashed upon the combatants with drawn sabres and forced them asunder.

The first blow dealt upon such occasions opens the artery of a whole nation, and the wild blood streams forth until strength is utterly exhausted, and the arm yields feebly to the bandage which often only conceals a new fetter.

On the third day the City looked as if some public festival were being celebrated. An inexplicable concourse of strangers thronged the streets; the trains arrived crowded with the inhabitants of the provinces; new bands constantly flocked to the City; the soldiers were consigned to the barracks, the places of business closed.

Still the demon of insurrection, imprisoned in every throbbing heart, waited until the scattered masses obtained a definite form, and then burst forth with all his long-repressed power; one mind in a many-limbed, gigantic body. Roaring and shouting he rushed forward with the wings of the storm, ever swelling and increasing, destroying all peaceful life as he dashed along. The breezes fled before and around him, the earth shook and whirled its stones upward to the glittering palaces; while shattering and crashing, groaning and roaring, was the accompanying harmony to the terrible, howling, and shouting song of fury of the unchained revolution.

Pale terror stared hollow-eyed at the passing desolation, while the Nemesis of the insulted law dashed after on snorting steeds. But the ghost of fratricide rested with paralyzing power upon the pursuers, and unreached, unchecked, a part of the mighty crowd rushed on to the arsenal. The guard stationed for its defense fell at the first tremendous assault; the huge doors yielded, and with an exultant roar of "Arms!" the combatants rushed in over the treasured emblems of battle-traditions centuries old, to prepare for the most important conflict--the victory of the new over the old time.

Vengeance hastened after with lightning and thunder; and the infuriated forces, crashing and shrieking, rushed upon each other and struggled in the most terrible of all conflicts--the narrow, crowded battle of the streets. Repeated volleys of artillery and new bands of soldiers at last forced a way through the throng before the arsenal was plundered. But, as a wave which the tempest lashes asunder always rushes together with redoubled violence, the crowd divided and grew denser here and there before the regular weapons of the troops. Hotter and more deadly grew the struggle. Darkness was gradually added to the thick smoke of the powder, which enveloped the noisy city and absorbed every ray of light. Barricades, those terrible fortifications of the populace, had risen, and around them the conflict raged, so that the walls of the houses groaned and trembled, and with the last gleam of day the last appearance of definite purpose vanished, darkness shrouded the heated brains, and both within and without all outline of form and plan vanished. Murder was no longer committed for the sake of a certain object, but became the object itself. Nature asserted her rights, not in a peaceful, normal manner, but with horrible degeneracy,--stupefaction in the place of sleep, the delirium of fury instead of dreams. The animal developed itself in forms of hideous distortion, and the most dangerous madness took possession of the soul: joy in cruelty, pleasure in destruction. Hour after hour elapsed in a wild tumult of excesses and crimes; anarchy writhed and twisted horribly beneath the superior force of fresh bodies of troops, clung giddily to her bulwarks, and defended them with convulsive energy as her last support. The struggle now became monotonous. Signals, volleys of artillery, and fierce howls, like those of wild beasts, alternated at regular intervals, while above them rose the notes of the alarm-bells, and only the crash of falling barricades, the glare of burning houses, interrupted the terrible rhythm with which the yielding revolution was uttering its last sighs. Limb after limb began to die, street after street became quiet.

At last, towards morning, the over-taxed strength was exhausted, the thirst for blood slaked. Death was gleaning in the houses where battle had cast its mangled victims, and trembling hands were busied in binding up wounds, while compassion and horror struggled for the mastery. The last shot died away, the insurrection was quelled. Silence spread over the scene the lassitude of death. Slowly the ever-patient heavens flushed with the rosy hues of dawn, and the still reeking city lay purple in its blood.

Ottmar stood at the window gazing silently, now at the glowing sky and now at the blood-stained earth. Horror had stupefied him. In the angles of the streets soldiers, who had fallen asleep while standing in the ranks, leaned against each other, shoulder to shoulder. Now and then a body covered with straw was borne past; pallid women stepped noiselessly over the barricades, urged on by the courage of despair, and crept along the streets to seek their husbands and sons; invisible angels of death floated through the air, guided them into the right path, and hovered around them when, in some lifeless body, they were forced to recognize a relative.

Heinrich gazed motionless at these changing scenes of misery; but his inmost heart was strangely stirred. The spirit of murdered freedom celebrated in him its resurrection, built a temple in his soul, raised its arches heavenward, and led him away from this sorrowful scene of his former unhallowed labors to his own home, where the lists stood open to the missionaries of national happiness, where he could obey the call which had appealed to his conscience in the death-cry of an ill-used country. All the frivolity and brilliancy that had formerly charmed him was swallowed up in the streams of blood he had seen flow,--all striving and struggling to assert his own merits vanished in the newly-awakened consciousness of the duties devolving upon every talented man for the development and culture of the masses. The solemnity of the moment had seized upon him and stripped off all that was false and superficial. He could not answer with sophisms the great question propounded by the times; he must at last be himself again, must acknowledge the truth, and from amidst all the horrors of vengeance, the rushing streams of blood, once more arose in its pure beauty the thought of the eternal rights of man he had so grievously profaned.

XXII
LIGHT AND SHADOW

A radiant morning sky arched over a green island which lay in the midst of a broad, ruffled lake. Blue mountain-peaks, veiled in mist, bounded the almost-immeasurable surface of water. Who can describe all the changeful lights upon the tide when the young rays of the morning sun play upon the dancing wavelets--the rising and falling, the sparkling and flashing, the confused blending of the reflections? A fresh breeze swept over the lake to the island and rustled the leaves of the lofty trees; with that exception, a deep silence, a sabbath-like peace, brooded over the scene.

A girlish figure stood upon the shore, gazing, in a trance of delight, at the starry shimmer of the waves, and inhaling with parted lips the cool breath of the water; dewy leaves and blossoms kissed her floating robes, and dragon-flies sported upon the tide at her feet. Her eyes followed with a longing look a bird of prey which soared in a majestic flight towards the pure, vaulted firmament. Just then the sound of the matin-bell rang out upon the silence, and at the same moment a tall man, in long, dark robe, appeared in the doorway of a peasant's house near by, and, standing motionless, gazed at the slender figure, whose marvelous proportions were sharply outlined against the sparkling lake! "Cornelia!" he called at last.

She turned and hurried towards him. "My dear Severinus! Oh, how happy I am! Here the free German air blows once more; here I again hear the rustling of German oaks and pines. Home surrounds me in this fresh, simple nature, speaks in the familiar language, looks from the kindly blue eyes. I live once more,--I am awake,--and what surrounds me is charming, bright reality."

"Have you only been dreaming while in our glorious Italy?" asked Severinus, gravely.

"Yes, Severinus; a beautiful, wonderful dream, but a dream after all. I was torn from my native soil; my heart could not take root anywhere; no dear relations with my past existed; no new ones were formed with the present. What I saw and experienced only enriched my intellect, not my heart; it afforded me pleasure without making me happy; occupied my mind without obtaining any hold upon my nature. I gazed, admired, learned, and reveled in a wealth of beauty; but I was not myself,--my individual life had no connection with my surroundings. What is this except a dream into which we bring nothing, and from which we take only a memory?"

"I had hoped you would not return so empty from a country of the loftiest revelations. I expected your great soul would there find its only true home, and the sorrow of finding myself mistaken shall be the last the world can prepare for me."

"Oh, do not talk so, Severinus, dear, pious father! Do not Look at me so sadly; do not be so stern and bitter, but enjoy with me the blessing of this peaceful morning. Let holy nature be the church in which our souls can unite in adoration of our common God. See, my friend, clearness of vision is as unavoidable a necessity to me as light and air; in clearness of vision God shows himself to me, while you only perceive him in mysteries. In order to see him I open my spiritual eyes; you close yours. I receive his manifestations with sharpened, you with artificially deadened, senses. I see him in each of these light clouds floating over the sunny sky; you darken your churches, and shroud yourselves in clouds of incense, that in the mysterious, rich-hued twilight you may paint a vague, fanciful picture. His natural and moral laws everywhere announce themselves to me in shining characters, and I serve him by cheerful obedience to them; you collect from the ambiguous writings of the Bible a book of church regulations, to which you slavishly submit, and exhaust your hearts and minds the superhuman effort of satisfying all your self-created duties."

"I hope this is not the only result of your observation of our sublime worship. It must be the short residence on this dull German soil which has loosened the strings that resounded so clearly in Rome."

"Do not cherish such a fancy, Severinus," said Cornelia, as she walked up and down the shore with him. "The forms of your worship, as I saw them in Rome, delighted me; nay, their grandeur and poesy aroused a wild enthusiasm. But it was the revelation of art, not that of the Deity, at which I gazed. All your miracles, all your lofty precepts, proved nothing except the grandeur of the human intellect, and in this the existence and influence of a God, which I never doubted, and which had been just as clearly revealed to me in every creation of genius. My God, to whom I pray in childish adoration, has remained the same; he has come from Rome with me the same as he went. You neither strengthened nor shook my belief; I cherish the deepest reverence for your worship of God; it is more beautiful, more sublime, than ours; my heart has opened to much that revealed a character of sincere piety, but I still see in it only a transitory *form*, liable to alter with the changes of centuries; while I bear within me the imperishable essence, ever the same through the lapse of ages."

"Oh, Cornelia, how I pity you!" said Severinus, as he leaned against an oak, covering his dark eyes with his hand, while his breast rose and fell as if he were struggling for breath. "Cornelia," he suddenly exclaimed, encircling her forehead with both hands, "free your mind, your godlike mind, from the clutches of this prejudice; cast aside the arrogance of independent judgment; bend your haughty brow in obedience to our church. Oh, if I could give you the blessing to be found in unconditional submission,--blind faith,--I would willingly sacrifice my life to save for the church this soul, which has no peer in human form! Cornelia, a fiend has taken possession of you; that of pride, doubt, indifference. He has concealed himself under the false lustre of an abstract reverence for God, to lull your conscience to sleep, in order that you may the more surely fall into unbelief and destruction." He suddenly threw himself at her feet, and gazed despairingly into her eyes. "Here I lie before you in the dust, and I plead in infinite anguish for the precious imperiled property of Christ. The next moment of time may perhaps decide your fate, and part us forever. Cornelia, join our church; believe me, she alone can save you."

"Oh, God, how hardly you try me! You wrong me, Severinus. No evil spirit, no prejudice, guides me. Have you ever seen me arrogant? If I were, should I not go over to you? for you have opened the most tempting prospects to my pride; you would halt my conversion with joy, and receive me with every kind of pomp and distinction. My self-love would be so greatly flattered that it would far, far outweigh the self-denial of an outward subordination to the church, while in my own congregation no one asks about Cornelia Erwing. But I cannot thus belie myself. Do not sadden my heart with entreaties and lamentations: convince me, Severinus; for so long as you do not succeed in that I can do nothing but weep, because I must grieve my best friend so deeply."

"Convince you!" cried Severinus, starting up. "If the whole gigantic structure of our religion, whose foundations certainly do not rest upon air, the marvels of our worship, the words of the fathers of the church, the historical proofs of our traditions which reach beck to the time of the establishment of Catholicism by Peter himself, could not convince you, there is nothing left for me to say."

"All that, my friend, even granting that they were proofs, could not make me forget the causes of the Reformation. The Reformation is the mother of my faith."

"Ah, do not utter these words in the same breath! What had your Reformation in common with faith? Were your dry, philosophical Melanchthon, your rough, sensual Luther, your chiding, physically and morally starving Hutten, representatives of a religious transformation?"

"They were men who had the courage to appear before the hypocrisy of your degenerate priesthood as they really were; who did not seek the halo of sanctity in the denial of human nature, but honored God and his wisdom in his laws. Besides, we too do not lack sainted martyrs, and the flames that consumed a Huss branded an eternal stigma upon your church."

"I cannot argue with you about the means the church was permitted to use against such apostates. I will only tell you, my child, that the Reformation of the sixteenth century was nothing more than a secular insurrection against abuses in the church, which unfortunately cannot be denied. But a secular revolution can never create a religion, and therefore Protestantism lacks the positive character the human heart needs, and where it strives to appropriate it, becomes a monster, for it is and remains nothing more than a--protest against Catholicism."

"Our Reformation was not to create a religion; its purpose was merely to free one already existing from abuse and error. Its task was to restore Christianity to its original purity, and if it did not wholly succeed, if in Protestantism it has only produced a transitory, imperfect form, we still thank it for the highest blessings of civilization, and most precious of all, that freedom of conscience which permits the dissatisfied mind to choose its own religion."

"And this much-praised 'freedom of conscience' leads directly to want of principle, and becomes the destruction of all virtue, all religion!" cried Severinus, indignantly. "The human race cannot dispense with a positive church discipline without falling into anarchy. And in you, Cornelia, unhappily, I have already had an opportunity to learn the effects of this emancipation."

"You have learned, Severinus," interrupted Cornelia, with noble pride, "that I resisted evil with the same power with which I now repel the flattering allurements of a church adorned with all the magic of fancy and attraction of rites, because it is at variance with my own convictions. Is this a want of moral discipline?"

Severinus walked on beside Cornelia in silence. The sun had risen higher in the heavens, and the bell for mass rang from the neighboring convent. Severinus paused and gazed long and earnestly into Cornelia's eyes. "Girl, does not that innocent voice fall upon your ear in tones of touching warning, like the pleading of a mother calling to her lost child?"

"Do not be such a bigoted Catholic to-day, Severinus," said Cornelia, gazing at him beseechingly. "All the joy of this earthly life is stirring in my heart, and must I constantly argue with you about the best means of reaching heaven? Oh, let me enjoy with a thankful soul the rich abundance of happiness my Creator has poured out for me! Do not cast the black shadow of your religious harshness over the sunny picture of this day. Severinus, my dear, gloomy friend, be mild and gentle. Look at me as kindly as you used to do. See, see, there is the glimmer of a smile upon your face! Ah, it has already vanished again! What a pity! Ever since the news of Ottmar's going over to the liberal party brought me back to Germany, and filled me with the blissful certainty of being reunited to him, you have become a different person. When I lost him, I gained you; and now that I am to gain him once more, I lose you. When I felt miserable and lonely, you were as loving and patient as a father; but since I have been animated with new hope, you have retired coldly into yourself, and you have hidden yourself behind the walls of your work of conversion."

"My task, Cornelia, is only to aid the afflicted; the happy do not need me." Severinus looked silently up towards heaven. His eyes were bloodshot; his wasted face, bronzed by the Italian sun, glowed with fervor.

Cornelia laid her clasped hands compassionately and beseechingly upon his breast. "Severinus, you are suffering; I see it."

For a moment he pressed her hands closely to his throbbing heart, then hurled them away, with an expression of horror, and hurried off.

Cornelia looked after him in astonishment, but did not try to follow, for she felt that the emotion which moved him was a secret she ought not to fathom. She turned towards the rural inn where she lodged, and now observed for the first time that one of the artists who came to the island to sketch was seated an a little hillock not far from the spot where she had been pacing with Severinus, and recognized him as the very person to whose talent she owed her first picture of Ottmar. She approached, and he hastily concealed in his portfolio the paper upon which he had been working.

"You only arrived yesterday evening, and are already sketching the scenery, Herr A----. Is it not a little hasty?"

"I have already made myself familiar with all its details," said A----, with evident embarrassment. "I am very much hurried, because I would like to finish the picture in time for the exhibition at H----."

"Then I will not detain you, but wish you all possible success. Au revoir, Herr A----."

"I will do myself the honor of waiting upon you at a later hour, Fräulein Erwing," said A----, bowing respectfully; and, as Cornelia turned away, he drew out his sketch, and eagerly continued his work.

Cornelia entered the public room, to ask if the newspapers had arrived. It was full of active life. Some twenty young artists were standing together consulting about a trip they were to take; most of them handsome young fellows, with large beards, boldly-curved Calabrian hats, open shirt-collars, and the general adventurous negligence of apparel with which the young representatives of the laws of beauty seek to remove the pedantic stiffness of modern costume.

A general "ah!" echoed through the room at Cornelia's entrance, and a movement took place which made the dense clouds of tobacco-smoke that filled the low apartment whirl as if driven by the wind. The hats were removed; the beer-glasses noiselessly set aside. All crowded around Cornelia.

"Fräulein Erwing!" cried one, to whom a waving red mane and widely-dilated nostrils gave the appearance of a lion, "we have at last caught you without your black guardian! You must yield to superior force, and let us steal your face. We are a terrible band of robbers, and a person for whom we once lay snares does not escape us so easily."

"Yes, but we must first have a fight, to decide which of us she will allow to paint her," said another, waving a staff in the air.

"Fräulein Erwing," cried a little black-bearded Pole, with a shrill accent, "I will shoot the first man to whom you sit!"

"That is not necessary," growled he of the lion's mane; "we will all paint her at once!"

"Yes, yes!" cried many voices at the same moment. "That's a good idea! We will all paint her at once!"

"That is, if I will sit to you," laughed Cornelia, "for I have not yet resigned all right of ownership in my own face, gentlemen."

"Fräulein Erwing," began the man of the lion's mane, with great pathos, "we do not know in what branch of Christian duty your reverend father instructs you, but he has certainly taught you that our advantages are only bestowed upon us that we may make them available for the profit and welfare of others; so you will perceive that it is your duty to pay the debt you owe Providence for your face, by using it to aid the development of youthful talent."

"Yes!" cried another; "you could not justify yourself before God if you displayed such a wealth of beauty to idle gazers, and grudgingly refused the struggling artist permission to use and perpetuate its lines in an inspired creation."

"You would make me unconscionably vain, gentlemen," said Cornelia, "if the fame of being the most beautiful on this little island were not so cheaply purchased."

A general "Oh, oh!" expressed the indignation of the enthusiastic artists at this modesty, and a torrent of eager protestations threatened to follow; but Cornelia cut them short by exclaiming, gayly, "Well, well, if you can make me of any use for a picture, I will give you a sitting; but one only, and at the utmost two hours long. So, whoever wants to paint me must take advantage of the opportunity."

"That is excellent!" they all cried, joyously. "It's a very short time, to be sure, but we'll see about the rest. But when may we draw you?"

"Whenever you choose, gentlemen. Perhaps the best time would be now!"

"Yes, yes; we will take her at her word," said one of the older ones of the party. "It shall be done now; and when the two hours are over, Fräulein Erwing shall see the sketches, and decide which of us she considers worthy the honor of another sitting for the completion of her picture."

"But our excursion," said a tall lad, whose whole vitality seemed to have run into an immense length of limb. "Shall we defer our excursion?"

"Let your chicken legs take you where you like, man," thundered he of the lion's mane; "but don't say you are an artist, if you talk about excursions while our eyes are permitted a glimpse into the holy of holies of beauty."

"Let him go!" cried another. "He can't help it; all his vital functions are expended in the use of his feet. It will be one the less to take up the room; there are twenty-three of us without him. The number is still too large. I scarcely believe that there were ever so many assembled on the island at one time before."

A long debate now followed concerning the place where they should sketch Cornelia, while the latter had meantime obtained possession of the newspaper, and was reading it in breathless suspense. Suddenly she started. She had found what she sought,--Ottmar's name as a candidate for the H---- Chambers. Her face was suffused with a rosy flush of joy, and her eyes sparkled as she laid the sheet aside and turned towards the artists, who were disputing violently because some thought it too hot out of doors, and others considered the room too small.

"Gentlemen," she cried gayly, "peace is the first condition I shall impose if I am to sit for you. We will go out into the open air and look for some shady spot; if you all want to paint me at the same time, we shall certainly need more room than there is here."

The proposal was accepted, and the whole party went out with Cornelia. On a lofty part of the shore, not far from the inn, was a large open space surrounded with lofty trees, beneath which stood wooden benches and tables, and where, in spite of the heat, it was cool and pleasant. The eye could wander undazzled over the rippling lake and the beautiful island, which rested on the waters like a large green leaf. The light surges gently rocked the boats fastened near by; in one of them, under the spreading branches of an ancient linden, a peasant lad was extended sleeping comfortably, undisturbed by the loud bustle of the approaching artists. It seemed as if all nature was slumbering in her sunny noontide brightness.

"Well, gentlemen," exclaimed Cornelia, "is it not delightful here? Have we not shade, fresh breezes, and comfort?"

"Yes, yes," cried the artists in one breath; "we will stay here. Out with the portfolios, and let every one take his place and go to work!"

They buzzed about Cornelia like a swarm of bees which are about to settle and fly from one spot to another, now alighting, now rising again, now dispersing, and anon collecting at the same point, scuffling with each other about places, and filling the inexperienced observer with anxiety lest they should never get established. Such were the preparations of the artists at the beginning of their work. Here several were disputing about the profile, yonder a group wished to sit opposite to her, not unfrequently a slight skirmish decided the matter, and those who did not succeed in conquering a place climbed up into the trees and established themselves and their portfolios among the branches.

"We must form the narrowest possible semicircle," advised he of the lion's mane, who, as the possessor of the strongest lungs in the company, undertook the duty of organizing the party, in which, by means of a great expenditure of voice and unwearied energy, he at last succeeded; and when, with the aid of the trees, a half-circle was formed in the shape of an amphitheatre whose extremities could not even obtain a full profile, but merely a portion of the cheek and ear, the zealous artist first perceived that he had completely excluded himself. His nostrils dilated to an unprecedented size as his large eyes wandered around the circle, while his broad freckled hands were thrust helplessly through his unkempt mane. A shrill peal of laughter echoed jeeringly from the circle and the trees, "Richard Cœur de Lion has no place!"

"Be calm, Richard," cried one; "we will get you into the exhibition after all. We'll paint Fräulein Erwing as the lion's bride, and you as the monster!"

"Jeer away, you mocking-birds!" he thundered. "Because I am an artist, I thought more of the subject than myself, and I'll show you what an artist can do. I'll paint a neck and heir such as the world never yet saw!" and with these words he strode majestically on, seated himself behind Cornelia, and began to work with the must grotesque movements.

Silence now reigned while the three-and-twenty artists struggled in the greatest possible haste to perpetuate her features.

Cornelia had watched the tumult absently; her thoughts were wandering far away, and the stillness that ensued was most welcome. She could give herself up to her dreams undisturbed. "She is marvelously beautiful!" suddenly cried one of the younger artists from his perch in the tree. Universal applause answered this naïve expression of delight. "The birds in the trees are singing your praises, Fräulein Erwing!" cried another. "Doesn't that flatter you?"

"Oh, certainly," she answered, smiling as indifferently as if she had not understood the compliment paid her.

"The best likeness will flatter her most," growled Richard Cœur de Lion from behind Cornelia. "Express your admiration by work instead of words, and she will value it more."

"Well growled, lion!" said the young enthusiast in the tree.

"Go on the stage and declaim verses; you are more fit for an actor than an artist," exclaimed Richard, without having the slightest suspicion that he was himself in his appearance the most theatrical of all; for naturalness, when carried too far, becomes as great a caricature as affectation, and the stage is certainly the home of caricatured forms.

"Come, gentlemen," cried Cornelia, laughing; "the time you spend in disputing you will lose in work; for I must tell you that I will not sit a moment longer than the two hours agreed upon! It is altogether too uncomfortable to endure the gaze of three-and-twenty pairs of eyes."

This threat re-established peace; for the artists once more devoted all their energy to their work, and henceforth nothing was heard but the wondering exclamations of several country people who stationed themselves here and there on the outskirts of the shaded spot to gaze at a proceeding utterly incomprehensible to them. The time agreed upon passed away, and Cornelia rose. Neither grumbling nor entreaties availed; she kept resolutely to her determination. The sketches were laid before her, and as she looked at them in succession she burst into a merry laugh. She saw her own face taken from some twenty different stand-points. "Dear me, can I be like all these?" she exclaimed, clasping her hands in astonishment. "If I ever knew how I looked, I should not from this day! Who can decide which of these many faces is mine? If this is, of course that can't be; and if this profile taken from the right is a good likeness, how can the one sketched from the left resemble me? The right side of my face must be entirely different from the left,--and that would be horribly abnormal. According to these profile views I should have two kinds of eyes, eyebrows, cheeks; nay, even my nose would consist of two dissimilar halves. Now, can you dispute this, gentlemen?"

The artists themselves could not help laughing as they looked at their pictures.

"Now you will get an idea of the variety and abundance of beauty your features possess, Fräulein Erwing," said one of the oldest of the group. "When compared with you the majority of the sketches seem passable likenesses, although so different from each other that one would almost doubt whether they all represented the same face."

"A very pretty compliment to me--and an admirable defense of your colleagues," said Cornelia, courteously.

"But, Fräulein Erwing," cried another; "you have not yet noticed a picture which is at all events unique in its way; and our Cœur de Lion, with unusual modesty, has already been waiting a long time for your opinion."

He handed Richard's drawing to Cornelia, and all gazed at it in astonishment, for it was a master-piece. A woman's upraised head, adorned with a wealth of hair so boldly drawn that one felt tempted to pass it through the fingers. A few curls which had escaped from the braids fell upon a most beautiful neck. Cornelia looked at the sheet in amazement. "You are indeed an artist," said she, fixing her large eyes with winning kindness upon Richard's rugged face. He blushed to the roots of his tawny hair with delight. "Fräulein Erwing," he exclaimed, "no praise ever made me so proud!"

"Yes, yes, Cœur de Lion, Fräulein Erwing is right," said several of the group; "this hair and neck irresistibly tempt the beholder to turn the head and see the face, which is concealed from us. You have produced a master-piece."

"If you go on so much longer, he'll get so vain that he will comb his hair to-morrow. Just see! he is running his fingers through his mane!" said others, laughing.

"Well," exclaimed the rest, "we will hope that at the exhibition Fräulein Erwing's features will yet win the victory over the beauty of her hair."

Thus each was cheered by the conviction that he alone would obtain the prize.

"So you will not sit longer to any of us?" asked Richard, as he placed his sketch in his portfolio.

"No, gentlemen. I was in the mood to enter into your jest; but if you ask me in earnest, I must tell you that it would not be at all agreeable to me to expose my face to the eyes of the whole public. I am both too proud and too modest."

"Is this your final decision?"

"It is irrevocable," said Cornelia, with courteous resolution.

"Well, we will not be ungrateful. In these two hours we have at least fixed the outlines of your features," said one of the quieter members of the party.

But the others would not yield at once, and began to plead again.

"If you understood the spirit that animates these features, you would beg no longer, for you would know it to be vain," cried Richard, with his usual artless pathos. Then he held out his hand to Cornelia and continued: "I should probably have the best right to entreat you for another sitting, since I was so great a loser; but I will not ask it after what you have just said."

"I thank you for your delicacy of feeling, Herr Richard," replied Cornelia, with unconcealed admiration. "You may be assured that if I sat to any of these gentlemen it would be to you; yet if you understand the reason of my refusal, you will not be angry if I make no exception, even in your favor."

Richard buried Cornelia's hand in his prickly beard to press a kiss upon it. "Angry with you? Who that had the heart of a true artist could be? For, although we are not permitted to make portraits of you, we still owe you thanks for a type of beauty which will be of service to us all."

"Yes, yes; he is right," they all assented. "You have not only enriched our eyes, but our imaginations! Long live Cornelia Erwing! Hurrah!"

At that moment the sound of the dinner-hell echoed from the inn, and at the same instant Severinus's black-robed figure appeared, coming from the neighboring convent. The artists wiped the perspiration from their brows, for the noonday sun and their zeal had made them very bot.

"There comes your pious father!" declaimed the young enthusiast, who always spoke in quotations. "Now, brothers, let us fly!"

And partly fear of the "black coat," partly hunger, drove the noisy group to the table. They departed waving their hats, nodding, and singing; and Cornelia was still looking after them with a smile, when Severinus approached with a pale, gloomy face.

"Such ovations certainly do not prepare one for the church," he murmured, somewhat bitterly.

"Ah, Severinus! I am so happy!" cried Cornelia, frankly. "What open-hearted, gay, magnificent men they are! How I laughed! It is a pity you were not here! Tell me, Father Severinus,--you are sincere,--am I really as beautiful as they all say?" she asked, with mischievous naïveté.

Severinus looked timidly away from her, and with a deep flush fixed his eyes upon the ground. "I do not know."

"You don't know?"

"I think only your soul beautiful, but not your body. Physical beauty is something so perishable that it is unheeded by one who perceives, and knows how to value, that of the soul."

Cornelia became embarrassed. She was ashamed of the want of reserve which had induced her to ask Severinus so inappropriate a question, and did not see the strange glance with which he gazed at her blooming cheeks and lips, and then clinched his teeth.

"Forgive me for disturbing your grave mood with such jests, my reverend friend; but I cannot help it. The gayety natural to my youth will sometimes assert its rights. I was very glad they thought me beautiful. The sight of a lovely face is always a pleasure to me, and the idea that my appearance could also rejoice the eyes and hearts of others pleased me. If this is vanity, is, at least, very innocent."

"Certainly, my child," said Severinus, and his tone gradually lost its assumed harshness. "I will not embitter the harmless little pleasures of your youth. I am sure they will not smother the earnestness of your nature."

"Severinus," said Cornelia, smiling, "isn't it a fact that you do not know what hunger is?"

"No, certainly not. But you seem to know; so come,--let us go to dinner."

Cornelia was glad to have put an end to the uncomfortable conversation, and hastened lightly on before him. Since her joy in life was once more awakened, and hope and cheerfulness again stirred within her, she felt Severinus's gloomy mood as a heavy burden. As long as she was at variance with her own heart and the world, the character of the ascetic priest suited her better than aught else; but now it began to form a disagreeable contrast with her mood, and cast a shadow over the newly-risen sun of her love. Yet she was too grateful to forget for a moment what consolation his assistance had afforded her in the time of her heavy visitation; so she maintained an unaltered, frank cordiality towards him, although he now began to torture her with a thousand contradictions and absurdities.

The scene with the artists, innocent as it was in itself, seemed to have made Severinus very thoughtful, in consequence of the pleasure Cornelia derived from it. Such impressions must be kept from her at any cost, for they were not adapted to aid his work of conversion. Even if he should remove her from the neighborhood, he could not prevent these young enthusiasts from traveling after her. He therefore went to the superior of the convent on the island, and, when he returned, brought an invitation from her to Cornelia to take up her residence in the cloister, "as it was not proper for a young girl, with an equally young companion, to remain in a country inn with a party of gay young men." Cornelia, who did not care where she lodged, easily allowed herself to be persuaded to fulfill Severinus's wish, and accept the friendly superior's offer. Her removal to the cloister took place immediately, and the astonished hostess told the artists, on their return from an excursion, that the beautiful Fräulein Erwing had just entered a convent. They were beside themselves at the news, for who could doubt that the poor victim of the black coat had been brought here to commence her novitiate? Thus Severinus's design of spreading a halo of inaccessibility around Cornelia, and cutting off any intrusive pursuit, was effectually attained; but that neither she nor her companion should betray the truth in their unavoidable walks, it was necessary that they should be taken away with all secrecy. On that very evening Severinus excited Cornelia's interest in the B---- Oberland to such a degree that she herself expressed a wish to continue her journey as soon as possible, and he was merely fulfilling her own desire when he proposed that they should leave the Island at daybreak, not to return. As no one saw or heard anything of this departure, Cornelia was, and remained, in the convent, whose strict seclusion made any inquiries impossible, and the young artists grieved deeply that the world was robbed of so much beauty.

Meantime Severinus took the supposed victim farther and farther away, and several months passed so quickly in the constant change from one beautiful scene to another, and in grave but intellectually exciting conversation with Severinus, that she was not conscious how skillfully he managed to cut her off from all society. Priests and nuns were the only persons with whom she held occasional intercourse; and she passed them by with friendly indifference, which rendered any advances impossible. Severinus's hopes of a conversion drooped more and more; he could not conceal from himself that a sorrow was gnawing at his soul which exhausted his best powers, and felt, with increasing despair, that he should succumb himself before he could conquer Cornelia's resolute temper.

XXIII
BETWEEN HEAVEN AND EARTH

Severinus entered Cornelia's room one evening when they were to spend the night in a peasant's house in the B---- forest. She was standing at the window, gazing out into the sultry night. The sky arched over the earth like a leaden-hued canopy; not a breath of air was stirring, not a leaf moved on the trees; here and there a star gleamed forth where the dense masses of clouds parted for a moment, and now and then a distant flash of lightning glittered in the horizon, revealing the dim outlines of the forest-crowned heights. "Severinus," she said, drawing a long breath, as she turned toward him, "let us go out into the open air before the storm breaks: the air is so oppressive here; perhaps it is cooler outside."

"I have come to speak to you about very serious subjects: it will be better for us to stay here," said Severinus. And now for the first time Cornelia noticed his gloomy expression, and looked with anxious expectation into his face.

"Cornelia, the time when your fate must be decided has arrived. The day of election is approaching. I must not allow Ottmar to move forward unrestrained upon the road in which he can only bring ruin upon our church. If he is elected to the parliament, a powerful enemy will arise against us. I have already told you what papers the order has in its hands: they must be used now, if they are not to become useless. Let Ottmar be a deputy; let him speak, and--as is to be foreseen--win the masses, and everything we undertake against him will be in vain. The last point of time is reached, when I must decide what is to be done."

"And that is a publication of his relations with Jesuitism, the destruction of the toilsomely obtained confidence of his party, in order to prevent his election. Am I not right?"

"Certainly."

"And do you not know that you will not convert a man like Ottmar by such means, but simply render him miserable?"

"We wish to make him harmless,--nothing more."

"But you do far worse," cried Cornelia, indignantly. "You bar the path upon which he might become a better man; hurt him back to the cheerless void of a life without a purpose: perhaps even entangle him in fresh snares of falsehood and hypocrisy; and thus destroy a nature which, in its own way, might accomplish great things for the world. Who gives you the right thus violently to interfere with an independent existence?"

"The same right which the government has to punish secular crimes, we, as the representatives of the kingdom of God, possess against him who sins against God and his servants."

"Severinus, when the government chastises, it represents the insulted law, and uses honest means; but you avenge only your own boundless pride, and your weapons are hypocrisy and deceit! Are you better than he whom you punish?"

"Cornelia!" cried Severinus, with flashing eyes, "do you dare say that to me?"

"I have never spoken anything but the truth all my life. You could not expect me to call wrong right; and if God should descend to the earth once more he would judge the zeal of those who commit sin for his honor, and misuse his name for selfish purposes, far more harshly than the errors of the men who have deserted him in form, but not in reality."

"It is only natural that the child of the world should speak in her lover's favor; and I will be patient now, as I have often been before. I cannot ask you to perceive the sublimity of a subordination to the will of a chief, as our order practices it. Our General alone bears the responsibility; God will call him only to an account; and he can lay it aside: for God is higher than the law, and whoever represents him on earth cannot have his acts measured by the standard of earthly justice!"

Cornelia gazed at Severinus long and silently. "You told me a short time ago that you pitied me. Now I must answer you in the same words: Severinus, I pity you! I am not angry; but you will perceive that from this hour our paths must lie apart. If you deal a blow which will destroy Ottmar's honest efforts, it is my duty to be at his side."

"Cornelia, it is in your power to avert this dangerous blow."

"How?"

"The order has determined to give up the papers to you at the price of your conversion to Catholicism. The order feels itself justified in resigning the pursuit of this faithless man; if it can thereby win for the good cause another soul, which will be pleasing to God."

"Indeed!" cried Cornelia, fixing a piercing glance upon Severinus. "Is it thus you advance your work of conversion?"

"We leave you the choice between the only church which can save souls and your lover's prosperity, or his destruction and our hostility. Can you hesitate?"

Cornelia stood before him with noble dignity. "And do you believe you can win me over to a religion which sanctions such means? Do you think to bribe me by any advantage--even the welfare of the man I love--to deny that which is highest and most sacred to me: the knowledge of the truth? No, Severinus; I feel I possess the power to make the man of my heart happy without being compelled to save him from your persecution by abjuring my own faith!"

"May you not trust to yourself too much? He whom we wish to ruin is not so easily saved by any one, even the bold spirit of Cornelia Erwing!"

"Severinus, you frighten me! I never saw you in this mood before. I feel as if in my sleep I had wandered into a tiger's den, and on awakening found myself shut up alone with the terrible enemy!" She paused and looked at Severinus; then growing calmer, shook her head: "No, no, Severinus; that is a bad comparison; forgive me for it! Those pure eyes give the lie to your threats; the dignity enthroned upon your brow cannot suffer you to become the tool of a base revenge."

"Cornelia, you will never learn to understand the nature of Jesuitism. I am no blind tool who mechanically performs what is imposed upon him, but a living part of the whole, who abhors what injures the order, and labors for its advantage. Our obedience is no mere form which we can outwardly satisfy without real sympathy: it is an allegiance in spirit and in truth, which makes the will it serves its own. Thus I hate Ottmar, since he became faithless to his obligations towards us, as the order hates him, and will destroy him as the order commands, if you do not comply with the condition upon which we will spare him."

He watched Cornelia for a moment, then drew out some papers and spread them upon the table before her. "Here are the documents which are to serve us as weapons against Ottmar; read them, and convince yourself whether they will be destructive enough to him to outweigh the sacrifice you must make to secure his safety."

Cornelia looked over the papers, the very ones with which years before Severinus had succeeded in intimidating Ottmar, and binding upon him the chains he now wished to strip off. When she had finished, she gazed sorrowfully into vacancy.

"This is certainly material enough to devise a snare for him. Oh, Severinus, throw these papers into the fire, and I will revere you as a saint!"

"It will only cost you a few words, Cornelia. Say, 'I will become a Catholic,' and these papers are *yours*!"

Cornelia drew herself up proudly. "I have already told you that I would drive no bargain with my convictions. This is my final resolution!"

"Noble woman!" thought Severinus, gazing at her in astonishment.

Cornelia gathered up the documents, restored them to the priest, then clasped her hands, and gazed into his face with her irresistible charm. "Severinus, give me these papers."

A long pause ensued. The priest was absorbed in watching the beautiful face, and made no reply.

Cornelia took his hand; he started back.

"Severinus, for once, be more obedient to the law of love and forbearance God has written in our hearts, than the stern commands of your order; destroy these proofs of Heinrich's, and also your, dishonor,--or give them to me that I may do so. You do not answer! Oh, let my entreaties move you, dear, honored friend!"

Severinus covered his eyes with his hand, and exclaimed, almost imploringly: "Cease, Cornelia; you know not what you are doing."

"I am well aware of it,--I am torturing you; for I am bringing you into a conflict with what you believe to be your duty. I see the struggle between your Jesuit's conscience and your heart. True, genuine manhood will conquer; it will burst the fetters in which your whole life is bound."

She rushed to the table, took up a light, and held it towards Severinus, that he might set the papers on fire. A gust of air that blew through the open window made the flame flicker to and fro, and her light dress float around her like a cloud. As she stood thus with the arm that held the candle raised high above her head, bathed in the red gleam of the flickering light, in the earnestness of her enthusiasm,--half pleading, half commanding,--she seemed like an angel; and without knowing what he was doing he threw the papers towards her, bent down, and pressed the hem of her dress to his lips.

"I thank you!" cried Cornelia. But ere she could gather up the scattered papers Severinus recollected himself, and caught her hand.

"Stop! these papers are not yours nor mine; they belong to the order which intrusted them to my care, and only an evil spirit could have so bewildered my mind that I wavered in my duty." He made the sign of the cross, pressed his hands tightly upon his heart, and softly murmured the "*Anima Christi, sanctifica me*,"[1] then collected the papers and went to the window. The rain was pouring in torrents; he leaned out and let the cool water drench his head. "Extinguish, oh, extinguish the fire!" he prayed, looking up with a deep sigh at the dark watery masses of clouds.

Cornelia watched him with mingled surprise and grief. "Severinus, you are playing a part with yourself, like all who hold ideas founded on sophisms and principles contrary to nature; you must do so, at a moment when your illusion forms so striking a contrast with the truth. I can only pity you; but may God let those who made you a Jesuit,--who robbed you of the world and the world of you,--reap the fruits of their deed!"

"Do not blame them," replied Severinus, turning calmly away from the window. "They were my parents, and both are dead. I, too, have often cursed them for giving me life; but since I became a Jesuit, I bless them."

"Unhappy man, what secret weighs upon the past which you have hitherto so closely concealed?"

"Disgrace, girl! To you alone I will confess it, that some day you may think of me more kindly when we are parted. I have no name save that the church gave me; no father save God; no home save the Casa al Gesu; no human dignity save that of my holy office. If I had belonged to the world, I should have been an outcast. But my parents turned the curse into a blessing when they dedicated to Heaven the life they denied on earth; and for the sake of that deed may God pardon the sin which gave me birth!" He raised his head, while his face kindled with enthusiastic feeling. "But I, Cornelia, will devote my strength, to my latest breath, to that Jesuitism which accomplished the miracle of making the child of sin the supporter of the highest and holiest cause, which produces everything great and noble that can be done for the honor of God, and desires nothing except by all means, both mild and gentle, to lead men to heaven."

Cornelia gazed thoughtfully into vacancy, then suddenly looked earnestly at the regular features of the handsome man before her.

"Severinus," she said, with strange eagerness, "who was your father?"

"I do not know; I never saw him."

"Did your mother tell you nothing about him? or did you not know her either?"

"She could tell me nothing except how she loved him, and how he had deceived her. His accent betrayed that he was a German, but he concealed his name and residence. When I was scarcely a year old he disappeared, and no longer gave my mother any signs of existence except the remittance, through some unknown hand, of money for my education upon the condition that I should become a priest."

"And your mother; what was her name?"

"Girl, why do you ask me all these questions?"

"You shall learn the reason after you have told me who your mother was."

"I have no right to expose the name of the unhappy woman, and have never mentioned it to any one."

"Not even to Heinrich?"

"I never disclosed the secret of my past to him."

Cornelia approached him; her breath came more quickly. "Was your mother's name Angelina, Severinus?" said she, her voice tremulous with some secret emotion.

Severinus gazed at her in astonishment. "Yes, yes; how did you know?"

"Was she the sister of a Carmelite monk in Compatri?"

"Where did you learn this?" exclaimed Severinus, greatly agitated. "What connection have you with my past? Speak; of what are you thinking? Your eyes sparkle, your cheeks glow; do not torture me."

"Are you your mother's only child?"

"So truly as she expiated all her remaining days in a cloister, the one error of her life."

"Then God has sent me to you to warn you at the right time not to commit a most grievous wrong. Do you know who the man is whom you thus inexorably pursue?"

A suspicion began to arise in Severinus's mind; he recoiled and extended his hands repellently, as if he feared the words that hovered upon Cornelia's lips.

"He is your brother!" she cried, tears gushing from her eyes.

Severinus involuntarily pressed his hand upon his brow, his fingers quivered slightly as they touched the broad scar upon it, and he gazed absently before him as if in a dream.

"Oh, do not crush the feeling that stirs in your heart! Give me your hand, and let me tell you how warmly I greet the brother of my beloved! Oh, God, to see the two men dearest to me on earth united, the souls which always struggled with each other, and yet could never resist the impulse of sympathy, reconciled in brotherly love! And it is I, I who am permitted to bring you together, to give you to each other! Ah, my friend, this is inexpressible joy!"

"And are you so sure you are not deceiving yourself?" asked Severinus, gloomily.

"Deceiving? Oh, you incredulous man! Heinrich's father is yours also. Ten years before his marriage in Germany he traveled in Italy. In wild, romantic Compatri he was attracted by the beauty of your mother, Angelina, who was living in the greatest poverty upon the products of her vines and the scanty gifts of the Carmelite convent in that place, then falling to decay. He took her to Rome, and remained there two years,--until his duties compelled him to return to Germany and desert Angelina, with her eleven-months-old boy. What afterwards became of her and her child, Heinrich did not know."

"And how did Heinrich happen to tell you this?"

"He told me a great many things about his father's life."

"And where did he learn this sad history?"

"From Anton, who, as valet, accompanied old Herr von Ottmar on his travels, and whose statements were confirmed by the dead man's papers. Heinrich did not then foresee how important this discovery might some day become. But if all this is not sufficient proof for you, question your own heart; remember what an inexplicable affection still bound you to Heinrich, even after you believed him lost to the church. Does not this impulse of the heart harmonize with all that has been so strangely revealed to you? Oh, you feel it yourself at this moment! I see it by the tears that will steal out from beneath your lashes; you feel, you believe, that he is your brother!"

Severinus covered his face. "He is! he is! Oh, God, and I must ruin my brother!"

"Thank God," cried Cornelia, joyously, "you are moved, touched! The voice of blood is again stirring within you; you will be reconciled to him, will spare him! Oh, say you will!"

Severinus raised his head and leaned against the window-sill; the tears that Cornelia had seen in his eyes were dried. "Do you believe that a pupil of Loyola will listen to the voice of blood? Do you know what the saint, who is our protector and pattern, did? He burned, unread, the letters from his own family, that he might break off all ties with the world; and I, should I spare the enemy of my church because he is related to me? Should I allow my zeal in God's cause to grow cold because my heart warms with a mere animal instinct? No, Cornelia, my brothers are in Christ; he who does not belong to him is no brother of mine."

"Cruel, hard-hearted man!" cried Cornelia, in horror. "I do not know whether it is compassion or terror that seizes upon me, but my soul trembles at the power of an illusion which can thus petrify the noblest heart."

"Petrify!" cried Severinus. "Oh, do not speak so, child that you are! Have you ever cast a glance into this 'petrified heart'? Have you a suspicion of the strength of the love I must tear away from earth and consecrate to God? Have you ever heard the outcry of the tortured man when he is obliged to accomplish his regeneration from earthly to heavenly things? Do you know how mighty nature writhes and struggles and groans under the prickly iron ring of the cilicium?[2] You are spared these agonies, because God requires only the easiest sacrifices from you; but we, who are appointed to be the imitators of Christ upon earth, are compelled taste them to the dregs. We must fulfill our great task, and no human eye is permitted to see that the sacrifice it admires trickles from the warm heart's blood."

"My poor Severinus!"

"Do not pity me; I want no one's compassion. I only want you to understand me; the more difficult the victory, the greater the fame. I shall one day be proud of my tortures. But I must labor without rest or sleep, and watch over myself at every hour, for the enemy is cunning, and if he chooses can clothe himself in the garb of an angel." His large eyes rested ardently upon Cornelia.

"Severinus," she answered, sadly, "do you take me for this false angel--me, who preach nothing to you except the first and simplest laws of Christianity? Do you think the 'foul fiend' is in me, because I oppose a belief which rejects the purest impulse of nature as a mere animal instinct, if it is not of use to its plans,--denies the tie God himself has hallowed, if it bars its progress; and acknowledges nothing which does not----"

"Redound to the greater honor of God," interrupted Severinus. "Yes, we do all for the honor of God. That is the word which permits no false meaning; the path from which we cannot deviate an inch; the object from which we dare not turn our eyes, even though we trample underfoot the bodies of our dearest friends. He who opposes us must fall, for we cannot allow ourselves to be stopped. For the honor of God we live, and are ready to die."

"And are you sure that in this you act only for the honor of God? Are you sure you do not abuse this great word as a pretext for an act of selfishness?"

Severinus looked at her inquiringly.

She struggled with her Feelings, and then began, gently: "Tell me, my friend, if in the execution of a punishment commanded by the order a Jesuit should also find the gratification of a personal desire for revenge, would he not profane the cause of God by making it his own?"

"Certainly," replied Severinus, in a hollow tone, fixing his eyes upon the floor.

"There are many kinds of passions, of which the man who ardently desires only what is right is scarcely conscious, because he does not even allow them to take the form of a thought; yet they are there, and the so-called foul fiend undermines in them the more securely, because concealed, the toilsomely-erected structure of virtue. Let me quote an example. Suppose a Jesuit hated an enemy of his order, not only because the order hates him, but because he is loved by a girl who is dear to the Jesuit himself?"

Severinus started; a deep flush suffused his face.

Cornelia continued: "Suppose he used against him the weapons the order placed his hands, not for the sake of the church, but to serve the instincts of his own jealousy, and should suddenly perceive what he had not confessed, even to himself, what would be his duty then?"

Severinus was now as pale as he had before been red. He stood like a marble statue, not a breath stirred his breast; but at last his delicate lips opened to utter the words, "Then it would be his duty to resign the work he would profane to another, who could perform it with pure hands, solely for the sake of God and the order."

"Well, then, Severinus, do what you believe to be your duty. I have nothing more to say."

A deep silence followed. Severinus still stood motionless, and Cornelia did not venture to look at him; she did not wish to read the pale face. She was terrified at what, for Heinrich's sake, she had done to this noble man, and involuntarily feared the results.

Severinus slowly approached her, laid his hand upon her head, and said, "Let us bid each other farewell."

Cornelia looked up. The pure features expressed no bitterness, no anger, only the repose of an immovable resolution. "Farewell?" she asked, in surprise.

"For life!"

Remorse suddenly seized upon her. She had overstepped the bounds of womanly delicacy, and pitilessly assailed the heart which, in spite of its errors, she had always seen rise superior to every weakness. She now felt for the first time how much she should lose in him, and, with sincere shame, bent down, and before he could prevent it, pressed her lips to his hands. "Severinus, can you forgive me?"

"I have nothing to forgive," he replied, gently drawing back.

"Where are you going?"

"To Rome."

"And what takes you to Rome so suddenly?"

"I had already resolved to return there some weeks ago; only the hope of still winning you for the church, and the hostile mission against Heinrich, detained me. This hour is the destruction of all my plans. Nothing is left for me to do except to place the papers intrusted to me in the General's hands, and explain to him that I am unworthy of his confidence,--that I am not fit for the business of the world."

"And then,--what will happen then?"

"Then the General will commit the office I held to another, and, if God wills, sanction the penance I shall impose upon myself of voluntary seclusion in the monastery during the remainder of my life."

"Will you retire from the world,--bury yourself within the walls of a cloister?"

"That I may the more surely rise again in God."

"And is such a resolution compatible with your zeal for the order? Suppose your office falls into the hands of a man who will not act with the wisdom and dignity you have shown,--who will perhaps injure the interests and authority of your association,--would you not reproach yourself for having been to blame for this injury by resigning the 'holy cause' into unworthy hands?"

"There are many among our ranks who are perfectly competent to fill my place; the General's keen eye will discover the right man. I can perform my duties to the order. Even in the silence of a convent-cell, I can write the words with which I should cheer souls and strengthen them in the faith, and, in undisturbed intercourse with the Highest One, they will gain more sanctity and power than in the profane society of the world. Nay, my writings may perhaps influence future generations long after spoken words have died away. Is not such an expectation edifying to true faith?--such a resolution the highest victory over our earthly nature?"

"A victory! Oh, Severinus, do not deceive yourself! A spark of the warm life you wish to deny still glows in your breast. Suppose, Severinus, you should perceive too late that you had formed your resolution too early? Suppose you should long despairingly for a breath of freedom, and in the suffocating agony of being walled up alive in the wild struggle of its contending elements, your soul should forget itself and God, and fall into the apparently liberating hand of Satan?"

Severinus recoiled a step in horror. "Stop, I implore you!"

But Cornelia's unfettered stream of eloquence would not allow itself to be repressed. "You go into the cloister, not because you have conquered, but because you fear to yield; you go there to fly from the battle, not to rest after the victory; but that which would have caused the conflict here will go with you, will disturb the peace of your devout solitude; and you must conquer it with anguish there as well as here, can succumb to it in the narrow convent-cell as well as in God's wide world."

Severinus's broad breast heaved painfully. "Oh, God! my God! let me withstand this last trial!" he prayed, fervently. "Cornelia, I do not retreat to the cloister on account of the danger, but to fly from the evil I abhor; that I may no longer see the world that stands between me and heaven, which I hate----"

"The world to you is mankind; if you detest the former it is for the sake of the latter. But why? What have men done to you? You are a servant of Christ. Does this humanity, which Christ so loved that he suffered and bled for it, deserve your love less than the Master's? Why do you scorn the race whose form a God did not hesitate to assume,--for which a God bore the tortures of life and death? Has it injured you more than him? It has not pressed upon your brow the crown of thorns; it has not nailed you to the cross; and yet he could forgive, while you cannot!"

"A God might do this,--but I am a man!"

"And do you know why you hate mankind? Because you dare not love like a human being. You curse your own earthly nature, because it always opposes your task. You are a man, and would fain be a god; you have human passions, and desire to practice a divine self-sacrifice. This is the fatality of your position, this the foul fiend you fear! Oh, I know my words fall upon you as the surges dash against a rock, but it seems as if a higher power urged me on to struggle again and again against the unhappy errors of your church!"

"Cornelia," cried Severinus, starting up, "my church does not err,--she is infallible!"

"But, I tell you, it is an error that Christ has required of his priests what the church demands from you. If Christ was God, it is presumption for you mortals to imitate his divine person, and attempt to give the world an example of what you do not attain yourselves. You are merely to announce it and show it in all its beauty in yourselves. But how can you do this,--shut off from life behind convent walls? Only when, like our ministers, in real life, before the eyes of a whole parish, oppressed by the same anxieties, pursued by the same enemies, assailed by the same temptations as all, you can practice the virtues you preach, will you become a true representative of the Christian religion, will you have a right to require of others what was not too difficult for yourself, and be what Christ desires, a true, perfect man!"

Severinus hastily approached the door: his whole manner betrayed tokens of violent emotion. "I dare not listen to you longer, terrible, dangerous woman! God sees my anguish that I cannot save your soul, make your noble powers useful to the good cause. In you all the hostile powers of the world assume a bodily form; in you I have convinced myself that I am no match for them, and only the repentance of a whole life can atone for the weakness!"

"Must I, then, lose you forever?"

"Forever! But my prayers will be with you,--implore the protection of the Holy Virgin for you." His voice trembled. "God cannot let such a soul go to destruction!" He turned and, with averted face, opened the door.

Then Cornelia's sincere affection burst forth in all its fervor; she rushed up to him, threw her arms around his neck, and with childlike contrition laid her head upon his breast. "Will you go without a farewell?" she cried, sobbing. "Ah, Severinus, a deep, inexpressible pity for you overwhelms me! Poor, noble man, I loved you so dearly!"

Severinus stood as if a thunderbolt had struck him; he did not move a finger, did not clasp Cornelia to his heart or push her from him. But suddenly a cry of anguish burst from his compressed lips, so full of torture that Cornelia's very soul was filled with terror, and she no longer ventured to detain him when, as if driven by some mortal dread, he hurried away.

Late at night, before she went to rest, she saw him wandering about in the storm and rain, and before dawn he entered the carriage which bore him away from Cornelia forever. He traveled without pausing until he reached Rome, where he delivered the papers to the General; confessed, resigned his office, and entered the Casa al Gesu as a monk, to atone by the strictest seclusion for the crime of being a man.

XXIV
REGENERATION

While Cornelia was confidently looking forward to a meeting with Ottmar, proud in the consciousness of having repelled all the attacks of his enemies, *Heinrich* was tortured by uncertainty in regard to her fate. Ever since his return home, he had lived exclusively on his estates, engaged in making preparations for his new calling. In this complete seclusion from the would, whose influence had been so hostile to Cornelia, engrossed by the ideas of which she was the charming representative, he fed his longing for her more and more. At every step in his new career he had expected some sign of life from her, but in vain. His hope began to waver. He knew that she was in the hands of the Jesuits, and trembled lest her young, susceptible soul, her easily excited fancy, should not remain closed to their influences, for then she would be irrecoverably torn from him. He had fulfilled every condition mentioned in her letter. It was not possible that she still loved him if, after all this, she still persisted in her obstinate silence. A deep melancholy began to overpower him once more; his prospects lay before him like a region destitute of sunlight; his whole career would lack purpose if Cornelia was not won again. As yet no success had crowned his efforts. He had no anticipation of the happiness he would feel if he could some day consider himself as the true benefactor of a whole nation. The quiet labor for his new vocation did not yet satisfy him, and he therefore founded all his hopes upon his entrance into parliament, and longed for the day of election as the last limit Cornelia had perhaps allowed herself. One day, in his restlessness, he drove into the city to divert his thoughts. He wished to visit the Exhibition, and as he went up the broad staircase of the museum he noticed with secret pleasure that people whispered to each other, "That is Ottmar!" and looked at him with interest and approval. He entered the large hall where reigned the solemn silence with which men receive into their souls the wonders of art. The first and second rooms were empty of spectators. The dead and yet lifelike forms upon the walls looked down upon him with their eternal laughing, weeping, or anger. An exhibition is a mute world of a brilliant-hued medley of times, customs, and passions, petrified as if by some magic, and imprisoned in frames, condemned to remain motionless in the attitude assumed at the moment when the spell began to work. There a Magdalen repents with inexhaustible tears; yonder a Roman maiden allures, ever unsuccessfully, with her motionless, half-opened lips; and here an Alva rages in implacable fury, while close by a Huss burns in never-dying flames; below a wolf snaps in unappeasable hunger at a child, which, fortunately, he will never reach; a mother seeks to tear it away, and cannot draw it to her protecting breast; the poor woman is condemned to perpetual dread, and the spectator with her. Not far away is--and will forever remain--a pair of lovers in the act of exchanging a kiss. Upon the other side ships struggle with waves, nations contend in a never-decided battle, a vanquished man awaits the death-stroke of the conqueror, and high up, an a golden background, flooded by the light that streams through the glass dome, is enthroned the Virgin, in her calm peace, surrounded by her heavenly glory.

All the passions, joys, griefs, and hopes of humanity, fixed and beautified by the power of genius, displayed themselves to *Heinrich's* wandering gaze, but his thoughts dwelt only with Cornelia; nay, it even seemed as if here and there he found some resemblance to her. One picture had her eyes, another her profile or her mouth,--her brow. He fancied he saw her everywhere; it was doubtless a trick of his excited imagination, or the likeness all regular beauties bear to each other. He passed on into the third hall, which was crowded. Two oil-paintings attracted the especial attention of the public, and the universal verdict pronounced them to be the best in the Exhibition. It was difficult for him to make his way in, but he could scarcely trust his eyes when he saw one of them,--for it was Cornelia again; the likeness was so speaking that no doubt was possible, and the figure of Severinus beside her was equally unmistakable. Both were really only minor accessories to a beautiful landscape, but painted in a most masterly manner. They were standing under lofty trees which formed the foreground, by the shore of a lake, which, surrounded by beautiful mountain-peaks, stretched out into the background. Severinus had one arm extended, pointing to a church-tower almost shrouded in mist. Cornelia, with clasped hands, was looking up into his face. In the catalogue, the work was merely named "View of the Ch---- See, by A----."

Heinrich could not understand it; and when an acquaintance came up and called his attention to the other famous painting, he turned carelessly towards it; but his astonishment was inexpressible, as here also he found Cornelia. The figures were life-size. The picture represented the moment before a novice assumes the garb of a nun. She was leaning upon the window-sill of a gloomy convent-room, gazing up towards heaven, whose brilliant blue gleamed through the bars, while a green branch, swayed by the wind, tossed against the rusty iron gratings. The artist, by a singular fancy, had drawn his principal figure with her back towards the spectators, probably to show in all its magnificence the beautiful brown hair which was so soon to fall under the scissors. But the bright panes of the window, which opened inwards, revealed the face, upraised in fervent prayer. This face was Cornelia's, as well as the hair he had so often stroked; the youthful neck, which the thin undergarment she was soon to cover with the nun's dress, lying close by, clearly revealed, and which he had so often admired. He rubbed his eyes; he looked again and again; it was still Cornelia. A gloomy, haggard prioress was in the act of advancing with the scissors, and a sweet-faced young nun was gazing with evident compassion at the beautiful, devout novice.

"Is it not a true work of genius?" said *Heinrich's* companion. "The expression of enthusiastic devotion in the face reflected in the window, and the wonderfully painted hair! One really dreads the moment when that stern, unfeeling prioress will cut it off!"

"By whom was the picture painted?" asked *Heinrich*.

"By a B---- artist of the name of Richard."

"Does any one know whom he had for a model?"

"No; he keeps it a profound secret. I could almost believe he has--Heaven knows how!--witnessed such a scene. People don't create such things purely from imagination."

Heinrich made no reply, and his acquaintance, perceiving his strange emotion, withdrew.

Ottmar went from one picture to another; but reflect and consider as he would, one thing only was clear to him, that Cornelia must have sat to these artists herself, for such a resemblance could not be accidental; and although the window-panes in one picture reflected her face but dimly, it was all the more unmistakable in the other,--and Severinus too. So in this way she had consented to make known to the world her connection with Jesuitism! She must consider these relations an honor of which she publicly boasted, and this she could not do unless she had been converted to Catholicism,--unless they had impressed upon her mind the dogma of the supremacy and infallibility of the one saving church. There was a mysterious connection of ideas between the two pictures; and although he would not give way to it, it oppressed his heart with a torturing dread. The words "people don't create such things purely from imagination" still rang in his ears. Suppose the artist had really taken the idea of his work from the fact that Cornelia, whom he perhaps painted a short time before, had entered a convent? In conditions of the soul like that into which he had cast Cornelia, where the whole existence is pervaded with pain, and every foundation is shaken, the seeds of the Jesuits thrive best; in such moods they most easily obtain a mastery over man. Now, for the first time, it occurred to him that her letter had been redolent of that pride of self-sacrifice, which, after great conflicts, chills so many a young heart, and drives it into the nursery of such virtues, the convent. Suppose Cornelia had gone so far? It was not impossible! Her enthusiasm in everything, especially her zealous desire to be of use, the inclination to sacrifice herself for great ideas which she had so often shown, her susceptibility to the poesy of religion,--all this seemed to him material enough to form an agent of the church; and as the psychological fathers would not have ventured to send such a fiery genius into the world, they had perhaps taken advantage of some moment of weakness to imprison her in one of the convents which lead young girls "to the heart of Jesus." The more *Heinrich* thought of this, the more probable and clear it appeared. Urged on by his agony, he hastened to ascertain the residences of the two artists. He wished to buy the pictures spite of their extremely high price,-- wished to learn some particulars about Cornelia. He would and must have some certainty; he could not bear this terrible doubt. He wrote to Richard and A----, but at the same time to Cornelia, addressing the letter to the Ch---- See. Perhaps the people there knew her present residence and could send it to her.

The reply of the artist A---- was extremely unsatisfactory. He would give no account of the manner in which he had succeeded in obtaining the portrait, for he had stolen her features on that first morning by the lake, when Cornelia, thinking herself unobserved, had walked upon the shore with Severinus. Richard wrote: "The lady had been painted from memory, and he had really taken the subject of his picture from the fact that she had entered a convent, where she had been kept rigidly secluded, since no information concerning her had been obtained."

So she had really entered a convent, and there was no possibility of learning any further particulars! *Heinrich's* condition was pitiable. To wait--to do nothing but wait--with this burning longing and uncertainty in his breast, for an event which perhaps might never occur, to hope for a fortunate dispensation that perhaps was already baffled,--such was his fate! He lived in a feverish dream, but forced himself to enter with all his powers into what would promote the decision of his fate, his election to the parliament. The newspapers mentioned his name connection with those of the most honored patriots; and if Cornelia still had free control over herself, she must at least be touched by the loyalty with which he struggled to reach the prescribed goal; if she were silent, then there could be no doubt that she was lost to him. Just at that time the blow Cornelia had vainly sought to avert suddenly fell upon him. The Jesuits executed their threats, but this time in a different way from that Severinus had adopted years before. The organ of ultramontanism in H---- printed an article headed, "Contributions to the Traits of Character of a New Candidate." This essay contained a biography of Ottmar, from the time of his entrance into the Jesuit college to that of his present change of opinions, which, animosity, distortion of facts, and compromising indiscretions, surpassed everything for which Ottmar had given them credit. The style was in the so-called interests of the nation, so often merely the cloak beneath which partisan writers strive to win the applause of the masses; but the worst part of all was that the author, Geheimrath Schwelling, who years before had played so contemptible a part as Severinus's companion in the interview with *Heinrich*, offered to exhibit to any one who might desire it written proofs of most of his accusations. There was no lack of credulous and doubtful persons who wished to convince themselves with their own eyes. The Geheimrath's house became the rendezvous of the curious of all parties, and the papers Severinus had returned to the General for a more worthy use passed from hand to hand. The matter made all the greater excitement an account of the great expectations which had been fixed upon Ottmar. The sheet containing the scandalous article had an immense circulation; and although the cultivated portion of the community turned with disgust from its coarse tone, the facts were not to be denied, and people shrugged their shoulders doubtfully. But the lower classes even gave credence to the charges, in consequence of the amusement the commonplace wit of the style afforded them. In vain Ottmar's friends printed articles in his defense; in vain his banker proved that he had spent the greater portion of his property in purchasing expensive agricultural implements, which he allowed all the country people in the neighborhood to use gratis, and for other national purposes; it was now an easy matter for his enemies to convince the suspicious masses that a man who had gone from rationalism to Jesuitism, then back again to the former, next to despotism, and finally to liberalism once more, was not to be trusted in any relation. "Hold psychological discussions about the motives which forced you to deny your convictions, you will be laughed at, and your name will be branded before all parties," Severinus had said contemptuously years before, and now the result proved how completely he had been in the right. The facts spoke against him, and he could not succeed in giving the people a correct understanding of them, because he had only words,--no contradictory proofs at his command. Even the sincerity with which in N---- he had stood forth in behalf of the constitution was no longer acknowledged, for the scandalous article rendered even this deed suspected as a mere prudential measure. He had perceived that he could no longer hold his ground against the progressive party, and therefore took sides with them in time. This belief appeared only too probable in the case of a man whose life had been so full of contradictions. The confidence which had just been obtained was shaken; the voters began to hesitate. Many forgot what they owed him since his return; others made all the acknowledgments of his services as a public benefactor which were his due; but even they did not wish to elect, as the representative of the most important interests, one whose politics were doubtful. The day of decision came and crowned his enemies' labors with success. Ottmar was defeated by a large majority. He saw himself scorned, insulted; all his hopes crushed, his honor lost; and she for whom he suffered such intolerable torments, who alone could repay him for what he had lost,--Cornelia,--was silent! For love of her he had sacrificed everything; for love of her entered the path which was to lead him to find an abundant reward for ignominy in her arms; and day by day elapsed without bringing any tidings, convincing him more and more that she was torn from him,--that he had gained nothing save the fruits of his sins.

Every morning he went to meet the postman, who brought the letters to his estate, and always in vain. Fourteen times since the election he had borne the tortures of renewed and disappointed hope, had rushed towards the postman in breathless haste only to return with empty hands. He had lain awake on his couch all through the long nights, and welcomed the first ray of light as a preserver from his feverish, agonizing impatience. One morning this restlessness drove him out even earlier than usual, for it was the anniversary of the day on which Cornelia had left him. Perhaps she would give herself to him again on this day; perhaps she had waited for it intentionally. One who has hoped and expected so long at last clings to every conceivable possibility. Thus Ottmar's feet were winged with double speed as he hurried through pleasure-grounds and woodlands, to obtain that for which he longed a half-hour earlier. Wearied with his haste, he emerged from the thicket upon the highway. A fresh autumn breeze was rustling through the tops of the poplars, bending their stiff boughs asunder like the fingers of menacing giant hands. The broad, level road, with its dazzling white sand, stretched before him, endless and empty,--the storm had swept it clean; nothing was to be seen on the wide plain, and Ottmar hurried restlessly onward. Just at that moment the dark figure of the postman appeared in the distance, and with a beating heart *Heinrich* quickened his pace. At last he reached the man, who was already holding out his bag; but again he was disappointed,--it contained nothing but unimportant business letters. The last possibility of hope had now disappeared; now he could no longer doubt that Richard had written the truth, that Cornelia was in a convent.

His measure was full. The Nemesis he had so long seemed to escape had overtaken him, and he must patiently endure her fury with fettered hands. Fortune, love, honor, all were lost, irrevocably lost, and every accusation he wished to heap upon others recoiled upon himself. He was the cause of his own misery, he alone. Fate had given him everything he desired; but he had only demanded that which contained the germ of his ruin. No disaster had befallen him which was not the punishment of a crime. Absorbed in these reflections, the deeply-humbled man slowly returned and reached the wood. The bright rays of the autumn sunlight fell through the branches and made the yellow leaves glitter like gold; the farther he went the more quiet and pleasant it became. The withered foliage, alternated with the dark-green hue of a dense grove of firs; the forest murmured and whispered to him in a soothing tone,--he did not hear it, did not remember that the enchanted ground be entered was his own property; his heart remained closed, no source of comfort could force an entrance. In silent agony the man was collecting his thoughts to pass a stern, hopeless judgment upon himself.

A bench stood beside a beautiful forest stream; he involuntarily turned towards it, and sat down with his face turned towards the rushing water. He did not think of going home: he had one no longer; the house in which he lived contained nothing dear to him; the whole world had no spot where love and joy awaited him, where he would be missed; if he remained away, society had no place for him to fill, no interests which it would confide to him. What was he better than an outcast, a homeless man? Could he endure the disgrace of such a life? Was it not more honorable to extinguish it in the pure current of this stream? Who would lose, from whom would he take anything, if he cast off the burden of a hated, purposeless existence? And yet God had so endowed him that his death must have made a void in the world, if he had been to it what he ought. He gazed down into the murmuring water, which incessantly glided by him pursued by the wind; his soul allowed itself be carried on by the waves like a loosened vine. The eternally changing movement before his eyes made him giddy; he looked away, and now, for the first time, became aware to what thoughts he had involuntarily yielded. Did no power then live in him except that of despising and destroying himself? Could he atone for his faults by committing a crime against himself? Should he steal away like an unfaithful steward who allowed the property intrusted to his care to go to ruin? Should he add to the dishonor which had fallen upon his name the eternal disgrace of suicide, incur Cornelia's contempt, because he could not bear the loss of her love? No, he had not fallen so low as not to repel such a thought with a blush.

But what could, what ought he to do now, since the only profession for which his education and studies fitted him--that of politics--was closed to him in every direction? A quiet, inactive, private life, which but a few hours before, in the hope of a marriage with Cornelia, had appeared endurable, now seemed to him a moral death. He did not understand nature, the occupations of an agriculturist had no charms for him. Should he turn his estates into money, and invest it in some other way? But in what? All the pleasures that can be purchased he had already enjoyed to the dregs; life could afford him nothing more. The egotist had reached the end of his career, and could neither advance nor recede. Crushed and helpless, he looked back upon his past life, and now the point at which he had turned from the right path revealed itself to his searching gaze. The hours stood forth before his soul when he had struggled in his first conflict between inclination and duty, and inclination had conquered. All the strange, feverish fancies once more rose before his memory, and he perceived that they were the voices of his own heart which had spoken to him in the forms of delirium. Now he understood--now, after it was fulfilled--what they had said. With the first false step to which egotism urged him, he was lost. The frivolity with which he had degraded the first woman he loved, to be the prey of his passion, robbed him of his best possession, respect for the sex. Thus every base materialism, which only sought the enjoyment of the senses and thereby often formed the sharpest contrast with the demands of his intellectual nature, developed itself. The more frequently this conflict occurred, the greater it became, the further the two extremes became separated from each other, and the more distinctly their characteristics were stamped. The more the feelings were severed from the intellect, the lower they sank into sensuality, the stronger the passions became, and the more peremptorily they demanded their victim; while, on the other hand, the more exclusively the intellect withdrew into its own sphere, the further it banished the feelings, the colder and more obstinate it became, the more dull to everything which did not concern its own advantage, and therefore the more unprincipled. From this sprang the crimes which *Henri* on the one hand, and *Heinrich* on the other, had committed, whose consequences now drove him to despair, and had even terrified and driven from him forever the only woman for whom both extremes longed with equal ardor. Thus the cause of all the evil in his whole mistaken life was the separation between the mind and heart; the pleasure-seeking of the one, the immoderate ambition of the other, was the curse which had sprung from this division, the form under which egotism had taken possession of both portions of his nature. And of what he had enjoyed and obtained--nothing was left! His life had been fruitless to himself as well as to others. He had deceived and sacrificed confiding natures, and brought a nation to ruin for the sake of tasting the delights of ruling; the pleasure was over, and the curses of the unhappy accompanied him. Everything life could offer was exhausted, drained, and worn out! All the threads by which the heart draws its nourishment from the world were cut off and withered.

He now felt the deep truth of what Cornelia had wished to teach him, what he had once in a dream bodingly anticipated: "Remember that the end of life is neither to enjoy nor to obtain, but to be useful and accomplish good works." But now, when this great knowledge seized upon him,--when he perceived the fruitlessness of all selfish efforts,--now when a powerful impulse urged him to do what mankind, and accomplish what God, could ask of him,--now it was too late; every path was closed, and the woman who alone could restore harmony to his nature, lost! The guilt of the past had destroyed the hope of the future.

He rested his forehead upon his hand and closed his eyes; he could form no plans for the future, while repentance and anguish stirred his heart so violently--the first true repentance, the first great sorrow, of his life. True, his powers rose and expanded in the struggle with the unknown enemy as they had never done before, and the mighty assault of the contending elements widened and swelled his breast, as if now for the first time he became a man, now for the first time there was room in his heart for lofty feelings, resolutions, and efforts; true, the consciousness of the strength ennobled and increased by sorrow conquered for a moment: but as if with this, the longing for the nature that had always guided him towards the right path strengthened, the thoughts of Cornelia's loss once more gathered in the depths of his soul to break over him with renewed violence. What could life still offer him? There was no longer any love like Cornelia's, any mind like hers, any woman who could compare with her. He felt that this sorrow would never die; that he might perhaps obtain honor, but never happiness again. He threw himself despairingly upon the bench, face downward. The stream hurried along at his feet, plashing and glittering;

the birds looked down from the branches at the tall, quiet man, turned their heads inquisitively, and softly twittered a timid question. Far above his head the summits of the ancient firs rustled and told the azure sky of the sorrow concealed beneath their shade.

Softly and slowly the bushes near him parted,--he did not hear it,--and a slender girlish form glided over the soft moss with a light step; cautiously approached, and as she stood beside him, bent down, holding her breath. Her glances beamed through tears, and she trembled like a wild rose under the morning dew. *Heinrich* heard a heart beating close beside his ear, felt his head raised and pressed to a heaving bosom; looked into a pair of eyes like two shining worlds. It was no dream, and yet he could not utter a sound; all that he thought and felt blended together in an unspeakable something, which swelled his heart with glowing warmth, rose higher and higher till it reached his eyes, overflowed as if his whole soul was gushing forth with it: he had wept his first tears upon Cornelia's breast, and holding her in a mute embrace reveled in this unspeakable bliss!

The noonday sun shone brightly and glowed through the ripe clusters of grapes which hung from a trellis that surrounded the steward's pretty little house not far from Ottmar's castle. A charming young woman stood in the doorway, looking with eager expectation towards the forest; the steward was working busily in the garden, but he, too, often glanced into the distance.

"I don't understand where they could stay so long, if they met each other," said the little woman, at last. "It would be a pity if she missed him. I grieve over every hour the poor master is obliged to spend in his sorrow."

"Yes," gasped the man, wiping his brow, "it was time for her to show herself; the master's melancholy manner and wretched looks were becoming the talk of the whole neighborhood and, after all, she couldn't have been kept concealed much longer: we were always in a fright." He threw his tools aside, went up to his wife, and put his arm around her neck. "You would not have borne seeing me suffer so long, would you, my Röschen?"

She nestled fondly to his side and nodded. "No, indeed, my dear Albert! But these great people are very different from us. Cornelia has a grand, noble soul, which we must not judge by our own."

"You are right; it would not be proper for us to apply our standard to them. Let us thank God we are made as is needful for our situation and welfare."

"Yes, thank God for it!" cried Röschen, joyously. "Oh, Albert! how unhappy these aristocratic people often make themselves with their over-refinement and their lofty requirements! I saw that in my poor dead princess. Heaven knows what sorrow was gnawing at her heart! According to my ideas, she might have been very happy; but it often seemed as if she did not wish to be. At any rate, it was a very aristocratic sorrow. If she had been in our condition in life, and had not had so much time to give way to her thoughts, she would undoubtedly be alive now."

"Well, those two at least are not making themselves wretched," laughed Albert, pointing to Cornelia and *Heinrich*, who were rapidly approaching.

The married pair modestly withdrew, and Cornelia and *Heinrich*, absorbed in delightful conversation, reached the house, and entered a pleasant little room on the ground floor.

"See, Heinrich, here is the hiding-place where I waited for three weeks. From behind the curtains of that window I saw you pass, day after day, and watched your face with a throbbing heart. Will you forgive me for becoming a spy upon you? I wished, I was obliged, first to discover whether you were at last a man to whom I might dare to intrust my fate, whether you still loved me, and whether in my affection I should offer you a welcome gift. I was obliged to give you time to collect your thoughts after the blow that had fallen upon you, and to raise yourself by your own might. If you had shown yourself to my secretly watchful gaze otherwise than I hoped, otherwise than I might dare to love you, I should have gone away as I came, unobserved by you; perhaps with a broken heart, but silently and forever."

"Yon would have gone as already many a happiness has fled from the threshold of him who did not deserve it," said *Heinrich*, clasping her closely in his arms. "Oh, God, my salvation and my ruin were both so near! Your eyes watched me like those of God, and if I had not stood the test you would have left me for the second time, and been irrevocably lost to me."

"Ah, I did not doubt that you would stand the test! A man has rarely made greater sacrifices for a woman than you for me in the course of this last year; for I clearly perceived that you would never have acted as you have done if it had not been for my sake. But for your love for me you would in a few years have conquered your longing for a higher satisfaction, and remained till the end of your days in the cold splendor of your position at the court of N----. Love for me--I may be allowed to say so, since it is no merit of mine--was the impulse that led you to take the first steps in another path. It guided you hither, and I did not fear that it would desert you now, when it was apparently leading you into misery. But a noble woman asks more than love from the man of her choice: she demands character, firmness in misfortune as well as prosperity, the power which is to be her support and protection, the greatness to which she can cheerfully submit, admiringly look up. It is a necessity of our natures to honor what we love; in this humility lies our pride. If we cannot truly consider the man to whom we belong far superior to us, we feel humiliated in acknowledging him as our master. That is why I remained concealed so long; I wished to investigate your whole life and conduct here, to see what influence you exerted, whether you did good and made those around you happy, what pleasures and employments you choose, how you would bear the misfortune that had fallen upon you. And what I saw and heard convinced me that you had entered upon your new calling not only in appearance, but reality; that you had become a man to whom I might confidently give myself. Yet the tears you have just shed told me more than all. With these tears a new and better man was born in you; they have atoned for every wrong, washed away every spot. Ah, if the bigoted priests who believe you a lost soul had witnessed that one moment, they would have understood that there is something holy outside their church!"

"Cornelia," cried *Heinrich*, "dear, precious girl, say no more to me about the Jesuits! Although I bear no towards the unhappy Severinus, whom you have taught me to know as my brother, although I forgive the intrigues they plotted against me, I will never pardon them for having torn you from me and attempted to make you a proselyte, for having intrusted you for so long a time to that handsome, dangerous Severinus, whose perhaps unintentional conquests over women's hearts are well known to the order. I can only consider it as a miracle that you remained faithful to me."

Cornelia smilingly shook the hair back from her brow. "The miracle is nothing more than that I have a faithful heart and a firm head."

"Those are the highest gifts a woman can possess. And this jewel has fallen to my lot, mine of all others; this loyal, sorely wounded heart clung to me; this proud firm brow, no power has ever humiliated, bent to me. Oh, Cornelia, strong, gentle, forgiving woman, no man ever yet repented more deeply, or was more truly grateful, than I repent my crimes and thank you for your love! A thousand others in your place would either have been dragged down by me, or cast me off forever; but you would not permit yourself to be misled by all my faults and sins, you believed a noble germ within me. Instead of punishing, you reformed me, have been faithful to me; and now give yourself to me as trustfully and freely as in the first moment of our love. Oh, girl, there is no word for this bliss my thoughts are whelmed in a sea of emotions!" He paused and laid his head upon hers, as if he wished to rest from his overmastering emotion.

"Heinrich," said Cornelia, with deep, loving, earnestness, "let the past rest; the Heinrich to whom I always belonged, and shall as long as I live, never wronged me; he suffered with me when that other came between and tore us from each other. That Count Ottmar, whose wife I never wished to become, has atoned for his fault; he is dead. Never conjure up his gloomy shade before me, even to arraign him, I beseech you."

"Yes, my angel, you are right. Never was it so clear to me as to-day that I bore my worst enemy in myself, and in the last few hours I have buried him forever. One complete in himself, Cornelia, receives you in his arms; it shall be his one task to live for you and your happiness; he no longer seeks or hopes for anything but you and a quiet family happiness, unnoticed, but rich in blessing."

Cornelia looked at him in astonishment. "Would you renounce politics and every manly profession?"

"How can I help it? What can I begin after this failure? My political credit is ruined here as well as elsewhere. What can it avail to convince myself more and more that I cannot make amends for my errors in this province? But here,"--he laid his band an Cornelia's shoulder,--"here, thank God, I can atone for the wrongs I have committed; here I can and will prove that I have become a different man!"

"No, Heinrich," cried Cornelia, deeply touched. "I thank you for these words, and for the cheerfulness with which you hope to find in me a compensation for all; but I think too highly of you to be able to share this hope. No wife, not even the most beloved, can make that superfluous for which her husband was born: to work in a lofty vocation. What you now feel, in the first ebullition of joy, you cannot always experience. The storm that now fills your heart now will subside in time, and the calm which will then follow would at last make you find a void in yourself. You are no 'shepherd,' Heinrich. An idyllic, private life would not long satisfy you; a quiet withdrawal into your own family circle, a limiting of yourself to that which is personally dear to you, would be again an egotistical, and therefore only a partial, happiness. You possess the power of solving comprehensive problems. Every power imperiously demands its right to assert itself; if the opportunity is denied, it turns destructively against the barriers imposed upon it, and that which is also within them. Thus it would be with you and our peace. Woe betide the wife who believes that she can and must be the whole world to her husband! She does not understand his larger nature, and will only make herself or him unhappy. I do not belong to that class. I pride myself in taking into account all the just demands of your character, thus only can I make you happy. I will not regret you in the hours your profession claims, for I shall take possession of you doubly in spirit, when I know you to be toiling for that for which I myself would fain strive with all my powers, and must not because I am a woman. I will not bewail the time you take from me to give to mankind, for I love all men far too much to grudge them what you can do for their welfare. And then, Heinrich,"--she laid her head on his breast, and gazed into his face with a bride's ardent love,--"then when you return home to your wife weary but joyous in the consciousness of duty then you shall rest in my arms, in my faithful love, and let me have the proud belief that my heart is the soil from which the roots of your life draw nourishment for the glorious fruits that you permit the world to reap!"

"Cornelia, glorious creature! What a picture you conjure up before the soul! These are divine revelations, and I will follow them unquestioningly. Yes, I will begin anew; guide me with your inspired, prophetic glance, lead me to the path upon which my first step faltered; you alone know what is for my welfare." He gazed long and earnestly into her eyes. "Oh, do not reproach me as unmanly because I give myself up entirely to you, since through you I first became what I am, through you alone I first learned to perceive in laboring for others a duty, an object, in life! The representatives of these noble ideas are principally women; for to labor and care for others is woman's mission, to sacrifice herself for others' interests her greatest power. The man who allows himself to be guided by a woman need not become womanish, nor the woman masculine. If, like you, Cornelia, she rises above her narrow subjective world to ideas which comprehend all humanity, she confers the qualities inherent in her upon them, and then doubtless becomes capable of guiding the more egotistical man to honest efforts for the race, self-sacrifice, and true philanthropy! Thus the strength of your love and virtue, in one word, your lofty womanhood, draws me upward." He threw his arms around her and pressed her ardently to his heart. "Cornelia, my betrothed bride, oh, tell me again and again that I can never lose you, that you are mine!"

She clasped her hands. "Forever! forever! and may God's blessing be with us!"

"Amen!" said *Heinrich*.

Thus the power of a genuine love had healed the secret conflict in Ottmar. Intellect and sensuous feelings, both equally attracted, equally satisfied, united in the same object, and in the soft atmosphere of a true happiness his shattered nature healed into a symmetrical whole.

The ghostly apparitions of his dual existence disappeared before the reality of an all-reconciling feeling which seized upon the inmost kernel of life, and from this brought forth the source of never-failing joy.

When the whole man was in harmony with himself, his long-scattered and dispersed powers concentrated in the depths of his soul, and now for the first time showed unity of purpose and noble, honest action: for the first time he became a man. And when he thus once more appeared before the world with head erect, he conquered; for real ability and honest convictions always find allies in the natural instincts of the people, and against these even the hostility of the Jesuits was powerless. The web they had entwined around him was only that of his own cowardice and duplicity. His manly conduct at last tore it asunder. He was now free, and his purified character afforded no opening for a new snare. After a few years he saw the noblest ambition gratified,--that of being useful and accomplishing some good result. He was the main support of the Party in favor of the constitution, averted a threatening reaction by his ready dialectics, felt the mighty breath of an applauding nation hovering like a vivifying spring-storm about his head, and everywhere, far and wide, saw the seeds springing up which his reawakened philanthropy had sown.

And with inexpressible joy he clasped his blooming wife in his arms, compared the lifeless splendor of the former minister with the warm, evermore richly developing activity of the simple deputy, and his full heart gratefully overflowed in the proud words, "Yes, my wife, you were right; it is not what the world is to us, but what we are to the world, that is the measure of our happiness."

FOOTNOTE

Footnote 1: A Jesuit prayer.

Footnote 2: An instrument used by the Jesuits for penance and punishment.